1001

Steve McQueen
Facts

THE RIDES, ROLES & REALITIES
OF THE KING OF COOL

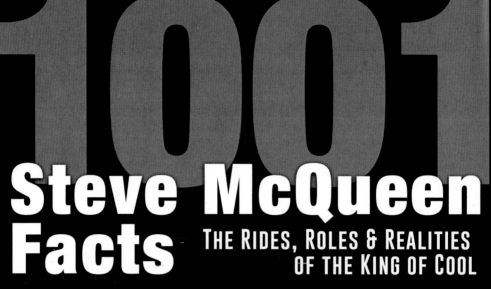

1001

Steve McQueen
Facts

The Rides, Roles & Realities
of the King of Cool

CarTech®

838 Lake Street South
Forest Lake, MN 55025
Phone: 651-277-1200 or 800-551-4754
Fax: 651-277-1203
www.cartechbooks.com

© 2020 by Tyler Greenblatt

Edit by Wes Eisenschenk
Layout by Connie DeFlorin
Cover and title page photos courtesy of Don Bok

ISBN 978-1-61325-473-8
Item No. CT654

Library of Congress Cataloging-in-Publication Data
Names: Greenblatt, Tyler, 1988- author.
Title: 1001 Steve McQueen facts : the rides, roles, and realities of the King of Cool / Tyler Greenblatt.
Other titles: One thousand one Steve McQueen facts
Description: Forest Lake, MN : CarTech, Inc., [2020]
Identifiers: LCCN 2019048950 | ISBN 9781613254738 (paperback)
Subjects: LCSH: McQueen, Steve, 1930-1980--Miscellanea. | Motion picture actors and actresses--United States--Miscellanea. | Stage props. | Automobiles in motion pictures.
Classification: LCC PN2287.M19 G74 2020 | DDC 791.4302/8092--dc23
LC record available at https://lccn.loc.gov/2019048950

Written, edited, and designed in the U.S.A.
Printed in China

10 9 8 7 6 5 4 3 2 1

DISTRIBUTION BY:

Europe
PGUK
63 Hatton Garden
London EC1N 8IE, England
Phone: 020 7061 1980 • Fax: 020 7242 3725
www.pguk.co.uk

Australia
Renniks Publications Ltd.
3/37-39 Green Street
Banksmeadow, NSW 2109, Australia
Phone: 2 9695 7055 • Fax: 2 9695 7355
www.renniks.com

Canada
Login Canada
300 Saulteaux Crescent
Winnipeg, MB, R3J 3T2 Canada
Phone: 800 665 1148 • Fax: 800 665 0103
www.lb.ca

TABLE OF CONTENTS

Dedication

This book is dedicated to the fans around the world who have kept Steve McQueen's memory alive since his passing in 1980. Thank you to the past, present, and future caretakers of his beloved cars, trucks, motorcycles, and aircraft for honoring his memory and allowing future generations to experience the Steve McQueen mystique for themselves.

About the Author

Tyler Greenblatt has been passionate about cars and motorcycles since day one. His parents hooked him on internal combustion when they had a jump seat installed in the back of their 1966 Sting Ray coupe so that a baby seat could be secured back there. The roar of a high-revving, small-block V-8 and the distinctly American smell of vinyl and gasoline had a lasting effect that led to a lifelong passion for cars, motorcycles, and off-road powersports vehicles.

Tyler spent eight years in various editorial positions with *American Iron Magazine*, during which time he wrote *1001 Harley-Davidson Facts*, which was published by CarTech Books in 2017. He followed that in 2018 with *The Corvette Hunter: Kevin Mackay's Greatest Corvette Finds*, which was a joint effort with longtime friend and world-class Corvette restorer Kevin Mackay. His latest CarTech project, *1001 Steve McQueen Facts* was his biggest undertaking yet, combining his love of both cars and motorcycles and his fascination with the King of Cool himself.

Tyler and his wife, Danielle, live in Madison, Wisconsin, with their labradoodle, Dixie, and tortoise, Rambo. In addition to his daily-rider Harley, he enjoys working on, riding, and showing his 1982 Honda CBX and 1975 Yamaha DT175. He works full-time as a classic car and motorcycle auction specialist with Bring a Trailer Auctions and contributes regularly to *Motorcyclist Online*, one of the world's leading motorcycle news sources.

Acknowledgments

Thank you to all the Steve McQueen biographers who laid the ground-work for this collection of trivia facts. My goal with this project was less about breaking new ground and more about honing in on the plethora of information that was already available. Unfortunately, many of the men and women associated with Steve McQueen are no longer with us, so again, I thank previous biographers for recording their testimony for generations to come.

Thank you to my wife, Danielle, who lost me for far too many nights and weekends. I also apologize for the slew of dirt bikes that made their way into the garage; thanks to the desert exploits of Steve McQueen, I've become obsessed with off-road motorcycle riding.

Thank you to my family too, for their support and motivation throughout this nearly two-year process and providing me with the will required to finish when I didn't think I could.

Thank you to Bob and Susan Bishop for allowing me to use their ex-Steve McQueen and Von Dutch Brough Superior SS80 motorcycle for my author portrait and the support with my automotive endeavors over the years.

Thank you to my friend Kevin Mackay. He's been called the "Mr. October of Corvettes" by Reggie Jackson himself. With the help he's provided me on this project I have to say that when it comes to Corvettes and 1960s era endurance racing, Kevin truly is the King of Cool.

Thank you to Franz Estreicher, owner of the 1966 Corvette used in Steve McQueen's *Sports Illustrated* sports car shootout, which he also owned for some time after. Hearing Franz discuss the research and documentation on the car and his inside knowledge of behind-closed-doors activities in Detroit in that era motivated me even further to do justice to this topic.

Last but not least, thank you to the team at CarTech Books for making this project happen and especially to my editor, Wes Eisenschenk. This was a tough project; thank you for seeing it through to the end with me and for the opportunity to swim around in the world of American icon Steve McQueen.

Introduction

Few people, if any, really knew the man known to the world as Steve McQueen. He lived one of the fullest lives of any man to walk the earth, and yet, he was an enigma to even his closest friends and family. He compartmentalized his worlds and friend groups in such a way that no one person truly saw all sides of him.

Steve McQueen competed for roles and screen time with the best actors of his time including Yul Brynner, Paul Newman, and Frank Sinatra. Meanwhile, he held his own against the legendary Mario Andretti in one of the world's toughest races, losing by only seconds in a significantly slower car. He rose to the top of Hollywood, and came crashing down with the financial failure of his magnum opus, *Le Mans*. Over the years, he built up one of the largest and most valuable collections of cars and motorcycles of the time, the contents of which today fetch several times the sale price of an identical vehicle without the Steve McQueen provenance. Toward the end of his life, when wheeled transportation couldn't get him to where he wanted to go, McQueen earned a pilot's license and took to the sky.

It seems as if every new biography written about Steve McQueen paints a different picture and brings in previously unknown perspectives, not all of them flattering. This collection of 1,001 Steve McQueen facts is less about breaking new ground or revealing scandalous information as it is a culmination of the life of a man who meant so much to so many people around the globe and still means so much today. Broken down into five categories: personal life, movie facts, movie automobile facts, automobile collection, and racing, this book contains everything that a Steve McQueen fan could ever want to know about his or her hero.

He died at the young age of 50 leaving behind two children, a widow, and grieving fans all over the world. He also left behind a legacy so great that even today, nearly 40 years after his death, his name is still used in daily conversation. His likeness appears in ads selling cars faster and more technologically advanced than anything of which he ever could have dreamt. His films, namely *Bullitt* and *Le Mans*, are still regularly watched and enjoyed by viewers who may not have even been born when the films were released.

1001 Steve McQueen Facts: The Roles, Rides, & Realities of the King of Cool is a tribute to the man Steve McQueen was and the legend he remains today.

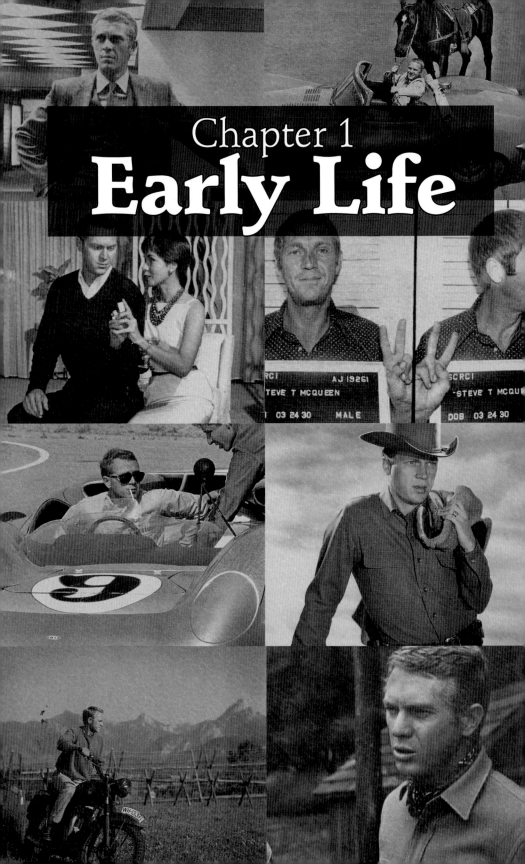

Chapter 1
Early Life

PERSONAL LIFE

1. Steve McQueen was named by his father, supposedly after a one-armed bookie friend named Steve Hall. McQueen commented later in life on his father's weird sense of humor, saying that his name-sake was one of the few things he actually did know about himself.

2. Both sides of McQueen's family can trace their American heritage to before the Revolutionary War. His first relative in the New World was Dugal McQueen, who arrived in Baltimore on August 20, 1716, as a prisoner of war held by England and became an indentured servant for seven years. On his mother's side, Samuel Thomson arrived in Virginia in 1717. Both sides of Steve's family originated in Scotland.

3. Just about every war in American history saw a Steve McQueen ancestor fight, including the Revolutionary War.

4. Steve McQueen became known in the film industry as a fighter when it came to getting what was best for him and his career. He likely received this trait from his uncle Claude Thomson, who virtually raised him as a young boy. Claude was a shrewd and disciplined hog farmer with a tough business acumen. He even pushed his siblings out of their family farm inheritance. Although this sounds terrible, it was because he was the primary person doing all the farming.

5. Uncle Claude was rumored to feed coal to his hogs before taking them to market. Since hogs were sold by the pound, the added weight fetched him more money. Steve definitely learned how to stretch a buck.

6. Steve McQueen's first address was 1311 North Drexel Avenue in Beech Grove, Indiana, following his birth on March 24, 1930. His mother, Julia Ann "Julian" Crawford, was living there at the time with her parents, Lillian and Victor, after moving from Indianapolis. Terrence Steven McQueen is recorded as living there at the time of the 1930 U.S. Census.

7. Although McQueen's mother is listed as Julian McQueen on his birth certificate and several other documents, there's no evidence that she and his father, William McQueen, were ever legally married. It has been suggested that because of Julian's Catholic upbringing, a wedding likely occurred as a religious ceremony that was never registered with any government office. When Steve was born, Julian was 19 and William was 23, and the Great Depression had set in just a few months prior.

8. With the Great Depression in full swing, and a young boy to care for, the Crawford family moved to Slater to live with Lillian's brother, Claude, on the family ranch. The town of Slater, Missouri, which now has a population of 2,000 residents, celebrates Steve McQueen as its most famous resident in a variety of ways. For example, on Saturday, April 24, 2010, the town dedicated the Steve McQueen Memorial Highway in his honor.

9. When Steve became old enough to help out on the family farm, his uncle Claude took on the role of his first real father figure. Although he dished out harsh discipline to the young boy, it was always fair. Steve had to earn everything through hard work, a principle that stuck with him throughout his life. It was through his farm work that he learned to ride a horse, which he did in several films, most notably in *Tom Horn*.

10. Steve McQueen was known as a cultivated collector of firearms and often carried one with him. He first learned to shoot when he was 8 years old and Uncle Claude let him use a rifle to go hunting in the woods. The catch: he was only given one bullet. He'd have to set up his shot perfectly to hit his target; otherwise, he'd walk home empty-handed. One day, he came back to the farmhouse carrying two dead pigeons. Steve told Uncle Claude that he waited to line up the perfect shot to get both at the same time. Claude was so impressed that he bragged to everyone in the town. In reality, Steve had snuck into a neighbor's silo, shot one pigeon, and the round bounced off the wall and hit another. He never told his uncle what actually happened.

11. Julian McQueen was away for most of Steve's time in Slater, Missouri, but she returned sometime in 1936 or 1937 to take her boy to Los Angeles, where she had met someone. As they were leaving, Claude handed Steve a gold pocket watch and told him that he wanted him to have it to remember him by. The inscription inside the pocket watch read, "To Steve—who has been like a son to me."

12. A new father figure in Steve's life was Hal Berri, who married Julian in Monterey, California, in 1937. Hal had only recently divorced his wife of 13 years and was 8 years older than Julian. The three of them moved to 1810 Ewing Street in Echo Park, and Steve took on the last name of Berri. A short while later, they moved to a nice home at 1966 Preston Avenue, also in Echo Park. Although the family seemed normal on paper, in reality Hal's previous wife divorced him because he was an alcoholic who disappeared for days at a time with other women, and he physically abused her many times.

13. Sharing a roof with Hal Berri was one of the most difficult times of young Steve's life. He was subjected to daily beatings "for the sheer sadistic pleasure it gave him, which included the joy he obviously derived from my pain," Steve later said. Although he vowed to bear the beatings until he was old enough to run away, he couldn't help himself from fighting back. Returning punches did little against the much-larger man, but it made Steve feel good, even though it often brought on even worse repercussions. "I would have borne any punishment, anything just for the pleasure of knowing that I had given back even a little of the pain he had inflicted on me," Steve said. Among the punishments for fighting back was being tossed into a pitch-black room with no food or water, not unlike the punishment he received in the film *Papillon*.

14. When Steve McQueen was young, he went by the nickname "Buddy." He even used the nickname on his social security card when he filled in his name as Buddy Steven McQueen.

15. In the early 1940s, young Steve was sent back to his uncle Claude's farm in Slater, Missouri. His mother had written Claude about the boy's behavior, and rather than send him to reform school, Claude offered to take him in. Claude enrolled the eighth grader at the Orearville School as Steve Berri, and he was the only blonde-haired, blue-eyed boy in his class, making him even more of an outsider from the get-go. He rarely attended school, opting instead to hang out in downtown Slater.

16. Among his familial and upbringing issues that handicapped his youth, Steve also had a few physical handicaps that added to his challenges. He had a mastoid infection behind his right ear that made it difficult for him to hear.

17. Steve was diagnosed in later years with dyslexia, which made reading extremely difficult as well. Between that and the mastoid infection, school would have likely been quite difficult for him.

18. When Steve was 13, he incurred the anger of Uncle Claude when he and some friends shot out the windows of a local restaurant with a BB gun. Rather than accept his punishment, he got a job with the traveling carnival that happened to be in Slater at the time. When the carnival left, Steve left with it, not telling anyone. Claude searched for him for days before accepting that Steve had actually run off. This was Steve McQueen's first great escape.

19. His carnival days didn't last long, and he quickly found himself living back with his mother and her husband, Hal Berri. Hal's beatings picked up right where they left off for 13-year-old Steve, but by May 1943, the couple separated. Julian and Steve moved into an apartment at 3266½ Descanso Drive in Los Angeles. Rather than work and go to school, however, Steve became involved with a "bad crowd" and was once again a juvenile delinquent.

20. After his mother and her husband Hal Berri separated, she made 13-year-old Steve apply for a social security number so that he could get a job and help with the rent, although there's no evidence that he ever did actually hold a job.

21. Steve McQueen was sent to the Boys Republic School in Chino, California, on February 6, 1945, by a court order obtained by his mother. The school was set up as its own little society in which the students were responsible for every facet of everyday life including running their own government. Students were responsible to themselves and their classmates, which taught respect and inspired confidence.

22. Boy's Republic School is a well-known, popular reform school today, but when Steve arrived, there were about 100 students, and he was given the number 3188. He lived at the John Brewer dormitory cottage and his mother paid $25 a month for his room and board.

23. Although he looked back at his time at Boys Republic with fondness, while there he and some buddies tried to escape. His friends made it as far as Long Beach, California, before getting caught. Steve had decided to go it on his own and was caught underneath the entrance bridge to Boys Republic. This was the last formal education Steve received, having never made it past ninth grade.

24. On April 1, 1946, Steve McQueen left Boys Republic, after his mother secured his release, and moved to be with her in New York. She was living at 240 Sullivan Street in Manhattan's Greenwich Village with artist Viktor Lukens. It was he who pushed for Steve to come live near them, and upon his arrival, Lukens took on a paternal role. They rented a room from an actor down the street for Steve to live.

25. At age 16, Steve joined the Merchant Marines after hearing about the adventures of a couple of sailors he met while drinking in a bar. He boarded a ship, the *Alpha*, in Yonkers, New York, and headed for the West Indies to pick up a cargo of molasses. Among the jobs he had on his maiden voyage were cleaning the decks under the hot summer sun, cleaning garbage receptacles, and cleaning toilets.

26. The ship caught fire just after leaving port and almost sank. The crew wasn't sure it could even reach the West Indies. McQueen jumped ship while docked at Santo Domingo in the Dominican Republic and quickly ended his career as a merchant marine.

27. While in Santo Domingo, Steve secured a job as a towel boy at a brothel, which he often recalled with a certain fondness. His tropical tenure lasted two months before he made his way back to the United States.

28. McQueen finally landed in Cedar Rapids, Iowa, working at another carnival. He slept on a park bench, an object that became sentimental to him later. "Sometimes, when I start to figure I've got the world by the tail, I think back to the bench and remember that it could've ended up a lot differently."

29. Did you know that Steve once worked as a lumberjack in Canada? He ditched the carnival while there, but his fear of heights led him to quit and return to the United States. He spent 30 days on a chain gang after being arrested as a vagrant, then celebrated his 17th birthday in Myrtle Beach, South Carolina.

30. In April 1947, living back in New York City, Steve reached out to his mother to sign a waiver so he could enlist in the Marine Corps at the age of 17. "I suppose I had heard enough of the stories about how tough the Corps was that I considered it somewhat of a challenge," he said. Interestingly, he likely had no knowledge of his family's extensive military service or that his father served in the Marine Corps from 1927 to 1929! On April 28, at the USMC Northeastern Recruiting Division District Headquarters at 90 Church Street, he filled out the official application, falsely saying that he had never been in jail or at a reform school.

31. Although his relationship with his mother was tenuous, he signed over 75 percent of his Marine Corps enlistment pay to her and received the military number 649015.

32. When discussing his time in the military in his later years, McQueen often joked that he had been "busted back down to private about seven times." However, his service records don't show a single demotion. In fact, his former drill instructor even said that he had been promoted at an impressive rate for peacetime service. The real joke is that one of his few friends in the Marines nicknamed him "Tough Shit McQueen" because the name on his uniform read "T. S. McQueen."

33. Although Steve's documented birthday is March 21, his mother claimed it was really March 24. Interestingly, he always celebrated on the 21st even though the 24th is considered the accepted day.

34. Steve's Civil War veteran ancestor, Pike Montgomery Thomson, was captured by the Union army and awaiting execution when a Union captain decided otherwise. Rather than hang him like so many others, he exiled Thomson, his wife, and their child from the country. While on their way, the bloody war ended, and they decided to return to Saline County in Missouri. The most interesting part about the whole ordeal? The captain who spared Pike Thomson's life went by the name McQueen.

35. While growing up on his uncle's hog farm, Steve noticed that whenever he called, one particular hog came and jumped on him like a dog. Uncle Claude warned him about his relationship with the hog, saying that one day, when the hog grew up, they'd have to eat it. However, Uncle Claude saw how much the animal meant to young Steve, who didn't have much else in his life, and allowed him to keep it as a pet, sparing its life in the process. Can you guess what Steve named his pet pig? Well, Pig, of course! Every time he called out for Pig, the animal came trotting right up to him.

36. Marine boot camp on Parris Island was rough for McQueen until he was discovered as a potentially good boxer. In his first fight, he went up against the biggest Marine there, who would later end up in Leavenworth Prison for punching several officers. The wiry McQueen got knocked down and got back up to fight nine times before being physically unable to get back up after the tenth knock-down. That fight proved his toughness to his officers and fellow enlistees, and proved that he belonged in the Marine Corps.

37. While living in New York, barely able to make ends meet, Steve entered a professional boxing match. Although he was knocked out in the third round, he earned $65 for the fight.

MOVIE FACTS

38. Steve and Claude's relationship continued to grow as they developed a mutual respect and appreciation for each other. Although Claude was a tough-as-nails farmer and businessman, he made time on Saturdays to take Steve to their local movie theater, the Kiva Theater on Main Street in Slater. Westerns were his favorite, but in the late 1930s, he would have also been exposed to some of the greatest films ever created in one of Hollywood's most glamorous and exciting eras.

39. Steve's favorite actors growing up were James Cagney, John Wayne, Spencer Tracy, Gary Cooper, and Humphry Bogart. "Bogie" (as Steve called Bogart), was his favorite, and an actor from whom he developed much of his own direction. He was later quoted as saying, "Sometimes kids ask me what a pro is. I just point to the Duke." Another of his quotes is, "Listen, in Taiwan most people don't know who Lyndon Johnson is, but they sure as hell know who John Wayne is."

40. While at Boys Republic, Steve developed a relationship with his guidance counselor, Lloyd Panter, who was one of the earliest adults to see great potential in young Steve McQueen. "No one seemed to give a damn about my future life as an adult," Steve said. "But he did, and it meant a lot to me." Panter first introduced Steve to Shakespeare and other literature, which he said "laid the foundation for my later interest in the theater."

41. Carnival life gave McQueen some insight into the entertainment industry because of the variety of performers and the opportunity to study them for days on end. Always the loner, he watched them interact with one another and with show attendees. It's believed that this is where he learned some of his natural acting ability on how to react to specific emotions and physical cues.

42. Although he seemed much taller in his films, his height was only 5 feet 9½ inches. He'd likely be much smaller if it weren't for the training and dietary regimen he received while in the Marine Corps. When he entered the Marines, at 17 years old, he was only 5 feet 6½ inches tall and weighed 135 pounds. In addition to the extra 3 inches, he also gained 30 pounds by the time he left the service!

43. Steve learned his shooting skills and natural gun-handling ability while in the Marines; it wasn't just acting! He qualified as a sharpshooter with both the M-1 rifle and the Colt .45 pistol. He worked with firearms in many of his films, and unlike other actors who needed to learn how to use them for the job, it was already a part of his skillset.

44. When Steve was living in Los Angeles and running the streets, a Coke bottle was thrown at his head and he received a serious cut to his lower lip that never healed properly. The wound, which had become a small mass, was discovered by a doctor during an examination while McQueen was in the Marines.

45. While serving, he also had the misfortune of falling off a tank and reinjuring the same spot, causing it to swell and scar even more, until a plastic surgeon removed it. What does this have to do with his films and acting? Even with the mass removed, he still had a slight mumble when he spoke and had difficulty pronouncing some words. This is why he speaks in monosyllabic dialogue in his films.

46. The same Marine buddy, Cliff Anderson, who nicknamed Steve "Tough Shit McQueen," learned of his former comrade's fame years later while flipping through a copy of *TV Guide* magazine. In it, there was a letter in which a fan asked about Steve McQueen. According to Marshall Terrill's book, *Steve McQueen: The Life And Legend Of A Hollywood Icon,* Anderson remarked upon discovering the letter, "Holy cow, that's Tough Shit McQueen! The son of a bitch is famous!"

47. On March 24, 1944, Steve's 14th birthday, Allied prisoners of war attempted the largest escape attempt of World War II and inspired the film *The Great Escape*, starring Steve McQueen.

48. Steve was born the same year as fellow film icon Clint Eastwood, and they even got their big breaks around the same time. McQueen's came in 1958 with *Wanted Dead or Alive* and Eastwood's was a year later with *Rawhide*.

49. Having starred in similar roles throughout their careers, although he was always one step behind McQueen, Eastwood's career provides an important insight into what Steve's could have looked like had he not died at a young age. Today, most fans remember McQueen from his most popular films in the late 1960s and early 1970s; it's strange to think that he'd be nearly 90 years old today. Using Clint Eastwood as a reference provides assistance in that thought process.

50. Thanks to his stern upbringing on a Midwestern hog farm under the tutelage of his tough uncle Claude, Steve always felt that acting was not an appropriate job for a man. Much of his show of masculinity throughout his life and his desire to excel in racing came from the fact that he considered male actors, himself included, as sissies. After he had become an accomplished actor and he and wife Neile (prounced *kneel,* as in to kneel down) visited Uncle Claude, they never once spoke of Steve's acting career.

51. One of Steve's favorite actors as a young boy was James Cagney, who was well known for gangster movies. Similar to a character McQueen eventually played, Josh Randall, Cagney's characters were always small but tough and not afraid to stand up to bigger foes.

52. Steve once used his best Cagney impression while running on the streets when he was approached by a bigger, older street kid. The older kid was so impressed by young Steve's toughness that he invited him to join his gang.

53. Making James Cagney and Humphrey Bogart impressions became lucrative for a young Steve McQueen when he stood on a street corner and started acting for money. He put his hat down in front of him and people dropped in a few coins here and there as he ran through skits. Even though he was able to show that he earned money from it, Uncle Claude didn't approve of acting as a profession for men.

AUTOMOBILE COLLECTION

54. Growing up in Southern California, McQueen fell heavily into the hot rod scene. His first car was a hot rod with a Model A frame and a Ford 60 engine with Edelbrock manifolds. He remembers that car accelerating "like the J-2 Allards that some of the sports car people owned." His hot rod didn't handle all that well, but it did have "stark acceleration; when the engine stayed in it."

55. One of young McQueen's first experiences with motorcycles came when he was a young teenager in California and he hopped on a police bike that was parked outside a restaurant in Hollywood. He tossed the officer's gloves and helmet on the ground and made "vroom, vroom" noises according to a friend who was with him at the time. When he got off, he snapped off the bike's radio antenna and took it with him. His friend thought they'd be arrested on the spot!

56. As an homage to his student number at Boys Republic, 3188, when he was in his late 40s, he used a custom license plate on his everyday cars that read MCQ3188.

57. Because of Steve's interest in and experience with engines and automobiles, he was assigned the job of a tank crewman/driver on an M4 Sherman tank. "I'd often wonder if a tank could be speed converted," he said. "We figured on havin' the fastest tank in the division. What we got was plenty of skinned knuckles. I found out you can't soup up a tank."

58. After receiving disciplinary action due to going AWOL in the Marines and winding up in a civilian jail, Steve was assigned to a work detail in the engine room of a ship. His primary responsibility was cleaning and renovating it, and it was further life experience that he could use later on, such as in the movie *The Sand Pebbles*.

59. Part of Steve's job while in the brig was removing ripped asbestos liner from the pipes and ceilings. He recalled that the air was so thick with asbestos particles that he could hardly breathe. Experts later pointed to this experience as a major cause of his death from mesothelioma.

60. A love of automobiles ran through the Thomson family long before Steve McQueen came to be. His grandmother, Lillian, was one of the few women of the day to not only drive a car, but own her own car! This was especially uncommon in the rural area in which they lived, where roads were barely glorified horse trails and most people couldn't afford a car. Lillian drove her Ford to her work as a stenographer and typewriter.

61. Uncle Claude's stepdaughter, Jackie, began dating Huston Gigger after he got out of the Navy following World War II. When Huston came to the farm to take Jackie out, a young Steve complained that he wanted to go too, and certainly to the young couple's dismay, Eva, Claude's wife, made them take Steve with them. They quickly devised a way of keeping Steve out of their business by sharing a bottle of wine with him and putting him in the trunk of the car once he passed out. They'd check on him every so often, but he'd be safely fast asleep in the trunk. When it came time to head home, the booze had worn off and Claude and Eva were none the wiser.

62. Steve may have been well known for his off-road racing Triumph motorcycles, but he also owned a 1938 5T Speed Twin. The 500-cc, 355-pound machine was one of the sportiest and most attractive motorcycles in its day, a fact not lost on the actor when he purchased the bike in the early 1970s.

63. Perhaps most notable about the Speed Twin is that it was beautifully restored by famed racer, stuntman, and Triumph dealer Bud Ekins at McQueen's request. In addition, it is believed, but has not been proven, that the intricate pinstriping on the bike was done by the legendary Von Dutch. Recognizing the motorcycle as not only a monument in itself but also a machine with historically significant provenance, it was purchased at a Bonhams auction in 2019 for $175,000!

64. Even a bike as rare and beautiful as his 1927 Indian Big Chief could not escape McQueen's desire to make engines run better and faster. While undergoing a complete restoration in the late 1970s by personal mechanic Sammy Pierce, McQueen requested that his Big Chief be upgraded with racing cams, a later-model Linkert carburetor, wasted spark ignition system, and a later-model headlight. A few additional odds and ends received a chrome treatment.

65. Pierce hid a toggle switch under the tool box as a security measure. Only someone who knows to engage the hidden switch was able to actually start the bike. Steve's Big Chief was originally sold at the 1984 estate auction and most recently at Bonhams in 2006 for $42,120.

66. One day, Steve and his Marine tank crew discovered that the vehicle's hot exhaust pipe could be used to heat up a can of pork and beans. At the time, they were on a cold-weather training exercise in Labrador, Canada, where everyone was simply given K-rations, which were eaten cold and became boring rather quickly. McQueen's crew noticed a case of canned pork and beans in their inventory, which must have seemed like a fancy gourmet meal at the time! One Marine held a can over the exhaust pipe while Steve kept the engine RPM up and another Marine kept watch for officers or others who might not be sympathetic to their cause. After becoming comfortable with the process, they eventually let a can heat up for too long, at which point it exploded and covered the entire area with pork and beans, including several other tanks and the unit's gear.

67. McQueen's fascination with vehicles and his calling to find trades that involved engines continued after his time in the Marine Corps. Following his honorable discharge from the Corps, he worked as a cab driver in Washington, D.C., before saving enough money to get himself back to New York City.

68. Steve first got hooked on motor vehicles while living with his Uncle Claude in Slater, Missouri, where he grew up working with tractors, and his uncle drove a Jeep. It was while riding in that open-top Jeep that he fell in love with motoring. In his words to author Michael Munn, "Feeling the wind in my hair and on my face was like the most free feeling I ever had. And the faster we went, the better it was. That feeling of freedom and the feeling that wherever you were going, you were leaving behind something. I've always loved that leaving something behind."

RACING

69. On Steve's fourth birthday, his uncle Claude bought him a red tricycle to help him burn off his extra energy. Soon after, he began racing the other kids in the neighborhood on it. "There was a dirt bluff behind the farm, and I'd challenge the other kids in the area," he said. "We raced for gumdrops. I usually reached the top first. Got some skinned knees, but I sure won a lot of gumdrops!"

70. While working in the traveling carnival at age 13, young Steve's favorite pastime was walking away from his job to watch the car races put on by the carnival. "Man, you should've seen those smashers get knocked dingy on the track," he commented later.

Chapter 2
1950–1955

PERSONAL LIFE

71. When studying to be an actor in New York, McQueen used the Stanislavski system developed by Russian theater practitioner Konstantin Stanislavski. The principle stated that an actor's training and preparation should go beyond simply line memorization and dramatics. An actor should actually experience the role that he or she is to play beforehand, so as to make actions and reactions more natural.

72. In his young acting days, McQueen read an article in a celebrity magazine about an actor who commented that he often had a difficult time deciding which of his cars to take to work on a particular day. As a car lover himself, Steve got mad reading the article. Later, once he could afford any car he wanted, in multitude, he commented that he doesn't "get sore at the stories about all the automobiles the stars own and the choices they have to make."

73. In his early days as an aspiring actor, while he still needed women to pay for his meals, Steve befriended a cook at a popular Greenwich Village spot called Louis' Tavern. The cook's name was Sal, and Steve made the deal with him that if Sal would feed him, Steve would pay him back once he landed paying acting jobs. True to his word, Sal fed Steve when he was hungry, and Steve payed him back in full whenever he got work.

74. McQueen had his first real experience with children when he occasionally babysat for one of The Neighborhood Playhouse faculty's baby daughter. It must have been an incredible experience for him to witness first-hand what a traditional family was like. This may have been a major factor in being considered a great parent once he had children.

75. In late 1954, McQueen and fellow actor Richard Martin left New York in search of work in Los Angeles. The only offer they received while there was to sail on magician John Calvert's yacht for a two-year tour. Although they'd be paid for the time, neither was willing to make the two-year sacrifice.

76. About the only thing that Steve and Richard did accomplish on their mission to Las Angeles was earning the notoriety of being kicked out of the famous hotel Chateau Marmont for skinny-dipping with a couple of actresses. This story spread throughout the acting community back in New York, and when they returned, the job offers began to roll in.

77. While on the set of *Two Fingers of Pride,* Steve had affairs with two female castmates: Peggy Feury and Olga Bellin. Each filled a different void that he needed in his life. His relationship with Feury was largely based on attraction while Bellin provided more on the emotional support side of things.

78. While living in The Village as a carefree, rebellious youth on a motorcycle, Steve's nickname in the neighborhood was "Bandido." In her memoir, wife Niele recalls being referred to as "Bandido's Girl" when they first started dating.

79. Critical and audience reviews of his performances never seemed to bother Steve while he was doing stage work, who understood that he was still a student actor. The one reviewer who did intimidate and frighten him was his very own teacher, Lee Strasberg!

80. Steve disliked classes and performing skits because he felt he got more out of live performances for patrons. Of being reviewed by Strasberg in class, Steve once said, "I would rather take my chances with the paying public." By his reasoning, at least he was getting paid!

MOVIE FACTS

81. When the Broadway production of *Time Out For Ginger* moved to Chicago in 1954, producers cast Steve as Eddie Davis. McQueen starred alongside several of the original cast members, including Melvyn Douglas, Nancy Malone, and Philip Loeb. The play focused on a girl, Ginger, who wanted to try out for her school's football team and the blowback that affected her supportive father. Steve would have been fired outright from the production if not for his agent, Peter Witt, stepping in and convincing Douglas and director Shepard Traube to let him resign. Getting fired from his first paying job would have had damning effects on his career.

82. McQueen's first known performance was in the play *Molly Picon*, which was put on by a Jewish company in New York in 1952. His one line in the play was: "Allez iz forloren," which is Yiddish for "All is lost." This role earned him $40 a week. McQueen said that he got the part thanks to his roommate's sister who was an actress and talked the producers into hiring him. He was fired after four performances, which he jokingly blamed on his "lousy Yiddish."

83. In the summer of 1952, McQueen dusted himself off and got back on the stage, this time at the Country Playhouse in East Rochester, New York, for the week-long production of *Peg O' My Heart*. The play required him to use an English accent; however, he was so nervous that he forgot some of his lines on the show's opening night.

84. A cast mate approached him after the show and said, "I want you to know that your performance was just embarrassing." McQueen recalled feeling like the wind was taken out of his sails. After that, he contemplated getting out of acting altogether.

85. Steve's first on-screen performance was in a 1952 TV short called *Family Affair*. The 27-minute film was originally intended for AT&T employees and select public groups to show the necessity of having multiple phones in a modern household. McQueen, credited as Stephen McQueen, plays a goofy sailor named Freddy. While on leave, he plans to propose to his girlfriend, but in order to connect with her he must use the household's additional phone. McQueen has four scenes, in all of which he wears a Navy uniform.

86. McQueen's second on-screen performance came in the form of an uncredited extra in the 1953 film *Girl On The Run*. The film is a murder mystery in which police investigate a murder in a burlesque theater. Although he has no lines, he can be spotted in the background in two scenes. The one-hour and four-minute film was his first involvement in a feature production.

87. Steve's credited TV debut came in the 1955 Goodyear Playhouse production of *The Chivington Raid.* The one-hour live to TV broadcast was based on the true story behind the 1864 Sand Creek Massacre. Colonel Chivington led his 675-man Colorado Volunteer Cavalry in an attack in Cheyenne and Arapaho territory to kill an estimated 70 to 163 men, women, and children as revenge for the suspected killing of two white men.

88. In the summer of 1955, the play *Two Fingers of Pride* was presented at the Ogunquit Playhouse in Maine with the intention of moving to Broadway. Steve was the only unproven actor among a well-known cast, and he played the second lead of Nino alongside Garry Merrill, who played the lead. The play was about corruption on the New York City docks, a dark theme that McQueen could play well. The writer, Jim Longhi, said of his performance, "This original, primitive, self-taught kid gets up onstage every night with these terrific pros and wins the race."

89. Upon his discharge from the service in April 1950, Steve headed back to Myrtle Beach to rejoin his former flame Sue Ann. She had numerous well-connected, wealthy friends and the pair often attended fancy dinner and dance parties. It was a world he had never known, and by all accounts he enjoyed it, if only because he knew every next meal was coming and he'd have plenty of time to lounge around.

90. Sue Ann's wealthy father approached Steve one day with a promising job offer and a life free from want if he would marry Sue Ann. Steve was so shocked that he left town immediately and never saw Sue Ann again. Bad for Sue Ann, good for Steve McQueen fans.

91. After leaving Myrtle Beach, McQueen worked his way back to New York City where his mother arranged for him to rent a room for $19 a month. His roommate was photographer and playwright Gene Lesser who went on to write several successful plays and films.

92. In typical cool, casual Steve McQueen style, he often credits his early interest in acting to a part-time actress he dated named Donna Barton, who was also a dancer at the Copacabana nightclub. She paid for the meal on their first date, and Steve moved in to her apartment the next day. She was taking classes at The Neighborhood Playhouse at the time and suggested that Steve should try it.

93. In all likelihood, Steve's mother's boyfriend Viktor Lukens played an even bigger role in his introduction to acting. Viktor was the one who introduced him to Sanford Meisner, who was on the faculty of The Neighborhood Playhouse.

94. Until he applied to The Neighborhood Playhouse on June 25, 1951, McQueen was still introducing himself as Steve Berri. Viktor Lukens was the one who told him to go by Steve McQueen, as he considered it to be a great name for an actor.

95. Further evidence that Viktor Lukens was the primary driving force behind McQueen's acting career was that Steve listed Lukens' 19 Barrow Street address on his application in addition to listing him as a professional reference. Lukens also paid for Steve's application fee and the first year of classes.

96. McQueen officially started acting school at The Neighborhood Playhouse in August 1951. Among the required list of items was a leotard and a set of ballet slippers. That doesn't exactly paint an image of the Steve McQueen we know, and according to his old instructor, Steve often complained about the attire. That is until she grabbed him by the groin and lifted him off the floor to teach him how to stand up straight.

97. In an informal poll conducted by fellow actors, Steve McQueen placed dead last as to who would be most likely to succeed.

98. Although not technically a paid production, McQueen's first real play was The Neighborhood Playhouse's year-end showcase entitled *Truckline Café*, which was originally a Marlon Brando production. Naturally, Steve played the Brando role and did so to perfection.

99. His performance was noticed by agent Peter Witt, who approached Steve after the show about becoming his agent. Steve later accepted the offer, making Peter Witt his first agent of record.

100. One of Steve's co-actors on stage in the *Truckline Café* production was Al Hedison. After the performance, Steve told him, "Al, you and I are going to be stars!" About seven years later, the two of them attained stardom when Steve took the lead in *The Blob* and Hedison took the lead in *The Fly*. Marquees displayed both titles along with the names of the actors. Steve was right again!

101. McQueen began his second attempt at drama school with a low-key operation run by Herbert Berghof and Uta Hagen. The $3 daily fee was simply collected by one of the students, although oftentimes students who couldn't afford the fee were allowed in anyway. The school focused on stage acting and heavy drama rather than big-screen cinema acting. Steve struggled in this setting, and with his instructors, who didn't find his antics or attitude very amusing.

102. Until his death in 1954, Steve considered James Dean his biggest competition when it came to scoring parts. They were similarly method actors with a one-year age difference and they were born 80 miles apart. They even dated the same woman at one point! Oftentimes, Steve stared at the mirror trying to emulate James Dean or Marlon Brando in an attempt to nail down their personas. Steve considered Dean's death an opportunity to take some of his roles.

103. After his "resignation" from *Time Out For Ginger*, Steve had a tough time landing paying jobs. To stay in the entertainment industry, and make some rent money, he posed for popular pulp magazines such as *Crime Detective* and *Homicide Detective*. Even though he was just about on the bottom of the acting business, he still insisted on choosing his own photographer for the shoots: Roy Schatt, who had previously done well-known pop-culture shoots with James Dean and Marilyn Monroe.

104. When Steve earned his part in *Two Fingers of Pride*, he was unable to produce an Actor's Equity Card, which is required for working actors. The producer and director were shocked upon hearing this news, and even more shocked when Steve asked for the money so that he could go get one. They each pitched in $17.50 to the worthy cause, after which Steve informed them that he also needed an agent, which is another requirement for getting an Actor's Equity Card. He even asked them to find him one. Because an agent represents the actor's interests against the executives, the request was a peculiar one, but necessary to continue production of the show.

105. MCA agent John Foreman agreed to represent Steve McQueen so he could get his card and continue his role in the play. Afterward, Foreman dropped him as a client. Whoops!

106. McQueen's role in *Two Fingers of Pride* was that of an Italian longshoreman working on the docks of New York City. To get a proper feel for the part, an arrangement was made to put Steve to work on the Mafia-run docks in the rough Red Hook neighborhood of Brooklyn. He stacked wooden crates for a few weeks, and at one point was worried that the crew had forgotten he was only an actor because they had been working him so hard. He asked the play's producer to call his contact who orchestrated the experience and confirm that the other workers knew that Steve was an actor studying for a role.

107. *Two Fingers of Pride* was shut down after only a week, but to Steve, it was a huge success. Although the play received harsh criticism, McQueen's performance was regarded as "truly excellent" by *The Village Voice*. Producer Jack Garfein was also impressed with his work, and he continued as a mentor to Steve, helping him to harness his talent and navigate a difficult industry.

108. In 1955, McQueen tried out for and successfully gained entry into Lee Strasberg's The Actor's Studio. In his final audition, and with Jack Garfein there for support, Steve delivered an incredible performance and was accepted on his first attempt, a rare feat. Only he and actor Martin Landau were accepted into The Actor's Studio that year out of the 2,000 actors who applied.

109. Although any direct evidence has yet to come to light, it's believed that a young Steve McQueen first appeared on camera in some Viktor Lukens films as early as 1951. Steve's application to acting school not only listed Lukens as his stepfather, but cites previous acting experience in his films.

110. At one point early in his acting career, McQueen began following James Dean around New York City. He took notes and copied his every move, trying to match and understand that special factor that made James Dean a Hollywood star. Steve's friends even called him "the shadow," because it was so obvious what he was doing. Dean knew what McQueen was up to, but never said anything, perhaps enjoying someone looking up to him like that.

111. Even though Steve played the second lead in the play *Two Fingers of Pride*, and excelled in the role according to critics, his name wasn't listed on advertising posters or billboards outside the theater. All the other actors in the play had more experience, and were represented by their own agents fighting for them. Although Steve had an agent, he was of little importance and therefore had nobody looking out for his best interests.

112. Rather than wait in the cold as an extra on *Somebody Up There Likes Me*, Steve decided to rest in a parked limo where he ended up falling asleep. It turned out to be Pier Angeli's limo, and her husband, Vic Damone, was irate to find the young man sleeping in it. Steve was briskly kicked back out into the cold.

113. Steve McQueen and his Actor's Studio partner, Peggy Feury, chose a scene to perform in which a catholic nun falls in love with one of her students and leaves the convent. To prepare their characters, Feury, dressed as a nun, and McQueen strolled the streets of New York, often taking breaks to show their affection for one another. According to Peggy Feury, Steve was in a panic throughout the walk thanks to his strong catholic upbringing. He thought that somebody, or somebody up there, would forcibly put a stop to their portrayal.

114. When McQueen and Feury finally performed the scene in front of Lee Strasberg, a nervous Steve couldn't take it anymore when Feury slipped out of her habit to reveal sexy lace lingerie underneath. He burst into tears at the sight and couldn't continue the scene.

115. While struggling to find work as an actor in New York City in the early 1950s, Steve, and many other actors and actresses, posed for detective and crime magazines. Photographers proved to be a wonderful resource for unemployed actors, as the work guaranteed a couple of bucks and could be done only when needed.

116. Steve's future wife, Neile, posed for the same kinds of magazines when she was a young up-and-comer. Chances are they crossed paths at some point or another before actually meeting.

117. Although most critics of *A Hatful of Rain* disliked Steve's performance, *Variety* made the important distinction that it was a very difficult role for anyone to play and that McQueen did fine for his Broadway debut. In her memoir, Neile mentions that his youth, compared to on-stage wife Vivian Blaine, hurt the performance since it didn't appear real for him to be with the more mature actress.

MOVIE AUTOMOBILE FACTS

118. Although *Time Out For Ginger* didn't feature any cars or motorcycles, the playbill relayed McQueen's love of riding and racing motorcycles. It reads, "Steve McQueen (Eddie Davis) was born in Los Angeles and when he is not acting he races motorcycles. He prefers the stage, which he considers only a little less hazardous. When questioned he said, 'Well, motorcycles may break your bones, but the theatre can break your heart.'"

119. Steve McQueen worked as a motorcycle mechanic while he attended acting school and was beginning his career. James Dean was out riding his motorcycle one day when it started acting up, so he limped it to the nearest shop in the area, which just happened to be where Steve was working that day. At the time, he was still under the belief that James Dean was taking all the roles that were otherwise meant for him. Although Dean likely had no idea who the young man working on his motorcycle was, Steve definitely knew who James Dean was!

120. While Steve was on tour in Chicago with the *Time Out For Ginger* production, he helped co-star Nancy Malone buy her first car. Since he had recently purchased an MG, he suggested that she do the same. Malone paid $2,500 cash for a brand-new 1953 MG at the Arnolt dealership in Chicago. Steve told her he would give her driving lessons, which he unfortunately wasn't able to do because he left the production shortly thereafter.

121. McQueen reported for duty at the Ogunquit Playhouse in Maine for *Two Fingers of Pride* on his motorcycle, naturally. He rode 300 miles through a rainstorm with his girlfriend on the back.

122. The yellow 1951 Chevrolet Styline Deluxe convertible driven by Ralph "Papa" Thorsen in *The Hunter* was purchased by McQueen after filming. Although it never took on quite the persona and following as the *Bullitt* Mustang, the Chevy was driven by McQueen at length throughout the film, and the fact that it was in his collection at his death makes it an important car. The vehicle remained in the limelight through the years and was even featured on two episodes of the popular TV series *Pawn Stars*. It was purchased at Barrett-Jackson's 2018 Scottsdale auction for $126,500.

AUTOMOBILE COLLECTION

123. McQueen bought his first sports car, a red 1948 TC-MG, in 1954 while on tour in Columbus, Ohio, with *Time Out For Ginger*. Although he wasn't earning much from the play, the crew played poker every night and he was the usual winner. The MG cost $750, so McQueen put $450 down and sent the seller money every week until it was paid off.

124. He had the car delivered to Chicago, where the play was based, and then took it back to New York with him after he was fired. "I thought I was kind of Jack L. Warner's son, you know," he said of the MG. "I didn't have any dough and lived in a cold-water flat, but I had that MG parked outside." He eventually sold it to pay the rent.

125. While living in Greenwich Village, Steve became somewhat of a local character by riding his motorcycle around shirtless, much to the joy of the girls in the area. Perhaps it was this display that caught the affection of actress Susan Oliver, whom Steve dated in 1950. She recalled riding around the Village on his motorcycle, although eventually grew tired of loaning him money for gas and food.

126. One of Steve's friends in his early acting days in Greenwich Village was fellow actor Richard Martin who owned an MG sports car. One day he let Steve drive it, which certainly made a young, broke Steve McQueen a happy man. He went on to buy his own MG a few years later, possibly because of this first experience in the British lightweight.

127. McQueen once rode his motorcycle into Louis' Tavern, his favorite hangout spot. Because the bar was below the sidewalk, he rode down the stairs and right into the barroom. You can assume he wasn't doing this slowly, since he crashed through a glass door once inside and landed on the floor. At the time, there just happened to be a couple of wiseguys inside, who removed Steve and his motorcycle from the bar.

128. Although McQueen rode a motorcycle as his only form of transportation, he didn't have a license! This wasn't a problem until his girlfriend, Janet Conway, hit her head into the back of his head after he hit a pothole. She had a serious cut over her left eye and they had to go to the emergency room. They couldn't tell the doctor that the accident had occurred on a motorcycle, so she fibbed and said that she had fallen so that Steve wouldn't get in trouble.

129. Steve purchased his first motorcycle in 1950, "a mean old" 1946 Indian Chief with sidecar.

130. Right after buying it he rode over to show it off to a girl he was dating at the time. Naturally, he was proud of his first major purchase. She told him, "You don't expect me to ride around with you on that?" He got her to try it, but she hated the bumpy sidecar and told him, "Either the bike goes or I go!" In his own words: "The girl went, but the bike stayed." His 1946 Chief sold at auction in 2013 for $143,750.

131. Steve once handed down an old, beat-up motorcycle helmet to fellow actor George Peppard who had just started riding. The helmet had deep gouges in it from when Steve had slid on a set of railroad tracks and crashed into someone's front porch one night. The helmet had seen much use and abuse; it obviously was worn by a motorcyclist who had seen and done a thing or two. The novice Peppard could throw a leg over the old, leaky BSA, and even though he was still learning to ride, McQueen's helmet made him look as hardened of a biker as anyone.

132. Broadway's famed Lyceum Theater used to have a little, easily-accessible yard behind it where NYPD mounted police could leave their horses and go on break. This spot also provided a place where Steve and fellow actor Ed Julien could park their motorcycles while working on *A Hatful of Rain*. The Lyceum Theater still stands strong as one of Broadway's oldest theaters; however, access to the back alley by motorcycle is now prohibited.

133. The 1952 Chevrolet 3800 pickup truck that eventually took Steve McQueen on his final ride was custom-built by Harold Van Hoosen in Yreka, California, in October 1952. The camper truck, known as "Dust Tite," was made of galvanized metal and aluminum and was originally meant as a track rig for a motorsports enthusiast. The heavy-duty platform on the top was strong enough for people to stand on to get a great vantage point of a motorcycle or car race.

134. Steve was out driving his MG convertible one day in New York City when he drove it right into an excavation hole on Sixth Avenue! He did so much damage to the fickle little British sports car that he got rid of it rather than fix it. He decided that two-wheeled transportation was the right way to go for the city and purchased a BSA motorcycle to replace the car.

135. When Steve moved in with then-girlfriend Neile, he kept his BSA motorcycle at the garage across the street from her apartment. In that same garage lived a new Bugatti. After making the daily trek past one of the most beautiful cars ever to grace the Earth, the temptation became too great and Steve decided that he needed to borrow the French sports car to see what it was all about. He grabbed the keys while the attendant wasn't looking and quickly pulled it out of the garage. He called Neile from a payphone around the corner and told her to come down. As soon as she saw the expensive car she knew that he had stolen it, or as he corrected her "borrowed" it from an owner who would never find out. They took a ride around Central Park and then drove it right back to the garage where Steve handed the keys to the stupefied parking attendant.

136. As soon as Neile's boss, George Abbot, found out that she was dating a guy with a motorcycle and that she was actually riding on the back of it, he requested that she stop. Or as she puts it, Abbot clarified specifically not to ride on the back of Steve McQueen's motorcycle. She had just begun starring in the Broadway play *Kismet*, and if the leading lady were to get hurt and not be able to dance, it would wreak major havoc on the production. As you may be able to guess, she silently denied Mr. Abbot's request and continued riding with Steve.

137. Steve McQueen is known for owning and driving some pretty whacky automobiles over the years, but can you imagine him driving a hearse? Before he purchased the red MG in 1952, he drove a hearse that he ended up crashing in New York City's Columbus Circle. He flipped the car upside down and totaled it, but he was able to walk away unhurt.

RACING

138. Not only did Viktor Lukens play a huge role in getting Steve interested in acting, he is also responsible for getting him interested in racing. A serious racer himself, through his team Racemasters, Lukens competed in the 24 Heures du Mans in 1955 and the 12 Hours of Sebring in 1957.

139. Most of the racing Steve did in his early days in New York City was of the stoplight-to-stoplight variety. His 1946 Indian flathead sported 80 inches of American power and since it was equipped with a sidecar, likely also had lower gears to make the heavy outfit less noticeable. With the sidecar removed, however, the big Indian became quite the challenger on short straightaways.

140. What's believed to be McQueen's second motorcycle, a Harley-Davidson K model, which was produced from 1952 to 1956, was one of the best racing bikes of the day. The lightweight motorcycle was one of the first to utilize hand-clutching and foot-shifting and had a quick-revving unit powertrain that made it the star of racetracks around the country. It remained the star of Harley-Davidson's race team until the dominating XR750 was introduced in 1970. Virtually nothing is known about the specific K that McQueen owned other than he was likely very difficult to beat on the track, strip, or street.

141. He must have owned it at least in early 1952 because people report him riding it at that time. He bought it with money from his truck driving wages and immediately began hopping up the engine.

142. Steve nearly stuffed his new K-model racebike into the back of a Lincoln while drag racing on the West Side Highway in New York City. He was leading his opponent when he pulled off onto the planned off-ramp at about 100 mph, and looked behind him to see that the other rider had missed the exit. When Steve turned his head around, traffic had come to a standstill at the bottom of the off-ramp. He slammed on his brakes and skidded right up to the back of a Lincoln, saying that he even tapped the bumper. This incident must have occurred higher up on the West Side Highway, near Harlem, where there are actual on- and off-ramps.

143. In addition to the street racing in Manhattan, McQueen also took his K-model Harley to Long Island City, in Queens, to compete in cycle runs held there every weekend. The prize money averaged about $50 a race and Steve won a couple of races each weekend. With that money, and whatever he could win that week playing Poker, he made enough to quit his truck driving job.

Chapter 3
1956–1960

PERSONAL LIFE

144. Steve McQueen first met Neile Adams in May 1956 at Jim Downey's Steakhouse in New York City. After a second meeting at the restaurant, he stopped by her show on Broadway and then asked her out. Rather than the typical date she was expecting, Steve showed up on his motorcycle to take her to Greenwich Village. Because she was wearing a dress, Neile rode sidesaddle as Steve sped along.

145. He later pawned the watch that his uncle had given him to buy an airline ticket to Los Angeles to ask Neile to marry him. The pawnbroker told him, "They don't make watches like this anymore," to which Steve responded, "They don't make men like the man who gave it to me."

146. Steve proposed to Neile Adams in October 1956, putting a $25 down payment on the ring and having Neile pay off the balance over the next two years. Neile was as surprised as she was confused, since she had left for California and Steve had refused to come along just a few weeks earlier.

147. Steve and Neile were married on November 2, 1956, at a Lutheran church in San Clemente, California. The original plan was to drive to Mission San Juan Capistrano in a rented Ford Thunderbird. When Steve stopped to call the mission on the way, the nun informed him that they only marry members of their parish.

148. After that, they were pulled over for speeding at 11:30 p.m. in San Clemente. Steve told the state troopers that he and Neile had to get married that weekend, so the troopers called the local pastor who married them that night. The state troopers acted as witnesses for the ceremony.

149. Steve's uncle Claude, who helped raise him as a boy, died on November 28, 1957. Although Steve didn't attend the funeral, he was lucky enough to spend some time with his uncle earlier that year when he took Neile to Slater, Missouri. Neile gained some important insight into Steve's upbringing, and had her one opportunity to meet Uncle Claude. After that trip in January 1957, Steve never returned to Slater again.

150. After a particularly bad fight between Steve and Neile, and the subsequent makeup, Neile gave Steve a St. Christopher medal. She had it inscribed "To part is to die a little." He rarely took it off over the years and it even made appearances in several films. He later commented about the gift, "She knew I felt like a gigolo, and she thought this might help. He only stopped wearing it after they divorced. *Le Mans* was one of the final movies in which the medal made an appearance.

151. Steve always dreamed of someday finding his father, William, who had abandoned him so early on. He finally tracked him down in February 1959. With Neile by his side, they went to his apartment in Long Beach, California, just a short drive away from where they lived. They were greeted by the landlady, who informed them that William had passed away three months earlier on November 11. She told Steve that for the last few months of his life, he spent every Saturday night in front of the television watching *Wanted Dead or Alive*, and wondering out loud if that was his son on the screen.

152. The only things Steve's father left him was a picture of himself and a Zippo lighter engraved "T.McQ." Steve told his friend Bud Ekins that he had tossed the lighter into some weeds after receiving it, but in truth, he kept it. No one knew that he had retained the only link he had to his father until he died, and his daughter, Terry, discovered it in his jewelry box. Of course, the T on the lighter stood for Terrence, so it's fitting that William's granddaughter, Terry, was the one to find it after so much time had passed.

153. Steve and Neile had their first child, a girl, on June 5, 1959. Terry Leslie McQueen was named after her father, whose real name was Terrence Steven McQueen, and by default her grandfather, William Terrence McQueen. Although Steve quickly fell in love with his newborn daughter, he didn't hold back in admitting that he had really wanted a boy. "I was a little hacked when the old lady bore me a daughter, but this kid is really gonna be a gas," he said. "I wanted a boy, but now I want another girl."

154. After he decided that he wanted another girl, the universe blessed Steve and Neile with a son on December 28, 1960, whom they named Chadwick Steven McQueen. According to Neile, "When the children were little, when they were first born, he really couldn't relate to them yet. He just sort of dissed them until they were able to become little persons. As soon as their personalities started evolving, then Steve could relate to them as children. He was wonderful with the children and he was wonderful with children in general because he saw the world through the eyes of a child. Consequently, it was always playtime when they were together."

155. In 1960, with his payday from *The Magnificent Seven*, Steve and Neile purchased a home at 2419 Solar Drive for $60,000. The Hollywood Hills estate overlooks downtown Los Angeles, and is situated near popular Runyon Canyon Park. With the move also came a name-change of McQueen's production company to Solar Productions from Scuderia Condor Enterprises. His company remained with this name from then on.

156. Before the filming of *Wanted Dead or Alive*, Steve spent many hours over the course of a few weeks practicing with firearms to develop his draw. However, because the gun used in the show was an actual, working firearm, he had to get a special permit to remove it from the studio.

157. It was extremely important to Steve that he was able to draw and handle the gun properly, just as his character, Josh Randall, would have. At the time, he claimed to be the fourth fastest gunman in California. He said, "I can put a book of matches on the back of my hand, drop it from waist level, draw, and fire two shots into it before it hits the ground."

158. Steve and Neile were invited to participate in Bob Hope's annual Christmas show entertaining soldiers stationed in Alaska. Although filmed primarily in Colorado, Steve still had to request leave from the filming of *Wanted* to be on the show. CBS encouraged him to do the show, even though it would be stuck paying even more overtime for the crew of *Wanted*. Steve's appearance not only brought even more public attention to his television show, but promoted *Never So Few*, which opened just a few weeks later. His successful appearance led to numerous other guest spots to promote his projects.

159. McQueen and co-star Yul Brynner may have bumped some serious heads while filming *The Magnificent Seven*, but that didn't stop Dorris and Yul Brynner from sending the McQueen family a telegram on New Year's Eve that read, "Happy New Year happy new baby."

160. The first strike in Screen Actors Guild history began on March 7, 1960, and nearly destroyed the possibility of making *The Magnificent Seven*. Everyone in Hollywood was under a mad rush to have contracts signed and projects initiated before that date to avoid being caught up in the strike. This worked out to McQueen's benefit on *Wanted,* where he was contractually given permission to make *The Magnificent Seven* in addition to a doubled salary.

161. The Screen Actors Guild strike almost lost *The Magnificent Seven*, the movie Steve had fought so hard for, since director John Sturges didn't complete casting until the day before production began and a week before the strike began.

162. Because .44-40-caliber rounds didn't look that big sitting in Randall's cartridge belt, .45-70-caliber rounds were used for a more striking visual effect. Since the large firearm required its own unique draw style, Steve turned to actor/singer Sammy Davis, Jr., whom he knew from his time in New York. Davis was a serious Old West pistol enthusiast and reportedly practiced his draw technique for hours a day. He helped McQueen develop Josh Randall's characteristic draw.

163. Folks all over the country tuned in to watch CBS's *Wanted Dead or Alive* to see Steve McQueen as bounty hunter Josh Randall. Among them was a five-year-old girl named Barbara Minty who sneaked out of bed on Saturday nights to secretly watch without her grandparents' knowledge. About 20 years later, Barbara and Steve met, fell in love, and married. When they actually did meet, McQueen was fresh off his portrayal of Dr. Thomas Stockman in *An Enemy of the People* and she didn't realize until well after the meeting that Josh Randall and Steve McQueen were the same person!

164. It's no shock that Steve used trickery to convince store owners that he was returning an item for cash while he was scrounging his way around New York City in his teens and early 20s. But can you imagine that he pulled the same trick on the night of his daughter's birth in 1959. He had already hit it big financially with *Wanted*, but he never gave up the habit of not carrying any cash. Needing something to toast his first-born's birth, he walked into a wine store, picked up a bottle, and simply asked if he could exchange it for another one. The clerk obliged the TV star's request and Steve walked out with a free bottle of wine!

165. Even though Steve McQueen's relationship with his mother was strained at best, Neile's introduction into their lives helped ease the tension and provide them both with an outlet of communication. Steve always kept his mother at arm's length, but with her fondness for Neile it's no surprise that Steve told her about his plan to propose before anybody else.

166. Ever since he was a boy growing up on Uncle Claude's farm, Steve McQueen loved animals and was always determined to someday have a dog of his own. On his 27th birthday he made that dream a reality when he stopped in a pet store and purchased a German Shepard puppy named Thor. It was his first dog and since they were all living in a tiny New York City apartment at the time, Steve, Neile, and Thor all slept on the floor together. After Thor, Steve always had a dog by his side.

167. Steve had hearing problems stemming from a double mastoidectomy when he was a young boy and a scuba diving accident when he was 20 years old. He often raised his hand to his ear to show that he was hard of hearing.

168. However, being a street-smart guy, he eventually learned that the signal of cupping his ear, and public knowledge of his hearing issues, could be used to his advantage. If a journalist asked a question he wasn't prepared for, he could simply cup his hand around his ear and think about a response as the journalist repeated himself. He would also use the motion if he were bored in a conversation in the hope that the other person would grow weary of repeating themselves and give up the line of conversation. Chalk this one up as another one of Steve's signature tricks!

169. When McQueen first started as Josh Randall on *Wanted Dead or Alive*, he had access to his first press agent who's responsibility was promoting the show and in turn, him. In addition to the show's publicist, Steve also hired his own publicist for the purpose of separating him from the show. *Wanted*'s publicist wanted to promote Steve McQueen as Josh Randall, but Steve's own publicist worked to separate him from Josh Randall and show him as a multifaceted actor. The investment in building his brand paid off as Steve's reputation continued to grow.

170. In 1960, after shooting *Never So Few*, Steve returned to Louis' Tavern to see Sal. He brought Frank Sinatra and Peter Lawford with him, surely making all those free meals worth the effort and giving his old friend a lifelong memory.

MOVIE FACTS

171. Steve McQueen made his Broadway debut in 1956 in *A Hatful of Rain*. His character, Johnny Pope, was originally written as being Latino, which McQueen was not. Because of his noticeably European features, stage manager Ed Julian nicknamed him "Cornflakes." Although his performance was good, the actresses who played his wife, Vivian Blain followed by Kim Hunter, looked much older than he did. Critics suggested that they appeared old enough to be his mother.

172. While working on *Wanted Dead or Alive,* McQueen filmed three television ads for Viceroy Cigarettes. The commercials took place on set, with McQueen in costume but playing himself. His commercial catchphrase was: "Viceroy is the cigarette with the thinking man's filter, and the smokin' man's taste." The commercials began airing in 1958.

173. Steve's first feature film was *Somebody Up There Likes Me,* which came out in 1956. The film is about the early life of boxer Rocky Graziano, played by Paul Newman, from his childhood until he won the World Middleweight Championship in 1947 at 28 years of age. McQueen's uncredited performance as Fidel was limited to only a short scene, of which his wife, Neile, thought he was terrible in the part. At least he was paid $19 a day for his work!

174 Interestingly, the lead role was originally meant for another famous gearhead, James Dean, but he was killed just weeks before filming was set to start.

175. McQueen's first credited feature film was *Never Love a Stranger,* which came out in 1958. He played the role of Martin Cabell, a Jewish district attorney, in a film where the other primary characters are also Jewish. His first credited film sure sounds a lot like his first role back in New York in 1952! The low-budget film was a flop, and Steve failed at playing the upstanding, good-guy gentleman.

176. In 1957, Steve acted in a two-part television series called *The Defender,* which was part of CBS's Studio One series. The first part aired on February 25 and the second part on March 4, both of which received critical appraise for several actors, including Steve. CBS Executive Herbert Brodkin even wrote Steve a letter on March 5 thanking him for his fine work on the program.

177. Thanks to his role on *The Defender*, Steve received his first bit of fan mail. Not only did he get his first letter, the CBS studio also fielded several calls from people saying they were "fans of Steve McQueen."

178. Steve McQueen, billed as "Steven" for the last time, earned the lead role in *The Blob* after impressing the directors with his work on *The Defender*. Unfortunately, at 27 years old, they thought he was too old to play a high school student. He ran into one of the directors in New York and convinced him that he could play the role after reading a few lines from the script.

179. From his very first day on set, Steve made his presence known by throwing firecrackers at the crew and riding his motorcycle around. He insisted that he needed a bigger dressing room than the other actors and oftentimes brought his dog to the set. Because the crew of *The Blob* was so religious, they held daily prayer meetings where they prayed for a variety of things on the movie to go well. Every meeting concluded with one final prayer for the day: "God save us from Steve McQueen!"

180. There's a popular rumor that McQueen was initially offered $2,500 or 10 percent of the profit for his work on *The Blob*. It makes for a funny story, but it's false. He was paid $3,000 for his work and the option to appear in the studio's two next films.

181. At the time, *The Blob* was made for only $130,000 and wasn't expected to do all that well. It ended up shocking everyone and went on to become a symbol of 1950s popular culture. That first year, *The Blob* brought in a $6 million profit and is estimated to have grossed more than $40 million over the years.

182. One of the first people outside of the production staff to see *The Blob* was Dick Powell, head of Four Star Studios, who asked to see a rough cut of the film. The purpose of his viewing was to look at Steve McQueen and potentially cast him in an upcoming television show. Jack Harris, even with all that the crew went through on set with McQueen, gave his recommendation. The show Powell went on to produce? *Wanted Dead or Alive.*

183. Steve fired his horse on his first day of work on *Wanted Dead or Alive.* He was initially supplied with an older horse that he claimed had to be put on roller skates so it could get around the sound stage.

184. He asked Dick Powell if he could pick out his own horse, saying, "We're going to be doing this series for a while; I'd kind of like a horse I got something with, you know?" He decided on a black one named Ringo who bucked him off during his first ride. Ringo bit all the other horses in his first week on set and destroyed several pieces of equipment.

185. McQueen also insisted on picking his own gun for his character of Josh Randall to use in *Wanted Dead or Alive.* The cut-down .44-40 Winchester Model 1892 rifle that he used was created by his friend, artist Von Dutch. Where a sawed-off shotgun is often referred to as a "hog's leg," Steve wanted his creation to instill fear without being "mean." The name "Mare's Leg" was chosen for the thigh-mounted rifle.

186. By the time filming on *Never So Few* had wrapped, Steve had so much practice handling firearms that he challenged the industry's best, Sammy Davis, Jr., to a draw-and-shoot contest. The prize was a nickel-plated memorial Colt .45, otherwise known as the Peacemaker, plus a few side bets Steve took that were all going for Davis. McQueen ended up beating Davis, taking the show gun and some cash, but most importantly, the respect.

187. Steve McQueen's method acting style meant that his characters and actions were based on some level of real-life experience or emotion. His character of Josh Randall in *Wanted Dead or Alive* was based on a cop he knew when he was a kid in New York. "There was no monkey business with him," he said. "When he said he'd shoot, he meant it. Well, I think of him, and pretty soon I'm Josh Randall."

188. The Federal Bureau of Investigation kept tabs on many Hollywood actors and businesspeople during J. Edgar Hoover's term as director. The FBI created its first dossier on Steve McQueen with the airing of *Wanted Dead or Alive*, giving it the classification of a "Gangster Glorification Movie." McQueen remained on the FBI's radar in this manner until his death.

189. In 1960, Steve and Neile starred in an episode of *Alfred Hitchcock Presents*, "Man from the South." The grisly tale features Steve as a gambler and Neile as a woman he meets in a bar and wants to leave town with, except they're both broke. He takes a strange bet with an older man that if he can light his lighter ten times in a row, he'll give him his new convertible. If he fails, the man gets to chop off his pinky finger. The episode was so macabre in fact, that CBS postponed the original January 1, 1960, air date to January 3 so it wasn't so close to the holiday season.

190. Steve and Dick Powell had made a verbal agreement that if a movie opportunity came along for Steve, every possible option would be exhausted to make the scheduling work. For someone like Steve, who grew bored easily and had a burning desire to be a film star, an arrangement like this was extremely important. It actually paid off after the first season of *Wanted*.

191. Originally, Sammy Davis, Jr., was cast for the role of Corporal Bill Ringa in *Never So Few* after Frank Sinatra went to bat for him. Regular casting of people of color in Hollywood was very uncommon at the time, and Sammy's $75,000 payday made a big splash in the industry. What also made a big splash was when Sammy criticized Sinatra's manners in a radio interview. Just like that, he was out, and a replacement was needed.

192. Director John Sturges' wife, Dorothy, was a fan of Steve McQueen on *Wanted Dead or Alive*, and thought his style would fit the role perfectly. Her husband agreed, and McQueen was cast with a $25,000 salary. An internal telegram announcing the switch to key people read, "Chicago replaced by Detroit."

193. Early in filming of *Never So Few*, Frank Sinatra snuck a firecracker into McQueen's belt loop while he was reading a script. The firecracker went off, sending Steve jumping backward and causing Sinatra to laugh. Never one to be outdone, Steve grabbed a nearby Tommy gun, loaded it with a magazine full of blanks, and fired right back at an unexpecting Sinatra, who jumped quite a few feet himself. He earned Sinatra's respect with that comeback, and throughout filming they played similar pranks on each other, such as tossing surprise firecrackers at each other or playing with the production's pyrotechnics equipment.

194. *Never So Few* was a critical disappointment considering the hype and star cast. This proved to be a blessing in disguise for McQueen, who delivered a stand-out performance and received numerous positive comments. Several reviews even suggested that he would go on to become a major star, although it's unlikely they guessed how quickly that would happen. Sinatra was also impressed with Steve's performance, and invited him to do more films together.

195. Although working with Frank Sinatra seemed like a huge opportunity at the time, and would have likely earned Steve a lot of money, it would have hurt his own star power. In addition to supporting Sinatra in two upcoming films, Steve McQueen would also have had to put on a nightclub act doing comedy impressions. Being a part of the famed Rat Pack would be a dream-come-true for many actors and singers, but it would also mean constantly playing second fiddle to someone else.

196. As part of McQueen's publicity duties for *Wanted Dead or Alive*, he had to visit state fairs, festivals, and rodeos to promote the show. His first event was at a rodeo in a small town in Texas. He had no idea what to do so he rode out on his horse and had his manager, Hilly Elkins, throw a coin for him to shoot with the Mare's Leg sawed-off rifle. After he fired, they quickly exited the arena, got in their car, and drove off. Neither had any idea as to whether or not Steve actually hit the coin.

197. Steve's antics on the set of *Wanted* are rumored to have led recovering alcoholic director George Blair to start drinking again. Oftentimes, during 15-minute breaks, he went for a ride on his motorcycle for 30 minutes, costing money and causing headaches. When Blair approached him about it, McQueen responded, "Hey, I'm enjoying my bike better than a little TV show!"

198. When the opportunity came up for Steve to play a role in a new western called *The Magnificent Seven* for $65,000, he once again turned to his *Wanted* contract and that little verbal agreement. This time, however, the shooting dates coincided and the studio refused to release Steve to film the movie. Manager Hilly Elkins knew that nothing could stop Steve from doing the film, so he gave him instructions on how to get out of the TV show. He told him to have an accident convincing enough to feign an injury, but not so bad that he would be seriously hurt.

199. Naturally, Steve McQueen pushed the limit and drove a rented Cadillac, with Neile in the car, into the side of a bank in Hartford, Connecticut. He returned to Los Angeles in a neck brace. The accident angered Four Star Studios, which right away assumed that it was done on purpose. However, it showed the lengths that McQueen was willing to go, so they agreed to let him do the movie before he actually got himself hurt or simply never returned to the set. Hilly Elkins also pushed for a pay raise to $150,000 a year, twice Steve's current salary, and got it.

200. Much of the onscreen tension in *The Magnificent Seven* is largely due to the offscreen tension between the actors while filming in Mexico. Yul Brynner and Horst Buchholz, the big names, were put up in beautiful private homes and were fully catered to. The rest were put up in a local motel called Posadas Jacarandas. Steve McQueen hung out with friend Charles Bronson, whom he had worked with on *Never So Few*, while Robert Vaughn and James Coburn stuck together.

201. While filming *The Magnificent Seven*, McQueen leaked information to the press about a supposed feud between him and Yul Brynner. It really wasn't so much a feud as McQueen trying to outdo his lead co-star while Brynner attempted to ignore him. The article infuriated Brynner as it positioned him and McQueen as equals, rather than star and supporting actor, as he saw it. He told McQueen, "I'm an established star, and I don't feud with supporting actors," after he told him to retract the story.

202. Even with a supposed feud going on between them, Steve still offered to help Yul Brynner with drawing his revolver. Rather than teach him a fancy move like what he did on screen, Steve taught him a rudimentary move that lacked any character. Once again, Steve McQueen was able to outshine the movie's "star" in the eyes of the viewers. Years later, after McQueen discovered he had mesothelioma, he made amends with Brynner by thanking him for not firing him from the movie that ended up jumpstarting his career.

203. Even after *The Blob* had been released, Steve McQueen was still a virtual nobody in the film world and actually preferred acting on stage to film where he felt more artistically satisfied. When he received a $400 offer for three days of work to play Bill Longley in a guest appearance of *Tales of Wells Fargo*, he took it, citing the money as his only motivation. He hated acting in the Western, and decried it to be "the last of these cockamamie cowboy shows for me."

204. While Steve was looking for work in the late 1950s, before his big break on *Wanted Dead or Alive*, he often went to the studio casting office and waited on line with the other actors hoping that he might be perfect for even the smallest part. As always, he figured out how to get a jump on the competition, although there's no evidence whether it worked. When he finally got to the front of the line (and like everyone else), he handed the receptionist his picture and resume. Except rather than leave after being turned away, he went straight to the back of the line. He was turned away several times throughout the day, but the idea was to eventually fool the receptionists into not only recognizing him, but thinking that they recognized him from television appearances.

205. New York City has long been known as one of the toughest places when it comes to gun laws. McQueen found this out first-hand when he flew into La Guardia Airport with Josh Randall's Mare's Laig sawed-off rifle in his luggage. He was detained by airport police immediately and simply informed them, "Where the gun goes, I go." In response, police took both him and the rifle to the station where he sat until a captain let him go.

206. *Wyatt Earp,* starring Hugh O'Brien, quickly became one of the most popular shows on television, and before Steve got his big break playing Josh Randall, he felt there was a good chance of getting a part on O'Brien's show. Hugh O'Brien was known as the fastest draw in Hollywood and if McQueen ever got his chance to go head to head, he wanted to be ready. He practiced and practiced but unfortunately never had the opportunity to face off against O'Brien before *Wanted Dead or Alive* came about.

207. Before he was finally cast in *Wanted,* or even had an agent for that matter, Steve hung around his wife's sets trying to get her to spend time with him. He also had a knack for using her money to buy cars and go out with friends to fill his days. Neile eventually had enough of this and begged her team to take him on and find him work. She had everyone on board including manager Hilly Elkins, agent Stan Kamen at the William Morris Agency, and publicist David Foster. They weren't enthused about taking on Steve McQueen, but if it kept their client on the rise and happy, they would do it. Elkins was eventually the one who came through with a pilot called *Trackdown* that morphed into *Wanted.*

208. To secure the part of the murderer on *The Defender,* a TV show starring William Shatner, Neile suggested that Steve go all out and pitch his case to the director, the producer, and the writer. Although the director held all the casting cards, she knew that he would be open to suggestions from the show's other important leaders. On his call-back, Steve did just that and whether it was his enthusiasm, skill, or just dumb luck, he got the role that thrust him into the limelight.

209. A far cry from what he would be making by his third season, McQueen's starting salary on *Wanted Dead or Alive* was $750 per episode. With 28 episodes having been ordered by the network right off the bat, Steve stood to make $21,000 that first season. He was still making half of what his wife made, but of course, the extra income went toward his 1958 Porsche Speedster.

210. Steve McQueen once got called out by a director in front of the entire crew for having to use the bathroom before a take on *Wanted*. In the director's defense, Steve was sitting around for 30 minutes while the crew set up the scene, and only when the scene was completely ready did Steve decide that he had to use the restroom. The director announced in a booming voice, "Everybody take five while Mr. McQueen takes a pee!" Not surprisingly, that particular director was paid the remainder of his contract and sent packing from the show.

211. The famous TV show *M*A*S*H* aired from 1972 to 1983 and was set in Korea during the Korean War. In one episode, *The Blob* is seen playing on a television set, undoubtedly a pop-culture reference to the 1950s. The only problem is that the Korean War ended in 1953 and *The Blob* wasn't even filmed until 1958!

212. Frank Sinatra took such a liking to Steve McQueen while filming *Never So Few* that he often instructed director John Sturges to focus on Steve instead of himself. He told Sturges that McQueen had "something that the kids will go for" and told him he didn't mind if he wanted to focus on the young up-and-comer for a particular scene. This was an especially big deal because on every other one of Frank Sinatra's pictures, he had to be the focus and the center of attention. Other actors wouldn't dare try to steal a scene away from him.

213. In 1959 Steve appeared as a guest panelist on the show *Juke-Box Jury*. A panel of judges listened to new popular music and then discussed their opinions of what they heard. While on the show, Steve said, "I went to two singing teachers and they both gave me my money back and they said, 'Go on outta here.' Ya know . . . I just gave up right then and there."

214. One of the skits McQueen performed on Bob Hope's 1959 Christmas USO tour was called "Operation: Eggroll" in which he and Hope played a couple of Japanese soldiers about to be captured by US forces. The special aired on January 13, 1960.

215. Steve was paid $7,500 to appear on *Kraft Music Hall*, otherwise known as *The Perry Como Show*, in 1960. He began a dance number that took place in an Old West saloon with him playing the town's sheriff. When it came time to do the actual dance, he just mouthed a couple of words, looked as if he would take a step, and then the number ended without him singing or dancing at all.

216. Steve appeared on the game show *It Could Be You* hosted by Bill Leyden in 1960 to promote *Wanted Dead or Alive*. As part of his skit, two women from the audience were invited to stand on stage. Leyden then told an embarrassing story about one of the women and Steve had to guess which one it was. The idea was to see if he possessed any of the traits that a real bounty hunter would have. McQueen easily identified the correct woman by how much she blushed at the relaying of her story.

217. Not many people know that it was actually Yul Brenner's son, Rock, who suggested Steve McQueen for the role of Vin alongside his dad in *The Magnificent Seven*. Like many kids, he was a fan of McQueen's from *Wanted Dead or Alive*. Brenner then watched an episode of the show and agreed with his son.

218. Can you believe that the actual blob used in the movie is still in existence and has never dried out? It's even still in the original pail used for transportation for the movie. It has made appearances at the annual Blobfest in Phoenixville, Pennsylvania.

219. McQueen's character of Vin Tanner in *The Magnificent Seven* never once made mention of being married in the film. Yet, he can be seen wearing a wedding ring throughout the entire movie, which you might guess was Steve's actual ring.

220. Steve disliked his movie *The Honeymoon Machine* so much that he walked out of the first public preview screening. He had yet to perfect his on-screen persona when he took on the role of Lt. Ferguson 'Fergie' Howard in 1961 and was uncomfortable watching himself in that role.

221. McQueen was a cast member in a 1957 episode of *The 20th Century Fox Hour* called "Deep Water." The plot was based on an actual event during World War II in which a team of high-strung Navy Frogmen (now known as the elite Navy SEALS) who didn't get along with each other were sent on a mission. McQueen played the role of Kinsella.

222. Steve McQueen appeared in a 1958 episode of *Climax!* called "Four Hours in White." In the episode he actually plays two characters: identical twins Henry and Anthony Reeves who have just been in an accident. One of the twins would die unless he received a kidney transplant from the other twin, which in the 1950s was a difficult and dangerous procedure. The surgeon must decide if it is worth risking one man's life to save the other from certain death.

223. McQueen has a solid role in a 1958 episode of *Tales of Wells Fargo* called "Bill Longley" in which he plays wanted outlaw Bill Longley. He joins forces with main character Jim Hardie (played by Dale Robertson) to retrieve money stolen from Wells Fargo for a $5,000 reward. Another outlaw working with them ends up stealing the reward from Hardie and the girl from Longley.

MOVIE AUTOMOBILE FACTS

224. Steve McQueen's car in *The Blob* is a blue 1953 Plymouth Cranbrook convertible with a red interior. The Cranbrook was updated for the 1953 model year, which saw an updated body and a few extra ponies, bringing the six-cylinder flathead's power from 97 to 100 hp.

225. For 1954, the Cranbrook was renamed Belvedere, making the convertible from *The Blob* a one-year-only item. The car's exact whereabouts are unknown today. In case you were wondering, the car has no special abilities to completely deflect the wind away from passengers with the top down as in the scenes where Jane's hair doesn't move while driving.

226. While on the set of *The Blob*, Steve was arrested in a nearby town for reckless driving in his MG. Producer Jack Harris had to bail him out, but under the condition that he clean up his act on- and off-set.

227. In the reverse drag racing scene in *The Blob*, what viewers actually see is the film going backward, not the cars. You can tell because even in reverse, exhaust actually billows out of the tailpipes, but in the movie, the exhaust smoke can be seen returning into the tailpipes.

228. In *Never So Few*, the fighter aircraft taxiing on the airfield is a Nakajimi KI-84 Hayate, and today that plane is the last surviving example. The KI-84, known to Allied forces as the "Frank," was Japan's most effective fighter used during World War II. Just over 3,500 of the single-seater craft were built. It was fast enough to run with the top Allied planes in combat and could fly high enough to intercept B-29 Superfortress bombers.

229. The KI-84 used in the film was captured at Clark Field in 1945 and transported back to the United States where it was sold as surplus in 1952. Edward Maloney, owner of the Ontario Air

Museum, treated the fighter to a complete restoration bringing it back to flight-ready condition. Since 2014 the plane has been on display at the Tokko Heiwa Kinen-Kan Museum in Kagoshima, Japan.

230. In the opening scene of *Never Love A Stranger*, which is stated as occurring in New York in 1912, the rear of a modern car is visible in the background. When Frances Kane is walking down the city street en route to the midwife's home, the car can be seen on the left side of the screen. A few years off, or even a decade, wouldn't have been all that noticeable, but considering the cars of 1912 were still virtually powered carriages, something from the 1950s definitely stands out.

AUTOMOBILE COLLECTION

231. Steve McQueen and two friends went to Cuba after his departure from *A Hatful of Rain* in September 1956. They hopped a ferry from Key West and rented motorcycles upon their arrival. They rode 967 miles from Havana to Santiago when Fidel Castro led an uprising against the Government, catching the three Americans by surprise.

232. They hightailed it back to Havana when Steve was arrested for selling contraband: American cigarettes. He spent the next couple of weeks in jail in Havana until he sold his motorcycle helmet to get out.

233. The very next Monday after their weekend wedding retreat, while Neile was working at the Tropicana in Las Vegas, Steve bought a Corvette … using her money, of course. The red car had white scallops and they didn't own it for very long.

234. After teaching Neile how to drive it, Steve went to St. Louis to work on a movie, and she crashed it into two other cars. Steve had only driven it twice, and shined it three times. He was able to fix the Corvette well enough to limp it back to LA where he continued to drive it for a little while. They then traded it for a Ford Fairlane convertible.

235. McQueen was once asked by Bette Davis why he continued to ride a motorcycle even after he had become successful because any damage to his face or body could cost him his career. He responded that it was "So I won't forget I'm a man and not just an actor." This feeling is likely why he'd disappear off set to go riding or driving one of his sports cars.

236. With the huge paydays coming in from *The Magnificent Seven* and *Wanted*, Steve bought what is perhaps his best-known automobile: a 1956 Jaguar XKSS. He paid $5,000 for it in 1958 but sold it in 1969. Knowing how much he loved the right-hand-drive street-legal race car, he must have regretted selling it.

237. After buying the Jaguar XKSS, McQueen got so many speeding tickets that his driver's license was suspended twice. One time, while en route to Phoenix, Arizona, he was pulled over going about 120 mph. With a six-month-pregnant Neile in the car, he told the officers that his wife had gone into early labor and he was rushing to the hospital. Rather than give him a ticket, they escorted him to the nearest emergency room, where, after the cops left, Steve told the nurse that it was just a false alarm.

238. Steve and Neile purchased a 1953 Siata 208S Spider in 1957 for $4,995 from Ernie McAfee Engineering in Hollywood. The small Italian sports car used a Fiat-built 2.0-liter V-8. Fiat only built 56 such drivetrain packages of which only 35 were turned into Spiders in 1952 and 1953.

239. McQueen sold the silver car, chassis number BS 523, almost a year after buying it because the studio didn't like him driving such a fast car. He sold it to a young doctor named Bruce Sand for $4,500. The Siata is currently restored in red and owned by Everett Anton Singer.

240. About six months after Bruce Sand purchased Steve's old Siata, McQueen happened to pull up next to the car in his Fairlane and motioned Sand to pull over. He got out of the Fairlane and simply said, "I want to drive." Sand's friend got out of the passenger seat to let the owner slide over and Steve got behind the wheel. He proceeded to punch his old car flat-out up Coldwater Canyon before turning around on Mulholland and heading back to Hollywood. He stopped back at the Fairlane and Sand's waiting friend, got out of the car, and drove away, never saying a word.

241. Did you know that Steve McQueen once got a ticket for driving too slow? His 1953 Siata had gotten stuck in second gear while traveling on the Hollywood Freeway. He was limping it to the shop on Sunset Boulevard when he was pulled over for going 40 mph on the highway, although he was overheard telling another actor that the ticket was for doing 150.

242. The first car that McQueen purchased new was his 1958 Porsche Speedster 1600 Super. The Speedster was based on the 356 coupe but with a serious amount of weight removed. The car had no windows, a cut-down windshield, and the top wasn't padded, since most customers didn't even put it up. Two models were produced, the 1600 and the 1600 Super, which had an additional 15 hp for a total of 75 hp. Since he intended to take it racing, and because he just plain liked fast cars, McQueen opted for the Super. He sold it in 1959 to buy a dedicated Lotus race car.

243. After buying the originally off-white-on-red Jaguar XKSS he had it repainted in its familiar British Racing Green and had upholsterer Tony Nancy redo the interior in black leather. In fact, it was the first car of McQueen's that Tony Nancy worked on—the first of many! Legendary fabricator Von Dutch built a little glove box door for him over the passenger side cubby since the car had no compartment for safe-keeping.

244. Steve went on to buy many motorcycles of varying brands from Bud Ekins' Sherman Oaks-based Triumph shop, which happened to be the largest in the nation at the time. No Steve McQueen book would be complete without giving proper honor to the shop mechanic, in addition to Bud Ekins, who kept McQueen's bikes running in top shape: Larry Harness.

245. Little is known of the McQueens' first Corvette, including its current whereabouts, but Penina Spiegel tells one story of the car in her book, *McQueen: The Untold Story of a Bad Boy in Hollywood*. Neile had convinced agent Cy Marsh to meet with Steve, so Marsh regretfully decided to make it a driving meeting, since he had a 30-minute drive to another meeting anyway and didn't want to actually take any time out of his day for Steve. Naturally, Steve McQueen insisted on doing the driving, and led Marsh to his "beat-up Corvette." McQueen raced the car through Coldwater Canyon as Marsh held on for dear life. Marsh never forgot that one drive with Steve McQueen, and three days later he had a job offer for him.

246. One of the biggest reasons Steve liked riding motorcycles in the desert and around Indian reservations was that it was like going back in time. There were no televisions or movie theaters, and no one there knew or cared about who he was. He could be himself. That was the case until one night, after driving through the desert all day, Steve and his buddies walked into a bar to find all the patrons huddled in a corner. They were shocked to discover that everyone was quietly tuned in to an old rerun of *Wanted Dead or Alive*. McQueen and his friends knew there would be no anonymity for him there, and slowly backed away. The bar patrons watching television never knew that the real Josh Randall had been right behind them.

247. Steve's 1958 GMC 101-series pickup truck had the best power-to-weight ratio of all the GMC trucks available that year. With a 336-ci V-8 engine and a 114-inch wheelbase, not only did the truck sport classic 1950s style, but it had some muscle car oomph as well. McQueen purchased the truck in the 1970s and it was his daily driver for a number of years. It was only one of ten vehicles that he brought with him when he moved into the Beverly Wilshire hotel in the late 1970s and was used often by him and third wife, Barbara Minty.

248. It remained in her possession after his death with the Idaho license plate number MCQ3188, McQueen's identification number at Boys Republic School. Barbara finally sold the truck at a Bonhams auction in 2006 where it hammered for $128,000.

249. Living in Los Angeles, you quickly become accustomed to the convenience of valet parking, especially for movie stars and other wealthy showbiz folks. McQueen, on the other hand, refused to ever valet his cars, claiming that every time he did so a new scratch or ding reared its ugly head. Considering the quality and rarity of the vehicles he drove, this was hardly a silly concern. He even got Neile hooked on parking her own car, rain or shine. She notes in her memoir that she continued to do even after their divorce.

250. Following his release from prison in Cuba and transport to the United States, Steve still needed to ride from Miami all the way back to New York City. With his helmet already having been sold in Cuba, he continued to sell the rest of his gear and belongings as he rode through the South. He eventually made it back to New York on his bike, and still with some of his possessions.

251. McQueen almost blew up the Thunderbird he rented on his and Neile's honeymoon in Mexico by accidentally launching a rocket at it. He liked driving the car on the beach every time he found a deserted spot (perhaps a future tie-in for *The Thomas Crown Affair*'s dune buggy scene), but one time he ran the car up a sandy embankment. Rather than keep driving, he felt it would be a good place to launch a rocket firecracker. The firecracker was supposed to shoot straight up in the air, but for whatever reason it turned 90 degrees and headed straight for the T-Bird. It hit the car, made a bang, then fizzled out. According to Neile, the poor Thunderbird got pretty beat up on that trip.

252. As soon as Neile was finished filming a movie in Los Angeles, she and Steve decided to head straight back to New York. Rather than fly as most people would, Steve convinced her to drive back in their new red MG. In his words, "You can't be a foreigner your whole life, you know. You've gotta see what this country looks like."

253. They made the 3,000-mile run in five days barely taking time to eat or sleep. Steve enjoyed leisurely drives to get his mind straight or blow off steam, but when there was a destination, driving turned into an endurance race for him. Neile recalls in her memoir that the entire trip was a blur and they actually got to see very little of the country.

254. Steve and Neile took a road trip from New York to Florida in their little Red MG in 1957 and found themselves stuck in the middle of a hurricane on the way home. While other drivers on the road pulled over for the storm to let up, Steve insisted that they press on in the lightweight sports car because if they pulled over the torrential rains might sweep the small car off the road. As it was with their cross country trip, McQueen felt the innate need to push his mind, body, and machine to their very limits. He eventually found a similar satisfaction with racing.

255. Police cars seemed to be ready for Steve McQueen wherever he went, and one time he actually led them on a chase, but not for the reason you might be thinking. A wildfire had broken out in Laurel Canyon near their home and was so dangerous that police cordoned off the entire area and wouldn't let anyone past the blockades for their own safety. Somehow, Neile and baby Terry were still at the house so Steve came rushing home and blasted right past the blockade in his Porsche. The officer on duty took chase, and by the time he caught up with the black Speedster at the McQueen residence, he could clearly see Steve escorting a frightened wife and child out of the house and into the car. The cop was stern with Steve for running the blockade but understood why he did it.

256. McQueen often expressed himself best to others while driving. He also became a pretty good listener while he was behind the wheel. On one such occasion, a *Wanted Dead or Alive* director, Dick Donner, and Steve were finding it difficult to communicate on set, and Dick decided to quit. McQueen invited Donner over and told him, "Nobody quits my show," then they went for a ride in his new Jaguar XKSS. Donner was so beat from the drive that he fell asleep on the McQueen couch as soon as they got home, but the next two episodes went off without a hitch and were finished ahead of schedule.

RACING

257. Steve McQueen entered his first race in May 1959 at Santa Barbara with his black Porsche Super. He had already spent time practicing with it at Southern California tracks and got interested in the competition side of things. When he entered the race that May, his fellow competitors didn't exactly welcome him with open arms. "Everybody was growling at me," McQueen said. "They'd all seen the actor who sat in a racing car for publicity." He remained calm and exhibited an honest willingness to learn from his competitors, who had imagined him to be a typical know-it-all actor.

258. Steve won the first auto race that he ever competed in. One competitor yelled to him before the race: "Hey, McQueen, you better make a hole when they drop the flag, because I'm coming through!" When the flag dropped, McQueen launched his Porsche off the line, passing other Porsches and some Triumphs as he went. After four laps he found himself in the lead, and continued to run as hard as he could for the remainder of the race. He won and became hooked on racing.

259. Having worked on *Wanted Dead or Alive* since 1958, when the studio found out about his racing hobby, they demanded that he stop. Like nearly all productions, the stars of the show are insured to cover the studio against potential losses if an actor can no longer do his job due to an accident. If McQueen had gotten hurt racing after the studio told him not to, the insurance company could have sued him for the cost of the production! He continued to race, even with that threat hanging over his head.

260. Steve McQueen was named Rookie of the Year by the Sports Car Club of America (SCCA) for 1959. As Steve often mentioned, the racetrack is the great equalizer where it doesn't matter if you're a major film actor or a backyard mechanic. Winning earns respect no matter who you are, and the Rookie of the Year title meant that McQueen had officially earned the respect he yearned for as a racer.

261. Soon after getting a taste of racing, and winning, McQueen sold his Porsche Super and purchased a purebred race car, a Lotus 11. It was in that car that he truly honed his racing prowess. "In that Lotus I really started to become competitive," he said. "I was smoother, more relaxed; the rough edges had been knocked off my driving. I was beginning to find out what real sports car racing was all about."

262. In 1959, famed British driver Sterling Moss went to California for a race and received a personal invitation to stay with Steve and Neile rather than at a hotel. Moss had never heard of the young actor/racer, but nevertheless took him up on his hospitable offer. The two connected immediately, although it was the connection between him and Neile that made the greatest impression because he had developed somewhat of a crush on her.

263. During a motorcycle race, Steve was forced to pull over because of a bad spark plug and had no wrench or replacement to fix it. A fellow movie industry racer, Hal Needham, who was a stuntman and director, pulled in behind him and loaned Steve his wrench and spare spark plug. The repair took less than a minute and the two men reentered the race.

264. Just five races later, the same thing happened again; this time it was Needham who pulled off. He watched as McQueen blew right by him, not repaying the favor. When he approached him after the race, Steve said, "I'm sorry, Hal, but I was running second, and I just couldn't afford to stop."

265. To make his new Porsche 1600 Super more competitive, Steve added a set of expensive Rudge knock-off alloy wheels, which were wider and lighter than the Porsche's stock wheels. He removed the bumpers and added a lower racing windscreen and single-hoop roll bar.

266. It may not be an important racing item, but Steve needed a way to light one of his favorite Viceroy cigarettes in his race car, so he clamped an accessory cigarette lighter to the steering column of his Porsche 1600 Super, which was about the only creature comfort the car had.

267. Steve and five other sports car drivers used to regularly meet up on Mulholland Drive after 10 pm to race their cars on the street. Each driver had a switch under the dash that turned off the license plate lights in case the police showed up. This was at the time McQueen was running his Porsche 1600 Super, which would have had no issues outrunning the bulky police cruisers of the day.

268. With the money starting to roll in from *Wanted Dead or Alive*, McQueen put it toward a number of investments, one of which was a high-performance auto shop in which he had become a co-partner. Not much is known about the shop except that McQueen had invested money into it, but since it came in before his Solar Production days, it may have doubled as a tax shelter for his racing program and vehicle purchases.

269. McQueen's first racing trophy was an engraved pewter tankard, which he won in his first-ever race in 1959. The 5-inch-tall pewter tankard, which was made in England by the company Manor Period, was engraved "E PROD. 1ST" to mark the class and position. It sold at auction in 2008 for $6,600.

Chapter 4
1961–1965

PERSONAL LIFE

270. A production secretary on the set of *The War Lover* received the task of helping Steve McQueen find a new place to stay after he was kicked out of his hotel. The two got along immediately, and she even mentioned that during the bombings of World War II, her father used to quiz the children about the old American West to keep their mind off the bombings. After seeing *The Magnificent Seven*, Steve McQueen became one of her father's favorite cowboys. Steve was so honored that he had a set of custom spurs made for her father inscribed with "For Bill from Steve McQueen" on them.

271. In February 1963, Steve and his family moved into what became his best known residence, a 5,560-square-foot mansion on 3½ acres in Brentwood. Steve nicknamed the heavily gated and secured stone residence "The Castle," which in essence, it was. Even the $250,000 price tag was imposing, with Steve remarking to fellow actor Ed Byrnes that he wouldn't be late for work one single day in order to pay for it.

272. McQueen was in Columbus, Texas, some 200 miles south of Dallas when President John F. Kennedy was shot. The cast and crew were busy filming *Baby, The Rain Must Fall* when a state trooper heard over his radio the news that the president had been shot. Filming immediately ceased and everyone gathered around the radio to listen. The news hit Steve especially hard because he had met JFK a few years earlier when he was running for office. After the assassination, filming in Texas was quickly wrapped and the rest of the movie was shot in a studio in Hollywood.

273. Another interesting JFK-McQueen connection is that Steve had a relationship with burlesque dancer Candy Barr, who had also had a relationship with nightclub owner Jack Ruby, who infamously shot Lee Harvey Oswald, JFK's assassin.

274. McQueen's favorite nightclub in Los Angeles was the famous Whisky A Go-Go located on the equally famed Sunset Strip.

After the opening in January 1964, Steve quickly became known as a regular and was often seated in the best booth in the house by owner Elmer Valentine, whom he befriended. McQueen's secret FBI dossier also mentions his tendency to be found at the Whisky a Go Go.

275. Steve founded the Steve McQueen Fund at the Boys Republic School in 1963, which provided a four-year scholarship to the top graduating student. Not only did he provide the school with monetary donations, even more important, he often visited the school to spend time with the students. He bypassed any official avenues and simply sneaked onto the school grounds to have conversations, shoot pool, or just sit on the floor of his old cabin and ask about their experience.

276. As one of the celebrities who usually steered well clear of politics, Steve couldn't stand by when the Los Angeles City Council revealed its plan to turn the natural Santa Monica Mountains into a dense residential and shopping area. Plans were in place for a highway, tall buildings, and subdivisions to take over the mountainside and double Santa Monica's population. The council pressed on with its attempt, despite many celebrity residents speaking out against it. In the next election, McQueen threw his full support toward an environmentalist candidate and unseated the incumbent leader of the build-up push.

277. Steve danced with First Daughter Luci Baines Johnson at a campaign event he co-hosted with Natalie Wood. Young Citizens for Johnson brought out the biggest celebrities to support the incumbent President, and one can assume that Luci loved every second of dancing the Watusi with Steve McQueen. A photo of them dancing made the cover of the *Los Angeles Times* as well as many other media outlets across the country.

278. Following his win, Lyndon Johnson wrote Steve a letter thanking him for the work he did to help the campaign.

279. After doing three back-to-back films in 1963, and only one finding any kind of success, Steve took a year off acting to promote the films he did, search for the next big hit, and spend time racing and with his family. At this point, he virtually had his pick of projects and no longer had to bite at anything that came his way. He could wait for the right picture that would advance his career.

280. Once Steve started making serious money as an A-list actor, he began supporting his mother. Although she didn't lend a lot of support in raising him, there were times when he was provided with the most basic of needs such as a roof over his head. He in turn did the same to her by having a business manager pay the $90 monthly rent on an apartment in San Francisco's North Beach area. He, however, took it one step further and also bought her a $400 Volkswagen, which she loved driving.

281. Not only did Steve assist Julian financially, but she played a somewhat involved role in his family's life. She became a proud parent, collecting all sorts of media about her son and seeing all of his movies multiple times. She was sent pictures of her grandchildren, Terry and Chad, and even given her own room to stay in when visiting. However, she didn't visit often or stay for very long when she did.

282. Julian Crawford McQueen Berri died on October 15, 1965, at 55 years of age, with her son, Steve, by her side. She had a cerebral hemorrhage the day before and went into a coma. Steve and Neile were about to board a flight for the premier of *The Cincinnati Kid* in New Orleans when they received the call. They canceled their appearance at the premier and flew to San Francisco immediately to see her.

283. She was buried in Gardens of Ascension, Forest Lawn Memorial Park, one of the most exclusive cemeteries in the world, located in Glendale, California. Only the McQueen family and Steve's agent and publicist attended the funeral with Steve delivering the only, and short, eulogy.

284. Steve McQueen announced his retirement from acting in 1964. His last intended appearance as an actor came at the 1964 Academy Awards where he presented the Oscar for Best Sound Recording. For the remainder of the year he turned down dozens of offers and devoted himself to spending time with his family, traveling, and racing.

285. The Louisiana location site for *Nevada Smith* was hit and mostly destroyed by Hurricane Betsy two days before the premiere of *The Cincinnati Kid*. Steve left Louisiana to attend the premier on October 15, 1965, and requested that the receipts from the showing be donated to the hurricane victims.

286. Upon arrival in Taiwan for the filming of *The Sand Pebbles*, Steve McQueen nearly found himself in handcuffs and behind bars. It turns out that he had a loaded .38-caliber revolver in his luggage, which was discovered at customs in Tokyo when he attempted to board his flight. He jokingly told officials that he brought it so he could do some "bear hunting" while there. Diplomatic officials from both the United States and Taiwan deliberated for several hours while Steve remained held up. Taiwanese ruler Chiang Kai-shek gave the order himself to allow Steve to continue on his way.

287. One of McQueen's favorite things to do once he was an established star was to drive by or visit places that he had previously lived as a struggling young actor. He even took an interviewer on a walking tour of Greenwich Village on a New York promotional stop to show the reporter his old cold-water flat.

288. One time, he and Neile stopped in the Silverlake neighborhood to visit the house that he, his mother, and his stepfather Hal Berri once lived in. McQueen walked right up to knock on the front door, and when opened he informed the current resident that he used to live there. The resident likely didn't watch TV or go to the movies because he slammed the door in Steve's face!

289. Steve nearly got himself fired from what became one of his biggest hits, *The Great Escape.* He continuously argued with director John Sturges about his role and didn't like anything in the script. Not only did he go so far as to quit once and return on his own, he was fired by Sturges twice!

290. Steve McQueen made history in February 1965 when he graced that month's cover of the fashion magazine *Harper's Bazaar.* He was the first male ever to be given that distinction. The photo was shot by Richard Avendon who also shot the inside feature that included both Steve and supermodel Jean Shrimpton.

291. Can you believe that Steve and Neile McQueen once spent a night in a Spanish brothel? It's true! En route to Mallorca, Spain, with some friends, the group became separated in the middle of the night, and by the time they found each other it was 4 a.m. The next sign of civilization that was open at that time was a small-town brothel where all the women working recognized Steve McQueen as soon as he got out of the car. The ladies took in the troupe, fed them, and let them use their rooms for the night. The next morning, they refused to accept any money for their kindness and Steve, Neile, and company went on their way to Mallorca.

292. Steve was asked to co-host an event for President Lyndon Johnson's re-election campaign. Vic Damone was already signed up to be a minor host. Steve refused to host the event if Damone was going to be there, a quick power play that proved who was truly the more important of the two. This time, it was Vic Damone who was kicked to the curb.

293. Steve McQueen appeared on the August 1, 1963, cover of *Life* magazine for a special about his outdoorsy nature. The photographer asked if he wanted to go camping so he could shoot him being one with the outdoors. Steve agreed; the only problem was that he had never been camping and didn't know anything about it. So, he invited Bud Ekins, Don Gordon, and James Coburn, thinking they would make him look good for the article. None of them knew how to camp either and they spent most of the time driving around in Steve's Land Rover and ordered burgers to be delivered to the campsite.

294. That issue of *Life* with Steve on the cover came out at the same time most other magazines covered President Kennedy's meeting with the pope on their covers. *Life* sold more copies than any other magazine that month.

295. In May 1964 an intruder managed to get over the wall at the McQueen residence in Brentwood and appear at the front door. He rang the doorbell at 3 a.m. simply because he wanted to talk to the man he saw in the movies. Fearing for his family, Steve grabbed his handgun before going to the door, and upon finding a stranger there instructed Neile to call the police while he made him hug a tree at gunpoint until the police arrived. Alfred Thomas Pucci was charged with "prowling," and it marked the first time Steve realized that perhaps some people could not distinguish that the man in the movies was just an actor playing a character.

MOVIE FACTS

296. As he became more deeply involved with racing, Steve McQueen knew that he had to go to Europe to learn from the best. "Motor racing in Europe is like studying medicine in Vienna," he said. In 1961 he got his chance when he took the film, *The War Lover*, which was set to be produced in England. He starred as Buzz Rickson, a World War II pilot who lived to take on the most dangerous suicide missions. Robert Wagner and Shirley Anne Field were cast with him, along with Michael Crawford who went on to be one of the biggest stars of Broadway.

297. While filming *The Great Escape* in Germany in 1962, Jack Linkletter of the *Here's Hollywood* show flew over to interview McQueen. Since Linkletter also rode motorcycles, McQueen borrowed three Harley-Davidsons for the two of them and James Garner to ride to Obermenzing for a folk fest. According to Linkletter,

"Neither Garner nor I had many cycle hours and the narrow streets, humped in the middle and made of cobblestones would have been scary enough, but then to have cars flying by within inches, made Garner and I think it was our last trip anywhere." Although none of them spoke German, they tried singing along anyways. The crowd even got McQueen up on one of the tables to sing along, since everyone had recognized him and Garner.

298. At the 36th annual Academy Awards, McQueen presented the award for Best Sound in a motion picture. Franklin Milton won the award for his work on *How The West Was Won*. Jack Lemmon hosted the awards ceremony that year.

299. McQueen again presented the Best Sound in a motion picture award at the 37th annual Academy Awards in 1965 alongside co-presenter Claudia Cardinale. George Groves won the award for *My Fair Lady*. Bob Hope hosted the awards ceremony that year.

300. In 1965, while on the set of *The Cincinnati Kid*, Steve filmed an ad for Christmas Seals. (Christmas Seals are labels affixed to holiday mail, the proceeds of which go toward charitable organizations.) Although money earned from Christmas Seals went toward a variety of important causes, he mentioned tuberculosis specifically. He said, "In 30 years we've moved ahead to deal with it. It's still here and it's still a threat, but we're getting closer to control, perhaps eradication."

301. The show that made Steve McQueen a household name, *Wanted Dead or Alive*, ran its last episode on CBS on March 29, 1961. Although Westerns were fading away, and *Wanted* was moved from its Saturday night slot to Wednesday, the show still held the second most-watched spot for its time slot until its demise. The only program that beat it for viewership was *The Price Is Right*. *Wanted* aired 94 episodes through its run, although neither producers, executives, nor McQueen were sad to see it go.

302. Steve gave his first real attempt at comedy with 1961's *The Honeymoon Machine*. It was a disaster, both for him and at the box office. Although both Steve and manager Hilly Elkins thought it was time for him to add a comedy to his resume, the format simply didn't work for him. Elkins later said, "It was a dumb move for both Steve and me. We were looking the other way, and we should have passed." Perhaps the one good thing to come of the film was McQueen's top billing on the poster.

303. Steve's agent, Stan Kamen, had to fly from Los Angeles to Germany and calm things down every time that Steve was fired or quit the production of The Great Escape. Upon Steve's final return, he was told in no uncertain terms that the next time he was fired, it would be for real and all his lines and sequences would be given to James Garner. He cleaned up his act after that.

304. Following the release of *The Great Escape*, McQueen became the first American to be voted Best Actor at the Moscow International Film Festival. The movie was a hit across Europe, Asia, North America, and even in the Soviet Union, which was responsible for liberating the prison camp in January 1945.

305. In 2001, *The Great Escape* was ranked 19th on the American Film Institute's list of the 100 most thrilling American pictures of all time. The film grossed $20 million domestically in 1963, making it one of the highest earning films of the year. With the star power behind it, and that legendary jump scene, it's easy to see how the film has attained its timeless, legendary status.

306. Following the massive success of *The Great Escape*, Steve used his newfound clout to officially bring control to the films he starred in. He was the first actor in Hollywood to demand, and receive, final approval on his films' producers, directors, writers, and costars. He was also one of the first to be paid $1 million for a movie, an amount that soon went up.

307. In the spring of 1963, McQueen returned to his old stomping grounds in lower Manhattan to film *Love with the Proper Stranger*. He hadn't spent much time there since really hitting it big in Hollywood, and took the opportunity to enjoy the moment. "It was a strange feeling to be playing scenes for a movie camera on the streets where I used to play ball . . . seeing the old and familiar streets gave me a fuller appreciation of how lucky I have been." Parts of the movie were filmed on East 11th Street and Third Avenue, around the corner from where he once lived on East 10th.

308. In *Baby, the Rain Must Fall*, Steve plays a parolee who attempts a singing career after returning home from prison. His wife and young daughter support his dream, and the family goes through hardship as McQueen's character's music career continues to fail. McQueen was a confusing choice for the role because he lacked singing ability and usually preferred characters who achieved some level of "win" in the story. One review said that he was "rather cast down as having to play someone who fails at becoming Elvis Presley," which is ironic as the real Elvis actually wanted the part but was stuck doing musical travelogues.

309. To prep for his role in *The Cincinnati Kid*, MGM gave McQueen $25,000 in cash to practice playing poker in Las Vegas when the film shut down for a month to find a new director. He and his friend Dave Resnick spent two weeks in Vegas partying and playing cards. Although MGM just wanted to keep McQueen happy and busy in the interim, playing high-stakes poker likely helped him develop his character and learn more about the game. No word on whether or not any of the money ever came back from Vegas.

310. While working in Louisiana in the aftermath of Hurricane Betsy, McQueen only ate whole chickens specially butchered and prepared for him by his personal chef. Reportedly, Steve refused to share his protected chickens with anyone else.

311. The hurricane had left the shooting location a disaster, allowing disease to run rampant in addition to the numerous other difficulties. There were no functioning bathrooms for the cast and crew, meaning that the only place to relieve oneself was in the very stream that was used for filming.

312. Steve McQueen once stood up to a delegation from the Paramount studio who walked onto the set of *Hell Is for Heroes* in an attempt to shut down the on-location film and bring all the equipment back to a Hollywood soundstage. Director Don Siegel and Steve refused the order, knowing that it would kill the realism of their movie. When the Paramount crew arrived, Steve drew a circle around the cameras with a stick in the dirt, turned to them, and said, "Anybody steps over that line . . . he gets the shit kicked out of him!" He had drawn an actual line in the sand, and it worked. The Paramount crew left him and Siegel to finish the movie on location.

313. In *The Great Escape,* McQueen plays Virgil Hilts, whose nickname is "The Cooler King," because of the amount of time he spent in solitary confinement, otherwise known as "the cooler." This was the early 1960s, and Steve McQueen had yet to earn his infamous nickname, "The King of Cool."

314. The barbed-wire fence used in the famous motorcycle jump scene wasn't actually barbed wire, as a crash could lead to some major injuries to stuntman Bud Ekins. The "barbed wire" seen in the film is actually just string made by knotting together black rubber bands.

315. Leading up to the jump scene, director John Sturges drafted the entire cast and crew to create hundreds of yards of the fake barbed wire during idle time on set. Even stars McQueen and James Garner helped out with the project!

316. Steve was one of the first actors to push for, and actually be awarded, script approval toward the end of his run on *Wanted Dead or Alive.* What pushed him to make such an outlandish (at the time) request was the increasingly unbelievable situations that his character, Josh Randall, was being placed in. His racing career was taking off at the time, while opportunities in film had to be turned down because of the television schedule. He had nothing to lose by requesting not only script approval, but more money at the same time. He got both.

317. Four Star, the producers of *Wanted Dead or Alive*, made an agreement with the producers of *Never So Few* that Steve would be released three days a week to film *Wanted*. If the film got in the way so much that *Wanted* would have to be filmed on the weekends, McQueen would have been held personally responsible for all of the associated costs. To protect himself in case this actually happened, he took out an insurance policy with Lloyd's of London that cost him $700 a week throughout the course of filming. Lloyd's agreed to insure him only if he agreed not to do any racing during the filming of *Never So Few*.

318. The promotional team marketing *Never So Few* repeatedly bragged about the film having been shot "extensively" in Burma to increase the exotic mystique of the film. In reality, only about 10 percent of the film was shot in Burma while most of it was shot in Thailand, Hawaii, and in MGM's Culver City studio.

319. As is often the case in Hollywood, *Hell Is for Heroes* wasn't the original name for the Steve McQueen movie, it was actually the name of another project that Paramount was working on. The film was initially called *Separation Hill*, which Steve didn't like. Director Don Siegel threw out *The War Story* at first, but Steve countered with the title of *Hell Is for Heroes*, which Siegel loved until he found out that the name already existed for a different project. McQueen went straight to Paramount head Marty Rackin and told him he wanted that title for his project. Rackin ordered the other project to change its name (it ended up debuting as *Man-Trap*), so that Steve could have the title he wanted.

320. When *Hell Is for Heroes* hit the box office, it included a special introduction by President John F. Kennedy. JFK was serving his first term as President when the film came out; however, the introduction was eliminated from future viewings after his assassination.

321. With some nominal successes under his belt and the Solar Productions brand developing some clout, McQueen wanted to try his hand at the business side of Hollywood. Of the several projects that he showed an interest in developing, you might be surprised to learn that one of them was the television rights to *Beauty and the Beast*, which had not yet earned its fame as an animated Disney movie. *Beauty and the Beast* has since gone on to be a major money-making title in various film and stage formats.

322. To save money and make filming easier on the cast and crew, the original idea for *The Great Escape* was to film it in California, which is far from the Bavarian forests as much in terms of looks as it is in distance. Assistant Director Robert Relyea was tasked with finding a location to shoot, and once he found a clump of six pine trees near Palm Springs, director John Sturges decided to try to make it work.

323. The bigger problem arose when the Screen Extras Guild wouldn't allow Sturges to use local extras in the film; he would have to bus Hollywood-based extras more than 100 miles to the location. The potential expense would have cost as much as if they just filmed on location in Germany, which is what they ended up doing. Once there, Sturges cut costs by using local students as extras rather than professional actors.

324. The 1965 *Baby, the Rain Must Fall* was Steve McQueen's last black-and-white film. Color films started to be popular in the 1950s (even *The Blob* was shot in color!), and by the mid-1960s, color films were the norm. However, even to this day many directors choose to shoot in black-and-white for artistic purposes.

325. McQueen appeared on several episodes of *Here's Hollywood*, a magazine-style show that featured celebrity interviews. For one of his appearances, host Jack Linkletter flew to Germany to meet up with Steve on the set of *The Great Escape*.

326. In 1963 Steve hosted an episode of *The Dick Powell Theatre*, a series that featured a different drama each week. Traditionally, a celebrity introduced that week's play and the actors in it. Steve introduced *Thunder in a Forgotten Town*, starring Jackie Cooper, Dewey Martin, Susan Oliver, Roger Emhardt, Edie Adams, Milton Burle, Joey Bishop, David Jansen, and Pat O'Brien.

327. Before production on *Hell Is for Heroes*, writer Robert Pirosh had to wait seven years for the US Army to declassify information relating to the screenplay he had written. The story of seven men holding their position against a massive onslaught of German soldiers is true, but the entire story wasn't known until the Army gave the okay. At that point, Pirosh was able to finish his script and, luckily, Steve McQueen needed an action vehicle to push his career forward. Unfortunately for Pirosh, he clashed on set with McQueen and was eventually replaced with Don Siegel.

328. Steve liked the idea for *The Cincinnati Kid* so much that he signed on for the lead role before a script was even written! Not only had he played a bit of Poker and done some hustling in his younger days, he relished the idea of having some involvement in the scriptwriting process.

329. In *Hell Is for Heroes*, Steve McQueen's firearm of choice was the M3 grease gun, which replaced the older Thompson sub-machine gun. Only special commandos and tank units carried the compact weapon that takes rounds from a magazine rather than a belt or drum. The one McQueen uses is an earlier model as evidenced by the charging lever on the side. He had to use this feature often to clear jams out of the gun because the studio purchased extremely low-quality blanks that kept jamming.

330. Although several Americans, including Virgil Hilts (played by Steve McQueen), are part of the mass escape in *The Great Escape*, no Americans, in fact, were able to escape from Stalag Luft III. That's not because they didn't want to, they were involved from the get-go on creating the tunnels.

331. Steve McQueen was paid $87,500 for his top-billed role in *The Great Escape*. It's doubtful he knew it at the time, but his friend and competitor James Garner earned $150,000 for the film.

332. Rolex watches have often been on prominent display in McQueen films, and *The Great Escape* is no different. He wears a Rolex Speedking model, which was very popular among POWs in German prison camps. Servicemen held in German prison camps, such as Stalag Luft III, could order a Rolex directly from the manufacturer while they were interned. The most popular model was the Speedking, and there are even reports of American POWs at Stalag Luft III wearing them.

333. Although Sgt. Hilts was one of the escapees in *The Great Escape*, none of the American officers actually held at Stalag Luft III attempted the escape. All Americans were moved to a different camp seven months before the actual escape because the Germans had become suspicious that something was going on.

334. Virgil Hilts was based on several historical American POWs from World War II. Major Dave Jones was a flight commander who took part in Doolittle's Raid before making it to Europe where he was shot down and captured. Colonel Jerry Sage was an OSS agent who was captured in the North African desert and was able to quickly find a flight jacket and tell his captors that he was a downed pilot. This quick thinking saved him from potentially being executed as a spy. Squadron Leader Eric Foster escaped from German POW camps seven times.

335. In the original script, McQueen's character disappears for 30 minutes while the other character plots are being followed. As you may guess, this was a problem for someone who liked being the star. A second writer, Ivan Moffitt, was brought on specifically to increase the importance of Virgil Hilts.

336. The incident in *The Great Escape* where Virgil Hilts proudly removes all of the wooden boards from his bunk and then comes crashing down on top of his bunkmate actually happened in real life at Stalag Luft III. The real POWs engineered a string system to hold up the bunks while they donated the boards to hold up the tunnels. The strings broke their first time using the bed and the man on the top bunk crashed down onto the man on the bottom bunk.

337. The baseball thrown and caught by Virgil Hilts while he was in the cooler was actually a baseball from the 1950s rather than the early 1940s when the film took place. The fingers on the ball in the movie were sewn together, a process that didn't start until about a decade after the war ended.

338. That's not really Steve McQueen singing in *Baby, the Rain Must Fall*. It's actually the voice of singer/songwriter Billy Strange who wrote songs for Elvis and played backup guitar for The Beach Boys and Nancy Sinatra.

339. In *Baby, the Rain Must Fall* McQueen's character is often seen wearing a denim shirt. The shirt is a Wrangler model 27MW, which is now a highly-collectable item among denim enthusiasts.

340. *Baby, the Rain Must Fall*, the title song of the film, was written by Elmer Bernstein and Ernie Sheldon and performed by Glenn Yarbrough. The song reached the 12th spot on the Billboard chart in 1965 and ranked number-two on the adult contemporary chart.

341. The big fight scene in *The Cincinnati Kid* was a result of Steve McQueen having written into his contract that there must be an action scene in the film.

342. The odds of two players having the poker hands in the final scene of *The Cincinnati Kid* are 45 million:1. The Kid is holding a full house, aces full of 10s, and gets beaten by The Man with a straight flush, 8 of diamonds to jack of diamonds.

343. *Hell Is for Heroes* met with rave reviews upon its release, which included many complimentary words written specifically about Steve McQueen. Perhaps the greatest review came from filmmaker Stanley Kubrick who sent Steve a telegram congratulating him on his performance. He told him, "It's the most perceptive and realistic performance of any soldier in any war film I have ever seen."

MOVIE AUTOMOBILE FACTS

344. While filming *Hell Is for Heroes*, Steve wrecked three rental cars in the forests of Redding, California. With primarily nighttime shooting and an easygoing director, he had plenty of time during the day to go out and drive. It didn't help that the rentals were among the finest sports cars of the day. One was a Mercedes 300 SL.

345. After wrecking the SL, Steve was told that if he crashed another car, the cost would be deducted from his paycheck. He didn't wreck another one after that. Co-star James Coburn rode with McQueen to the set every day, but after the third crash he sought alternative transportation.

346. Although Steve McQueen plays an American pilot in *The Great Escape*, when the film was released in England, the poster shows a Royal Air Force insignia on his jacket. This, combined with his known love of Jaguars and Triumphs, not to mention that the famous jump scene utilized a Triumph, Steve McQueen quickly became one of Great Britain's favorite actors.

347. In one of the post-escape chase scenes in *The Great Escape*, McQueen plays a Nazi soldier pursuing himself on a motorcycle. He was more than happy to spend time riding, and possibly even happier to sneak in a few extra seconds of screen time, although he wouldn't be recognized for it.

348. The big jump scene from *The Great Escape*, performed by Bud Ekins, was done on a modern Triumph TR6 Trophy Bird built to replicate a German World War II–era motorcycle. Ekins built two such machines for the film at his shop in California and then had them shipped to Germany.

349. Ekins' next task was figuring out how to jump a motorcycle over a barbed-wire fence without using a ramp. It was director John Sturges who suggested that the terrain's wallows could serve as a ramp. On his first attempt, Ekins flew for 10 feet and only achieved a height of 2 feet, not nearly enough for the scene. Ekins then tried digging a ramp out of the wallow, unseen from the camera angle, into which he was able to drop the bike and then launch out of it. He launched the Triumph 14 feet into the air and sailed for 65 feet before touching down again. He then nailed the jump on the first take with the cameras rolling.

350. While filming *Soldier in the Rain* in Texas, Ford loaned the production a "high-end convertible" that Steve ended up burning to the ground. He and co-actor William Claxton had a day off, so they took the car for a drive on a straight Texas highway. The car had 30 miles on it when Steve brought it up to 100 mph and smoke started coming out from under the floorboards. The floorboards heated up quickly, but Steve was able to stop the car and get out before it became fully engulfed in flames. Claxton and McQueen couldn't do anything but laugh as the car burned to the ground.

351. Although there's no mention of which "high-end convertible" Ford had loaned the production, Steve was actually in possession of a loaner Shelby Cobra (CSX2174) at the time. Could the car McQueen and Claxton burned to the ground on that Texas highway have been a Cobra? It's doubtful, since it's unlikely that the Cobra McQueen used would have only had 30 miles on it, nor would a Cobra have engine trouble at only 100 mph. We also know that a Cobra was returned to Los Angeles on a tandem trailer to the tune of $727.06. The car that the actors burned was most likely a Thunderbird because Ford had also given one to the show *77 Sunset Strip*.

352. *Nevada Smith* started filming in the bayous near Baton Rouge, Louisiana, where there wasn't much going on or much for the crew or actors to do in their down time. This lack of activity was especially tough for McQueen, who was used to going for quick drives or motorcycle rides while on breaks to blow off some steam. Director Henry Hathaway could see that his lead actor was restless, and a restless Steve McQueen could potentially bring down an entire film, or at least bring misery to those working on it. Hathaway quickly solved the problem by arranging for Steve to be given a small boat with a motor so he could explore the bayous.

353. John Sturges' assistant and future Solar Productions partner Robert E. Relyea was a pilot and doubled for James Garner's flying scenes in *The Great Escape*. For the part where the plane loses power and drops to the tree line, Relyea said that he flew low over a farm (in a plane covered with Nazi insignia) and the farmer happened to be working and threw his rake at the aircraft! On another occasion, he had problems with the plane and had to safely put it down in a field. The field happened to belong to a German aviation official, who had Relyea arrested. But it was the scene where the plane is shot down that caused the biggest scare for the amateur pilot. Upon crashing the plane as planned, he was knocked unconscious and had to be taken to the hospital. He was left with a lifelong back injury from the crash.

354. For the filming of *The War Lover* in England in 1961, McQueen convinced the studio to give him money for the purchase of a Land Rover to use while he was there. This is only half true; what actually happened was that the studio contractually agreed to provide the actor with a limousine and chauffeur to get him to the set. Steve didn't much like the idea of being driven around, so he suggested that the studio buy him a car, which actually saved them money!

355. He shipped the 12-speed Land Rover back home to California after production wrapped, where it was used as a family vehicle.

356. All of the planes used in the flying sequences in *The War Lover* were actual, fully capable aircraft rebuilt specially for the film. Royal Air Force Captain John Crewdson restored three Boeing B-17 Flying Fortresses via his company Aviation Services, which had previously been hired for Alfred Hitchcock's *To Catch a Thief*. He found the B-17s near Dallas, Texas, where they had been resting, unmaintained, for the previous decade and had them shipped to England to begin his work.

357. While filming *The Great Escape*, Steve McQueen was awarded 37 tickets by the German police, mostly for speeding, although one was for nearly hitting some stray farm animals and another was for crashing his car into a tree. Although it likely wouldn't have made a difference, because McQueen could drive anything fast, part of his problem had to be the "souped-up" Mercedes that was given to him to use. He found himself in court several times, along with a team of lawyers from the studio to ironically keep him out of prison.

358. His first appearance in front of a judge revealed that Steve had even forgotten his driver's license at home in California! Not wanting to risk the millions of dollars invested into the local Munich economy during the country's vital rebuilding years, judges refrained from actually throwing Steve behind bars.

359. The Shelby Cobra that was loaned to Steve, and which he had on set with him for the filming of *Soldier in the Rain*, made a brief appearance in the movie. Toward the beginning, Sergeant Eustis Clay (McQueen) admires the parked car, although it's unknown whether Carroll Shelby gave him the car for that purpose or he decided to add it on his own. It marks one of the few times that a real Cobra has made a film appearance, and possibly the earliest.

360. The whole world found out that its American hero, Steve McQueen, wasn't actually the one who performed the jump scene in *The Great Escape* when he appeared on *The Tonight Show Starring Johnny Carson.* The two didn't previously know each other, which usually led to a more serious, formal interview than Carson is famous for. One moment that should have brought the two together was when Carson congratulated McQueen on the motorcycle jump in *The Great Escape,* to which Steve simply responded, "It wasn't me. That was Bud Ekins." The studio was upset that he gave up one of the film's biggest fan draws, but Steve wasn't the type to take credit for something he didn't do, especially when it came to riding or driving.

361. It appears that there were a couple of mix-ups in *The War Lover* regarding the train that Captain Buzz Rickson, played by McQueen, rides in on. The film shows a V2-class steam engine with the identification number 60873 going under a bridge, but when Captain Rickson disembarks in London, it is from a B1-class engine with number 61378. The B1-class steam engine wasn't produced until 1951, well after the movie takes place. Also, the first shot of the V2 is a reverse image, as evidenced by the smoke-box door hinged on the left, when in reality it opened to the right.

362. At the airfield in *The Great Escape*, it appears that a fleet of German fighter planes sit at rest. Actually, those planes are American AT-6 Texan training craft that had been painted to look like German fighters. That's not to say, however, that they were inaccurate, as the Germans had commandeered many AT-6s from the French in 1940, which they in turn used as training craft. The German plane that you actually see flying is a Bucker Bu 181 "Bestmann," which is a correct German fighter plane.

363. The crew of *The Great Escape* had their own train to film those sequences, which had to be modified for the necessary cameras and equipment. They purchased two passenger cars that were taken out of service and added large arc lamps to the interiors and a swinging crane to catch the other famous jump scene in the film. The engine was rented, and the German National Railroad Bureau (GNRB) provided logistical assistance for the shoot. A radio operator from the GNRB kept the engineer informed about other pre-scheduled trains running on the tracks between Munich and Hamburg where the scene was shot.

364. Because of his racing accident with the Cooper at Brands Hatch, Steve needed several stitches in his lower lip, but had a series of close-ups to shoot for *The War Lover* over the next few days. Production would have to be delayed if they couldn't figure something out. Director Phil Leacock came to the productions rescue by allowing Steve to do his close-ups wearing the pilot's oxygen mask in the cockpit, which covered his mouth, nose, and chin entirely. Although it seems crazy to cover the star of the film's face during these important scenes, a pilot wearing an oxygen mask in a tense combat situation adds to the film's realism.

365. *Soldier in the Rain* may not have had any car chases, race scenes, motorcycle getaways, or all that much with an engine; well, except for the golf cart used in the several golfing sequences. Naturally, Steve had the motor in his cart souped-up for the handful of scenes. He can be seen in the film appearing to have fun weaving his golf cart around the course while Jackie Gleason drives his in a straight line. Steve said to his co-star, "Man, I bet this is the first time you've ever seen a golf cart burn rubber!"

366. At Steve's request, one major action sequence was written into *The Cincinnati Kid* that involved him escaping a crew of thugs by outrunning an oncoming train. It was a dangerous stunt, one that would usually go to a professional stuntman, yet McQueen insisted on doing it himself. He ran across 35 train tracks in Chicago and just nearly makes it to the other side before a train passes by. Steve learned from the train's engineer that if there was a problem, the train would not be able to stop in nearly enough time. One slip up on his part, or a miscalculation by the engineer, and it could have been the end. Luckily, McQueen made it through just in time, with the train coming within inches of hitting him.

367. Although the stunt bikes used in *The Great Escape* were late-model modified Triumphs, actual 1938 BMW R23 motorcycles were also used as props in the film, primarily outfitted with sidecars.

368. While filming *The Great Escape*, director John Sturges insisted that his actors wear their costumes at all times so that they'd begin to feel more natural. On the day Steve was set to play a German motorcycle soldier chasing him as Virgil Hilts, he left his house that morning in full Nazi uniform riding a modified Triumph that looked like a 1940s BMW. He ended up becoming lost on his way to the set and caused quite the commotion as he rode through a small German town, on a military-looking motorcycle, dressed perfectly as a Nazi soldier! Finally, he stopped, with a sizable crowd around him, possibly more confused than he was, to ask for directions. Since he didn't speak any German, and forgot the name of the town where the movie was filmed, he mimed a movie camera with his hands until someone caught on that he was looking for the large movie set in the town of Geiselgasteig.

369. Steve scammed yet another Land Rover out of the studios when he requested one to use while doing promotional work for *Baby, the Rain Must Fall*. Once he received the vehicle, the studio began booking events for him to attend with it and promote the movie; however, he was nowhere to be found. He and the big British four-wheel-drive were long gone and remained unreachable throughout the promotional campaign for the film.

370. Steve McQueen became one of the first actors in Hollywood to purchase his own motorhome for use while at the studio. He then charged studios to rent it from him, for him. His RV of choice was a Ford Condor that came fully equipped with a bathtub, shower, stove, and stereo, which also made it perfect for family trips. He was allowed to keep it on a studio lot when it wasn't in use.

371. While filming *Never So Few*, Steve was banned from riding his Triumph motorcycle on set, since the producers knew that he would likely get himself into trouble with it.

372. One day, he asked if he could borrow castmate Dean Jones' Triumph and take it for a spin to clear his head. Jones heard from director John Sturges shortly thereafter that Steve McQueen had driven his motorcycle through a fence on the studio lot and that he, too, was now banned from riding his motorcycle to work.

373. German police set a speed trap one day just outside the set of *The Great Escape*. Of course, a number of cast and crew were caught that day, including Steve. When cops finally caught up to him, the officer said, "Herr McQueen, we have caught several of your comrades today, but you have won the prize!"

374. All of Steve's motorcycle scenes were filmed in the town of Fussen, Germany, which is near the Austrian border and the Alps.

375. *The Cincinnati Kid* is supposed to take place in 1930s New Orleans; however, in several scenes, modern vehicles from the 1960s are visible. Also, the diesel locomotives from the opening scene are of modern manufacture.

AUTOMOBILE COLLECTION

376. The disk brakes on Steve McQueen's famed Jaguar XKSS cost a whopping $2,400. The front shoes contain six brake pads each while the rear shoes use four brake pads each. Considering the body and wheels are made of magnesium, that's a lot of stopping power for such a lightweight machine.

377. McQueen's second favorite car to the XKSS was his Ferrari Berlinetta Lusso bought for him by Neile for his 34th birthday. It was dark brown and had 15-inch Borrani wire wheels. In part due to his love of this car, he developed a huge respect for Enzo Ferrari and his engineering prowess. He said of Mr. Ferrari, "It would take a lot of persuading to convince me that Enzo Ferrari can do anything wrong. To me, he is one of the finest engineers in the world. When I am not working on the XKSS or driving it, I drive the Ferrari."

378. While shooting *The Great Escape* in Germany, McQueen purchased a red Mercedes SL300 gullwing to use as his transportation to and from the set. Immediately upon purchasing the car he had it refurbished by the Mercedes factory to like-new condition and garnered more than 40 speeding tickets with it.

379. The beautiful car met its demise one day when Steve was running late and a couple of farmers blocked the entire road to have a conversation. Rather than risk missing his call time, a serious offense for a rising star in the feature film world, he steered the sports car off the paved road and took off for the set through a field. At some point, he lost control of the car and planted it nose-first into a tree. He nearly cried at the loss of his beloved automobile, hardly caring that he was unhurt.

380. During the restoration process of McQueen's Jaguar XKSS, Von Dutch painted a tiny reproduction of the famed Mare's Leg rifle on the car. Steve always liked having personal touches on his vehicles, and Josh Randall's unique sidearm represented the work he did on *Wanted Dead or Alive* that allowed him to purchase the rare British sports car. Von Dutch painted small, personalized crests on several other McQueen vehicles, in addition to the Jaguar.

381. McQueen hated someone else driving him around, whether it was a friend in a pickup truck or a chauffeur in a limousine. On a shopping trip in New York City with Neile and some friends, something he couldn't have been all that excited about in the first place, he got so fed up in the back that he got out, pushed the driver into the passenger's seat, stole his cap, and drove the limo himself! You wonder how many people on the streets of Manhattan peered into the back of that limo for a celebrity sighting, when the world's biggest star was behind the wheel!

382. After the French premier of *Love with the Proper Stranger*, Steve, Neile, and a bunch of Steve's friends decided to drive from Paris to Mallorca, an island off the coast of Spain, for a little getaway. Rather than simply renting a van for everybody, they rented one Volkswagen van and one French sports car. McQueen was the only one allowed to drive the car, with his wife and friends taking turns enjoying the automobile.

RACING

383. Having taken a role in *The War Lover* to be closer to the epicenter of motor racing in Europe, specifically England, McQueen "scammed and shammed and used my juice as an actor to get a ride." He was, as he said, "a race bum." It likely also helped to have famed driver Sir Sterling Moss as a friend. While in England in 1961, Moss even tutored him in the fine art of racing and encouraged him to compete.

384. Steve McQueen competed in his first European race on October 1, 1961, at Brands Hatch circuit in Kent, England. The car he used was a Mini that had recently won the British Saloon Car Championship with Sir John Whitmore behind the wheel. Compared to the cars he had raced previously, he considered the Mini to be "underpowered," although he finished in third place that day. To him, racing in England "was a big thing." It didn't matter that he was doing it in a Mini.

385. At another event at Brands Hatch during his time in England, Steve drove a Cooper, which he locked the brakes on coming out of a turn, careening the car off the track and cutting his lip.

386. Not only did McQueen race a Mini Cooper, but he learned how to race from its namesake, John Cooper. In addition to building modified Minis, Cooper also developed an open-wheel racer called the Cooper T56 Mark II Formula Junior. Steve purchased a 1961 racer from John Cooper for $6,800 while he was filming *The War Lover* in England and continued the car's racing success back in the United States.

387. After selling it, the Cooper Formula changed hands and continued to race through the decades until it was purchased in the early 2000s and treated to a premier restoration. The T56 sold most recently in 2012 for $198,000.

388. McQueen ran his Cooper off the track at Cotati Speedway in 1962 while battling veteran driver Ed Leslie for the lead. The head on his engine split, which allowed water to leak into the combustion chamber, canceling one of the four cylinders. He pushed the car hard on the remaining three cylinders, taking turns harder than he should have to make up for his lack of power. Eventually he clipped a loudspeaker on the side of the track and wiped out.

389. Two weeks later, Steve was back behind the wheel of his Formula Jr. at Santa Barbara, California, where he made his racing debut in 1959 and also scored his first victory. "That was the worst thing that could have happened. I was really hooked after that," he told Bob Thomas of the *Los Angeles Times*. Steve won again in Formula Jr. at Santa Barbara with Ken Miles also atop the podium in his 3-liter Ferrari in the feature race for the large modified sports cars.

390. In 1962, McQueen entered the Four Aces Moose Run, a 150-mile cross-country motorcycle race through the California desert. Aboard his trusty Triumph 650, he finished in 45th overall out of 193 riders and third in the Open Novice class. His buddy and stuntman Bud Ekins also competed in the race; he finished 2nd overall. Since Steve was still somewhat new at riding in the dirt, some of the other riders tried to block the actor at the start. They quickly learned, just as road racers had, that Steve McQueen was the real deal.

391. Steve went to Sebring in March 1962 to compete in the famous 12-hour race. The day before the race, a three-hour warm-up race was held at the track, in which he was put in an Austin-Healy Sprite. It was, at the time, the longest race he had yet attempted, completing 239 miles without so much as stopping for gas. He finished 9th out of more than 20 entries.

392. The following day, McQueen raced with co-driver John Colgate (of the toothpaste fame) in a Le Mans Healey. After leading their class for the first seven hours of the race, engine troubles forced them behind the wall for the day.

393. McQueen's racing performance at the 1962 Sebring races led to an offer from John Cooper to race full-time for the British Motoring Corporation alongside famed racers Innes Ireland, Stirling Moss, and Pedro Rodriguez. He was given just a couple of days to decide between two completely different careers and lives. "I spent two full days in a sweat, trying to decide whether I wanted to go into pro racing, earning my money on the track, or whether I wanted to continue being an actor." It was a difficult decision for him, but as we know, he chose to continue acting and continued racing as a hobby.

394. In September 1964, Steve competed in the International Six Days Trials (ISDT) in East Germany. The United States team consisted of Cliff Coleman, Bud Ekins, Dave Ekins, McQueen, and John Steen (as an alternate). Three hundred of the best racers from around the world took part in the cross-country challenge that took riders through every type of terrain imaginable. They rode 250 miles per day to complete the stage.

395. McQueen was successful for the first half of the race on his 650 Triumph, earning bonus points for his team, until a spectator rode his motorcycle onto the track and sideswiped him. He was sent flying into a ravine and cut his face, injured his leg, and wrecked his Triumph. Unfortunately for Team America, Bud Ekins also crashed and broke his leg that same day.

396. In the 1964 ISDT, McQueen competed on a 1964 Triumph TR6SC, which ran in the 750-cc class. Teammate Cliff Coleman rode the same model. Bud Ekins, Dave Ekins, and John Steen ran in the 500-cc class on T100SCs.

397. For a long time, all five Triumphs were believed to be lost, having been sold as 1966 models out of the Ekins dealership. Motorcycle collector and restorer Sean Kelly had the opportunity to look through some of the Ekins' old paperwork and, although the specific identification numbers weren't available, he found pink slips for five 1966 motorcycles with 1964 identification numbers. The only bike he could actually trace down happened to be the one ridden by Steve. It turned out that the then-owner of the TR6SC had won the sidecar class in the Baja 1000 three times on it!

398. *The Great Escape* had yet to be released and send McQueen's acting career into the realm of Hollywood's A-listers when he read the script for *Love with the Proper Stranger*. He desperately wanted to play the role of musician Rocky Papasano, with whom he could closely identify. He felt so strongly about the role, and was so concerned about his career, that he agreed up-front not to do any racing during the filming in New York in order to be hired for the part.

399. Representing Team USA meant so much to actor/racer Steve McQueen that he insisted on carrying the American flag when the team walked out in the opening ceremonies at the ISDT. The event was held in Communist East Germany that year, don't forget. Steve had matching blue blazers made up with the American flag sewn in on them for the team to wear, further emblazoning the symbol of freedom in front of the communist audience. The patriotism didn't stop there, however, as he also commissioned a painter to paint the flag on both sides of the team's blue van that they picked up in London.

400. Bud Ekins added fairly basic modifications to the ISDT team Triumphs to handle the torturous off-road course. He left the engine and the rest of the drivetrain alone, but added some travel in the forks, trail-ready tires, and number plates. He put tools and spare parts underneath the seat; riders couldn't receive any help from their crews during the race. McQueen added a tool of his own to his bike: a pliers that he strapped to the handlebar with rubber bands.

401. Interestingly, the number plate was placed directly in front of the headlight, which was an unnecessary component to begin with because all racing took place during the day. However, ISDT rules stated that bikes must have headlights.

402. Hardly the typical lightweight armor worn by off-road riders of today, the American ISDT team did wear the ultimate in protection for the time: J. Barbour & Sons jackets. The waxed cotton jackets were built for the most rugged of uses and in addition to resisting water and scratches, they could also protect a rider in the case of a fall or slide. The many internal and external pockets had snap closures that could keep safe anything that an off-road racer might need on the course.

403. Head protection was provided by the supplied Bell 500-TX helmets that were painted by Von Dutch in a red, white, and blue theme. He also pinstriped each rider's name onto his helmet.

404. Several weeks before the International Six Day Trials (ISDT) began, Steve was unloading a bike at Bud Ekins' shop when he slipped on some oil and injured his left wrist. He wore a cast at the Academy Awards that year, but he was still able to put in the necessary practice to prepare for the ISDT. By the time he left for East Germany, he had the cast off and was ready to compete.

405. After his first minor accident in the ISDT, Steve found that he had dented his exhaust system, which was restricting airflow and limiting the bike's power. The bike still ran, so he pushed it as hard as he could until he rode past a local man with an axe. He stopped, asked to borrow the axe, and proceeded to smash a slit into the header before the indent. Now free of the constriction, he was able to continue running near top speed. Although this is a great story, it's also against ISDT rules, which stipulate that you can receive no help while on the course and can only work on your bike with the tools you carry.

406. Immediately following his last day of filming on *Love with the Proper Stranger*, McQueen went straight back to California to compete in the 1963 Greenhorn Enduro. The Greenhorn is a 500-mile race spanning two days that's held just north of Los Angeles. It's one of the more difficult challenges on the off-road racing circuit, with 300 of the top riders in North America showing up at the starting line. The course takes riders all over the southern Mojave Desert covering every type of terrain imaginable. Just 20 miles from the finish line, Steve lost a cylinder while running in first place in his class and had to limp the bike back in on one cylinder, losing the position by the time he hit the finish line.

407. After his first year of racing in the American Motorcycle Association's District 37 (the Southern California region was understandably the most competitive to boot), McQueen was able to move up in rank from Novice to Amateur. Only 1 in 10 new racers move up that fast on average, out of the 5,000 new riders who take up competition every year.

408. Steve McQueen once won two races in a row when he competed in the Pacific West Coast Championship at Hi Vista, California. He won the first race after encountering a big pileup in the fourth lap, and to avoid becoming entangled in it, he swerved and hit a tree. He split his mouth open and knocked a few teeth loose; most helmets at the time didn't provide the chin and mouth protection that they do today. Although banged up, he and his bike were okay, and he pressed on to win. "Then I entered a second event that same afternoon, ran it with my face all puffed and bandaged, and won that race, too!" he told biographer William F. Nolan.

409. The Four Aces Moose Run beat McQueen up considerably; he finished the first 12-hour day with bloodied, blistered hands. Most riders would find it impossible to ride a motorcycle of any type the following day, much less partake in another 12 hours of off-road racing, but Steve persevered. With 40 miles to go on the second day, he crashed his motorcycle at 70 mph. Although he didn't know it at the time, he suffered a broken arm in the crash but was more concerned with the fact that the bike had trouble shifting. He ended up taking third in his class when the dust settled.

410. Steve McQueen's 1964 ISDT international driver's license sold at auction for $42,700. As a requirement for his participation in the 1964 ISDT, he had to have a valid international driver's license from the Fédération Internationale Motocyclisme (FIM), which was only good for that one event in that year. The license had been in the collection of Steve's first wife, Neile, until 2009 when it was purchased by someone who now has an important piece of racing history in their collection.

411. While filming *The War Lover* in England in 1961, Steve befriended a young prop man who was assisting on the film and had previously been a dispatch rider in the Royal Signals. They bonded over their mutual love of motorcycles, and McQueen often noted the young man riding his old BSA at racing speeds without a proper helmet. Before he returned to the States, Steve gave him the helmet that he had been racing with throughout his time in England and wrote on the inside, "Wear it in good health. Steve McQueen."

412. Unfortunately, the Austin-Healey Sprite that McQueen drove in the three-hour warm-up race the day before the 1962 12 Hours of Sebring is known to have been destroyed. BMC San Francisco purchased the car after the race and sold it to Willy Striker, who did some racing with it before passing it to Peter Talbert. Talbert also raced with it until the Sprite was struck by an out-of-control drag racer at the Cotati drag strip and destroyed. That doesn't mean, however, that the remnants aren't still sitting in some Northern California junkyard waiting to be found.

Chapter 5
1966–1970

PERSONAL LIFE

413. While filming *The Sand Pebbles* in Taiwan in 1966, Steve and Neile McQueen met a Catholic priest named Edward Wojniak who ran an orphanage for young girls, many of whom had been victims of the sex trade. They donated $12,500 to Wojniak's mission while there, and continued to support his work until the late 1970s when Wojniak died.

414. *The Sand Pebbles* makeup artist Bill Turner married a Japanese dancer whom he met overseas, and guess who his best man was? None other than Steve McQueen. He certainly deserved the honor after helping get her out of jail six weeks prior when she was arrested for breaking Hong Kong's curfew laws. Movie superstar Steve McQueen simply used his charm and clout, and the police let her go.

415. Steve also stood in for the bride's father at the shipboard ceremony because the bride's family wasn't able to attend the wedding in Hong Kong. The couple remained married until Bill's death in 1992.

416. Did you know that Steve McQueen once dreamed of owning a restaurant? After filming *The Sand Pebbles*, he spoke with his friend, and Whiskey A Go-Go co-owner, Elmer Valentine about making his dream come true. The concept was a Spanish restaurant called Rebelion de Los Adolescentes, or Teenage Rebellion in English, and he wanted it centrally located on the Sunset Strip. Unfortunately for his fans and legacy, the plan fell through.

417. A prominent sign in the Solar offices read, "Today Hollywood, Tomorrow ... the world!" Nothing could have summed up the legend of Steve McQueen better. Although sayings like this are on display in business offices around the world, for McQueen, the film industry was just another challenge to not just overcome but also conquer and move on to the next challenge.

418. While shooting *Bullitt*, McQueen visited General Hospital in San Francisco to meet crime victims to help him add depth to his character. One patient he met in the intensive care unit had just been in a motorcycle accident and, upon meeting Steve, a well-known motorcyclist, said, "Take it slow, Steve." It was a warning of the dangers that can be associated with riding too fast. McQueen actually used the line in the movie.

419. McQueen believed that he had accidentally witnessed a murder while at an underground fighting venue in San Francisco's Chinatown. He thought it would be a karate match, but when one fighter went down after a single punch, it was announced that he was dead. The body was put in a bag, deposited into a 55-gallon drum, and taken away. The whole thing seemed like an act until he read in the newspaper a couple of days later that a body had been discovered in an oil drum. He never found out, and likely didn't want to, whether or not the two events were related.

420. Money had always been an important factor in McQueen's life, from having none to having more than most could ever dream of, even by today's standards. He had a lot of money before *Bullitt*, but after 18 months, the film had earned $24,950,447 for Warner Brothers, minus the $5,435,303 cost of production. Solar was entitled to 42.5 percent of the profit, which came out to a cool $8.3 million into the company coffers. With inflation, that would be nearly $58 million today. As Steve McQueen famously said, "You put in the work, you get the goodies."

421. Steve personally designed and patented a fiberglass off-road racing seat that gave the driver extra protection in case of a roll-over. With the massive influx of capital from the *Bullitt* earnings, Steve expanded the Solar brand, opening up Solar Plastics and Engineering. The new division certainly covered his personal interests as some of its primary products were accessories for dune buggies and motorcycles. About 30 employees worked at the Ventura-based shop under the oversight of noted automotive upholsterer Tony Nancy.

422. Solar Plastics and Engineering was also contracted at one point to produce a buoy system for the US Coast Guard. Steve McQueen the movie star was quickly turning into Steve McQueen the mogul.

423. Solar Productions moved its office to Ventura Boulevard in Studio City, across the street from CBS. The irony behind the location is that it happens to be the former space of Four Star Studios, which produced *Wanted Dead or Alive*, McQueen's first big break. The move coincided with a $20-million six-movie deal Solar entered with CBS's new film division, Cinema Center Films, in 1969. The massive influx of cash into the company was exciting, but the high level of responsibility made Steve nervous.

424. In 1969 Steve won the Male Star of the Year Award from the National Association of Theatre Owners. That same year John Wayne won the Academy Award for best actor in *True Grit*.

425. Steve began studying the Jeet Kune Do form of martial arts under the tutelage of his friend Bruce Lee. Before he became an international phenomenon, Bruce accompanied Steve to the set of *The Reivers* to work out with him every day. While on the set, he often approached producer Robert Relyea to try to convince him to finance his kung fu movies, which he claimed could be the next big thing. Eventually, Relyea blew up on him and told him only to worry about keeping McQueen in shape and stop with all the nonsense.

426. Young co-star on *The Reivers* Mitch Vogel broke his arm after falling off a horse on the set. The on-set doctor, attempting to keep the production rolling, simply asked Vogel if he could lift his arm. The boy couldn't. The doctor declared the injury to be a sprain and that he would be fine. McQueen was there for the examination, and being familiar with various injuries from the racing world, knew that the injury was worse. He drove Vogel to the hospital in his El Camino where an X-ray showed the arm clearly broken. In fact, had he not sought immediate treatment, the bone could have easily gone right through the skin. McQueen stayed by the boy's side throughout the hospital visit, even holding the bottle while he gave a urine sample.

427. On January 17, 1969, McQueen surprised co-star Mitch Vogel with a minibike for his 13th birthday. This was no ordinary minibike as it was customized and painted by Von Dutch, who painted Mitch's name onto the frame. The entire film crew had gathered to wish the young star a happy birthday, but it was McQueen who stood up, said a few words, and bestowed such a special gift on the boy. The whereabouts of the Von Dutch/Steve McQueen minibike are unknown today.

428. On August 9, 1969, Steve's life changed forever when his best friend Jay Sebring and former girlfriend Sharon Tate were brutally murdered by the Manson Family at Tate's Benedict Canyon home. McQueen was invited to the party that night and was planning on going until he "ran into a chickie and decided to go off with her instead," in wife Neile's words. Could Steve's street toughs and martial arts skills have saved his friends that night or would he have ended up among the victims?

429. After the Tate murders, McQueen began carrying a gun at all times; he even had one tucked into his waistband as he delivered Jay Sebring's eulogy. Even before the infamous Manson Family hit list went public with Steve's name at the top, he compiled the many firearms that he owned and placed them strategically around The Castle in case of an invasion. Indeed, all of Hollywood was rightfully freaked out. The McQueen family even invited friend Barbra Streisand to stay with them in the well-equipped fortress of a house.

430. On June 5, 1970, a week after Neile had returned to the set of *Le Mans*, she and Steve put out a statement to the press announcing their separation. She stayed with him in France for a while after the official separation, and they continued as though nothing was different for the sake of the children and the film.

431. Although Steve preferred to drive himself around rather than sit in the back of a limo, on occasion he did take advantage of a chauffeured service, which happened at least once in Taiwan during the filming of *The Sand Pebbles*. The dirt roads resembled those of a rally course and were too much for Steve to take sitting in the back seat. He asked the driver if he could take over, to which the driver responded by handing over the keys and letting him take the wheel. What had to be a fun experience for both Steve and his Taiwanese driver was cut short by the local police who pulled them over and laid into the poor guide for allowing the American actor to speed. Steve stepped up and accepted the blame and promised not to do it again. To settle any doubts the policemen may have had, he pulled a bicycle out of the trunk and pedaled all the way back to his hotel!

432. While living in Taiwan for an extended period of time surrounding the filming of *The Sand Pebbles*, the McQueen family had a pet goose named Ha-Ha. A venomous snake called the Bamboo Viper is native to the area and potentially deadly. At the very least, the viper's bite causes severe pain for 24 hours while the flesh around the bite area dies and turns black. Supposedly, the locals used geese to ward off the snake, so the McQueens brought their own goose with them. No one in the family was attacked during their stay, so Ha-Ha must have done a good job!

433. Steve was always into helping others through charitable work and donations. But unlike some who simply stopped at donations, or spent some time helping a local charity, Steve took it upon himself to go out and supply those in need himself. Most of the time, he never even told anybody and preferred that the recipients didn't tell anyone either. One impoverished group that he took it upon himself to help was the Navajo Indians in the Four Corners area where Arizona, Colorado, New Mexico, and Utah meet. Every few months he loaded up one of his trucks with food, blankets, and basic medical supplies and delivered them personally.

434. The McQueen family rented a house in the Boston suburbs for the summertime filming of *The Thomas Crown Affair* with the hope that suburban life would be good for their children and family. The plan backfired somewhat when the children's friends discovered who their father was. Soon, the family became swamped with neighborhood kids seeking autographs from Steve when he got home from work. "For the first time our children began to think of their father as someone special," Neile recounted. "And that made them start to feel and act special, which was wrong . . . That summer in Boston really frightened me; it showed me how difficult it is to raise children when their father is a public idol."

435. Steve invited a delegation of Russian editors to his home after returning from *The Reivers* shoot in Mississippi. He had brought home several mason jars full of moonshine whiskey and wanted to test the proficient vodka drinkers' tolerance for some real American drink. The scene that followed wasn't far off from the moonshine drinking scene in *The Great Escape* with the Russian editors coughing and glowing red in their cheeks. McQueen drank with them, although his previous experience with the firewater let him play it cool. By the end the Russians told McQueen that the moonshine was "a superior American beverage."

436. A rumor spread in 1967 that Steve McQueen wanted college students to charge long distance calls to his telephone credit card number. Kids took advantage of the rumored offer quickly, billing $50,000 worth of charges over the course of 13,000 phone calls to a Beverly Hills number. The problem is that McQueen didn't have a telephone credit card and he never suggested to anyone that anybody should bill calls to it. Either way, the phone company got stiffed for the full amount of the charges.

437. McQueen cherished his noncelebrity friends from the motor-cycle, car, and racing worlds because they rarely treated him any different than they did each other. Whenever Steve became a superstar in front of them, oftentimes through no fault of his own, they'd call him a variety of names. Everyone's favorite by far, and it became somewhat of a regular nickname for Steve, was "Supie," short for "Superstar."

438. While on the set of *The Reivers*, McQueen requested that his Winnebago trailer be given mirror-tinted window treatments that would make it impossible to see inside. What ended up happening is that extras and other crew would constantly stop in front of the mirrored glass and treat it like any other mirror. They checked their teeth, rehearsed lines, fixed their hair, basically anything one did in private in front of a mirror. What they didn't know was that Steve was usually inside watching them from mere inches away. Like any good actor, he was fascinated by the way people acted and reacted in everyday life. He sat for hours watching people from his trailer.

439. McQueen's associate Robert Relyea had what he termed a "Steve Switch" installed on his home phone. McQueen never thought twice about calling someone at any time of day or night to discuss something that was on his mind, whether it was an emergency that needed immediate attention, or a miniscule detail on something that was three weeks away from actually happening. Relyea, as his number-two at Solar Productions, was usually on the receiving end of these phone calls. Rather than have the phone wake him in the middle of the night through a ring or a button flash, he installed a cutout switch that allowed him to simply disable the phone at night. When Steve found out, he was so impressed with the mechanical ingenuity that he bragged about Relyea's Steve Switch to the press!

440. Steve McQueen celebrated two birthdays in 1966. As per the Chinese calendar, every fourth year has 13 months with a rotating 13th month. In 1966, the same year Steve was in Hong Kong filming *The Sand Pebbles*, March was the repeated month; therefore, he had two birthday parties that year. Can a guy get any luckier?

441. McQueen wore special shoes called Murray's Space Shoes that helped with the knee and foot pain he suffered from due to numerous motorcycle accidents. Before a friend suggested the Space Shoes, Steve was always in pain, and it largely went away once he made the switch. He had several pairs custom-made and wore them almost exclusively. Because of the thicker soles it was rumored that he was wearing lifts in his shoes, but really it was just the design of the shoe.

442. In the summer of 1968 Steve and Neile visited some friends in Rome and were forced to hide out above a nearby store, in the owner's apartment, when the paparazzi discovered them. The shock of seeing Steve McQueen on what would have been an otherwise uneventful day for them sent them into a frenzy. There was no way the group could go out and face them so they tried negotiating from the second-story window. They got the paparazzi to agree that if they came down and posed for pictures for a little while, the photographers would leave them alone. Everyone stayed true to their word and the couple was able to go about the rest of their trip in peace.

MOVIE FACTS

443. The concept for *Le Mans* began in late 1965 when McQueen and director John Sturges began work on a project titled *Day of the Champion*. At the same time, another studio had also begun working on *Grand Prix*, starring James Garner, both of which based the story on the book of photographs entitled *The Cruel Sport*. With delays on the set of *The Sand Pebbles*, Garner's film was able to secure a significant head start on production. Deciding that there was only room in the world for one racing film at that time, McQueen's *Day of the Champion* was canceled after $4 million had already been invested into the production.

444. Many fans consider *The Sand Pebbles* to be one of the finest films of Steve McQueen's career, and one of his best roles. Hollywood agreed, and he was nominated for Best Actor at the

Academy Awards in 1966, the only nomination of his career; the film was nominated for Best Picture and six other awards. He did, however, win the Photoplay Gold Medal Award for his work in *The Sand Pebbles* and was given the honor of World Film Favorite by the Foreign Press Association. Japan bestowed him with the title of Most Popular Foreign Star for the second year in a row after the film came out. Lee Marvin ended up winning Best Actor that year for *Cat Ballou*.

445. Long a supporter of the environment and conservation, Steve narrated a half-hour documentary called *The Coming of the Roads*. The program focused on local nature conservation and aired on September 17, 1966, on ABC.

446. On March 21, 1967, Steve McQueen literally cemented his legacy when he became the 153rd star to have his handprints, footprints, and signature immortalized at Grauman's Chinese Theater on Hollywood Boulevard. More than 2,000 fans and press witnessed the event, with much of the joy surely coming from watching Steve and Neile pull up to the red carpet in their Ferrari.

447. At the time, his were the only prints to be made upside-down relative to the others. The only other upside-down prints at the Chinese Theater belong to his then-future wife, Ali MacGraw.

448. Since he had become a star by the early 1960s, McQueen hadn't enjoyed the experience of having to convince a studio to cast him in a role of his choice. For the last five years of stardom, he was willingly cast in roles deemed perfect for him. That is, until *The Thomas Crown Affair* came along, which featured an Ivy League–educated, classically wealthy, privileged main character who wore three-piece suits, drove a Rolls-Royce, and played Chess on dates. Alan R. Trustman's script was originally written for Sean Connery, and director Norman Jewison had a list of elites in mind for the part. Steve persisted, even showing up at Jewison's home, begging for the part that was so unlike him and his previous roles. He wanted the challenge, got it, and lived up to it.

449. True to his mantra of doing as many stunts himself as he could and becoming as much of the character as possible, McQueen saddled up and learned the difficult sport of Polo in just a matter of weeks. One report says that he worked so hard at learning the sport that by the end of the day his hand was bloody. In the scene, he fits right in with the other players who likely had many years of experience.

450. *The Thomas Crown Affair* requested permission to film inside the FBI's Boston headquarters for authenticity rather than having to fake it in a studio. Upon reading the script, the FBI was outraged at law enforcement's portrayal as incompetent and a source of humor in the wake of a major crime. Even worse was that an attractive young woman who used sex and charm to catch criminals had to come in and help them with the investigation. The FBI refused the request, wanting nothing to do with such a film.

451. McQueen wore his own watch in *The Thomas Crown Affair*, and in his typical fashion, charged the studio a $250 rental fee. He used three watches in the film, including a gold Patek Philippe pocket watch notable in the opening scene, a gold Jaeger-LeCoultre Memovox, and a Cartier Tank Americaine.

452. The chess scene in *The Thomas Crown Affair* is certainly one of the most romantically tense scenes in cinema history, but did you know that it was the first on-screen tongue kiss? The scene's overt sexual references and passionate kiss were considered graphic by 1968 standards and even today isn't something you'd want to watch with your parents, or kids.

453. *The Thomas Crown Affair* has become a symbol of style that has persevered through the decades and many of the looks McQueen popularized in the film are still popular today. Even more popular are the actual artifacts from the film, namely the tortoise-shell Persol sunglasses he wears throughout the film, which have become iconic in their own right. McQueen was often seen wearing the fold-up Persols after filming with both blue and black lenses.

454. McQueen's role as Frank Bullitt is easily his most recognizable today, although readers can decide for themselves if it's because of him or the green fastback Mustang. Looking back, he was a perfect fit, but at the time, he was completely against playing a policeman. The culture in 1968, particularly in Los Angeles, was staunchly anti-cop, and McQueen was worried about alienating his younger audiences. In the end, he thought that playing a cop with his own brand of cool might actually benefit the country by casting a different take on law enforcement.

455. *Bullitt* director Peter Yates was actually the third director on the list of possibilities compiled by McQueen and his team and lucked into his most famous job simply by answering the phone. With typical McQueen impatience, the team called the first two directors on the list, wanting to sign someone immediately. The first phone call gave them a busy signal and the second continued to ring without anyone picking up. Since Yates was English, it was 3 am when his phone rang, but that didn't stop him from picking it up and getting the job.

456. Although movies had been shot on-location for years, *Bullitt* was actually the first one to not only be shot entirely on location, but to use an entirely Hollywood-based crew. This was done at McQueen's insistence and cost the studio an additional half-million dollars on top of the $6 million budget. As usual, his instincts were right on, as much of the *Bullitt* legacy lives on because of the real San Francisco locations.

457. *Bullitt* was the first action film to premier at New York City's revered Radio City Music Hall, which it did on October 17, 1968. Warner Brothers studio had already written off the movie as a failure and kicked Solar Productions staff off the grounds as soon as the work was done. Studio executives were as shocked as anybody about the Radio City invitation, but they stuck to their word not to work with Solar anymore and provided no initial promotion for the film. They didn't need to, as it turned out, *Bullitt* was an instant hit, grossing an estimated $80 million in the United States in just the first year.

458. One of the biggest fans of the film was in the audience at Radio City Music Hall during the initial run and immediately fell in love with the star. Her name was Ali MacGraw, and within five years, she became Steve McQueen's wife.

459. With *Bullitt* wrapping in San Francisco in May, and set to premier in New York in October, postproduction was given two thirds of the initial time allotment to turn the footage into a film. Editor Frank Keller not only accomplished the task, but won an Academy Award for Best Film Editing. You can only imagine how difficult putting together the final chase scene must have been.

460. There's no doubt that McQueen was perfect as Frank Bullitt, and he was immediately offered a slew of other cop movies. He smartly turned them down, keeping the spirit of Frank Bullitt alive and not giving audiences the opportunity to compare his performances. Among the most notable of projects he turned down was *Dirty Harry*, which helped propel Clint Eastwood into superstardom and is impossible to imagine anyone else in the lead role.

461. The year 1967 saw two attempts to pair Steve McQueen and Paul Newman together in what would undoubtedly be a blockbuster hit. The first attempt was for the film *In Cold Blood*; unfortunately, both actors had scheduling conflicts. The film did well, however, with a cast of unknowns securing four Academy Award nominations. The other film became a global phenomenon, even doubling *Bullitt*'s box office numbers: *Butch Cassidy and the Sundance Kid*. McQueen ended up passing on the role, not wanting to play a supporting part after having cemented himself as a lead actor. Movie buffs are likely to be happy as the Newman/Redford pairing is one of the greatest of all time.

462. Not even knowing if they would ever end up actually doing a movie together, McQueen and Newman had agent Freddie Fields develop a billing system that would put one name first and low and one name second, but higher. Either position could be perceived as top billing by the industry and audience. They didn't have to utilize this system for a few more years until they co-starred in *The Towering Inferno*. McQueen took the first spot, and as usual, carried the lead role.

463. When Mark Rydell was picked to direct *The Reivers*, no one on the production staff had any idea that he used to date a woman named Neile Adams, now known as Neile McQueen. In fact, Neile and Rydell were on a date when Steve came up to him and said that he was interested in Neile. Surprisingly, it didn't affect film production one bit, with McQueen and Rydell sticking it out to the end.

464. Although *The Reivers* didn't bring in the kind of money that had been hoped for, it achieved a significant amount of critical acclaim both as a film and for McQueen's performance. The film received two Academy Award nominations, for Best Score and Best Supporting Actor, but it was simply "too American" to do well overseas, which had always been one of McQueen's financial draws.

465. *Le Mans* might have been McQueen's personal project that he had been working toward for the past decade, but Cinema Center was the one funding it. With massive cost overruns, no script, John Sturges quitting, Steve and Neile separating, and no end in sight, Cinema Center executives flew to France to offer Steve an ultimatum. He had to give up his salary and profit points or the studio would cancel the production. Even worse, they had already touched base with Robert Redford about replacing Steve in his own movie so that the film wouldn't be a total loss.

466. McQueen's representatives proved to be virtually powerless against the serious threat of shutting down *Le Mans* or replacing Steve with Robert Redford, so he fired his longtime agent Stan Kamen and the William Morris Agency. The firing was as straightforward as they come: Steve sent a telegram reading, "Dear Stan, You're fired. Letter follows. Steve McQueen." Not long after that, *Le Mans* director John Sturges quit because he simply didn't feel like dealing with Steve McQueen any longer.

467. *The Sand Pebbles* was one of the most colossal undertakings Hollywood had yet seen. It was the first big-budget Hollywood film shot completely on-site in Taiwan. The 111 crewmen were brought to Taiwan, which included 47 actors and 32 interpreters, and thousands of extras were hired for crowd scenes. The original 80-day film schedule ended up taking seven months and cost around $12 million to produce. The bulk of that cost went to Steve McQueen's salary, clocking in at $650,000.

468. Every scene in *The Sand Pebbles* was filmed twice, two different ways. McQueen had so much input and requested so many changes to each scene that director Robert Wise suggested that they shoot one take in his vision, and one in Steve's vision, then Steve could decide which one he liked better during the editing phase. Shooting everything twice added a massive time strain to the already over-schedule film, and to top it off, not one of McQueen's requested scenes made it into the final version.

469. Both Steve and Faye Dunaway in *The Thomas Crown Affair* appeared to be excellent Chess players, maybe a little too good. The moves used in the movie were based on a real match between world-renowned champions Gustav Zeissl and Walter Von Walthoffen in Vienna in 1899.

470. Of course, the long kiss takes most audiences' attention, having taken eight hours to shoot. McQueen's and Dunaway's lips were sore for days after the scene was filmed.

471. Would you believe that the famous tweed jacket worn by Steve McQueen in *Bullitt* is still around today? The Bullitt look became an immediate hit in the fashion world, and as he often did, McQueen kept the jacket after filming was completed. While clearing out his closet soon after, he came across the jacket, and since he had already created the fad and was on to the next one, passed it along to his son, Chad. Chad kept the jacket in his possession for 46 years before it was sold at auction for $120,000.

472. Steve insisted that a pool table be installed in the apartment rented for him during the filming of *Bullitt*. There was just one small problem: There was no possible way to get a pool table into the 12th-story apartment with the building's awkwardly small elevator. McQueen repeated his simple request that he wanted a pool table. To make the star of the movie happy, producers arranged for a pool table to be lifted up with a crane and swung into the side of the apartment. To do this, a large glass window had to be broken and then repaired once the table was inside.

473. With McQueen's name having been rumored to appear alongside Paul Newman's in *Butch Cassidy and the Sundance Kid*, studios went wild over the concept. Bidding on William Goldman's script reached $400,000, which made him the highest-paid screenwriter in history just because of a rumor that Newman and McQueen would be working together. As we know, McQueen dropped out of the film, but it still went on to be one of the most successful of all time.

474. The day before the Boston premier of *The Thomas Crown Affair*, the Massachusetts State Legislature declared the day Steve McQueen Day. McQueen appeared at the legislature where he gave a speech and was awarded an honorary commission by the Boston Police Department. As part of that commission he was given a badge to carry, which would hopefully keep him out of trouble if the need arose.

475. Steve appeared in episode 841 of the game show *What's My Line?* in 1966. He was the mystery guest in which four contestants tried to guess who he was while they were blindfolded. Although he did a voice impersonation and gave only yes and no answers, the contestants were able to figure it out quickly. One reason for this may have been the audience's excited reaction to him walking on stage.

476. Although his appearance on *The Tonight Show Starring Johnny Carson* in 1964 to promote *The Great Escape* didn't go over all that well with the studio, he appeared on the show again in 1966 to promote *The Sand Pebbles.*

477. When the script for *The Thomas Crown Affair* was first being shopped around, McQueen wasn't even a consideration for the lead role. Sean Connery was the first choice, followed by Rock Hudson when he turned it down. Neile and agent Stan Kamen thought the three-piece suit-wearing, polo-playing Boston executive would be perfect for him, plus they thought he needed to get away from the military and cowboy roles that he had been typecast in. Neile and Kamen knew Steve wouldn't go for the role, so they told him that all of the great leading men were being considered but that director Norman Jewison didn't want him. The idea that a director didn't want him got to Steve, and he made a push for the role.

478. Although McQueen had discussed returning for a sequel to *The Magnificent Seven*, Yul Brynner was the only actor from the original to reprise his role in 1966's *Return of the Magnificent Seven*. McQueen's character, Vin, was played by Robert Fuller in the sequel.

479. In *Nevada Smith*, McQueen played a 16-year-old teenager when he was in fact 35 years old. He was only eight years younger than Gene Evans, who played his father in the film.

480. McQueen gave *The Sand Pebbles* writer Robert Anderson such a difficult time when crafting the script that he ended up quitting. Years later, Anderson wrote a play that Steve wanted to be in and refused to cast him.

481. In *The Sand Pebbles*, Jake Holman's Machinist Mate First Class patch worn on his left shoulder has the crow facing to the right, or forward. The crow on this patch didn't face to the right until 1941 when it was changed to face the enemy in front of the soldier. In 1926 when the movie takes place, that patch should have had the crow facing left, or rearward.

482. For *The Thomas Crown Affair* polo match, Steve wears the number 2 on his shirt. This isn't random, player numbers in polo are for their positions. The number 2 player is an offensive role responsible for scoring or assisting the number 1 player.

483. Detective Frank Bullitt's holster is a custom-made fast-draw shoulder harness modeled after the one worn by real-life homicide inspector Dave Toschi. Toschi was famous for his work on the Zodiac killings, and McQueen used him as a model when preparing for his role as a detective.

484. Robert Vaughn plays the memorable Senator Walter Chalmers in *Bullitt*, but he initially tried to pass on the role because he didn't like the hard-to-follow script. McQueen kept pressing for his involvement in the project, and it wasn't until the studio offered him too much money to turn down that he accepted.

485. The navy suit that Detective Frank Bullitt wears in the early scenes of *Bullitt* was custom made for Steve McQueen by Doug Haywood's shop, which was director Peter Yates' favorite tailor in London.

486. Frank Bullitt's gun in *Bullitt* is a Colt Diamondback revolver chambered in .38 special. It has Colt Detective Special grips.

MOVIE AUTOMOBILE FACTS

487. To support and promote the release of *The Sand Pebbles*, McQueen went to New York for appearances on all the major interview shows. A limousine was hired to chauffeur him around the city, which even then was notoriously difficult to drive around and park. After the first day of the trip, he refused the limo and instead rented a Volkswagen Beetle to drive himself around.

continued on page 169

Steve McQueen changes his daughter Terry's diaper at the family's Solar Drive home. (Photo Courtesy Sid Avery/MPTVImages.com)

Not only did Steve McQueen drive this 1951 Chevrolet Styline in his last film, The Hunter, *but he purchased it from the studio for his own use afterwards. It was sold as part of the 1984 Steve McQueen auction and was most recently sold at Barrett-Jackson Scottsdale 2018 for $126,500. (Photo Courtesy Barrett-Jackson)*

Steve McQueen is shown as bounty hunter Josh Randall on his hit television show Wanted Dead or Alive. *Between the sawed-off Winchester rifle known as the Mare's Leg and that icy, blue-eyed stare, fugitives in the Old West were in for trouble. (Photo Courtesy Gabi Rona/MPTVImages.com)*

Those .45-70 rifle rounds might add a tough touch to Josh Randall's look, but in actuality his Mare's Leg rifle used .44-40 rifle rounds. Wanted Dead or Alive *was McQueen's public launch vehicle that brought him into every household in America. He was on the show for three years before going all in on feature films. (Photo Courtesy Gabi Rona/MPTVImages.com)*

Once again behind the wheel, although this World War II–era Jeep is a far cry from some of the vehicles McQueen drove in his films. This is from Never So Few, *in which he co-starred alongside Frank Sinatra. (Photo Courtesy MPTVImages.com)*

His films often found him behind the wheel; one of his earliest ones was The Great St. Louis Bank Robbery, *in which he played the getaway driver. (Photo MPTVImages.com)*

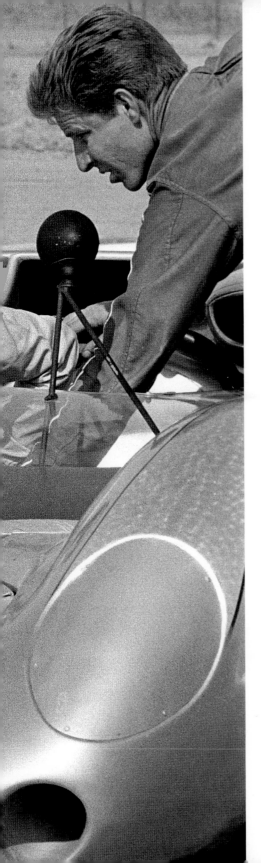

McQueen takes a quick break for a cigarette and a chat from the driver's seat of his Lotus 11 race car. The Lotus was his first dedicated race car and it allowed him to take his driving to the next level. (Photo Courtesy Chester Maydole/ MPTVImages.com)

Steve and Neile McQueen at their Brentwood home in 1967 with their Ferrari 275 GTS. (Photo Courtesy Gunther/ MPTVImages.com)

Steve and Director John Sturges check out McQueen's 1957 Jaguar XKSS while on the Goldwyn studio lot in 1960. The Jag is in its best-known green color, but it was white when Steve purchased it. (Photo Courtesy Sid Avery/MPTVImages.com)

Steve McQueen did most of the stunt riding in The Great Escape. *He was the one who pressed for the motorcycle escape scene, which wasn't in the original script. (Photo Courtesy MPTVImages.com)*

Stuntman Bud Ekins launches the late-model Triumph motorcycle he built for The Great Escape *over a fake barbed-wire fence. Movie goers thought it really was McQueen doing the jump until he stated publicly on* The Tonight Show Starring Johnny Carson *that it was his friend Bud Ekins. (Photo Courtesy MTPVImages.com)*

One of McQueen's early breakout roles was as Virgil Hilts in *The Great Escape*. He famously played catch with himself while in solitary confinement, known as "the cooler." His nickname in the film became "The Cooler King," which may have led to his nickname in real life as "The King of Cool." (Photo Courtesy *MPTVImages.com*)

Steve reaches in to pop the hood on his 1963 Ferrari 250GT Berlinetta Lusso. Or maybe he's lighting a cigarette? Neile bought the brown sports car for him for his birthday in 1964. (Photo Courtesy Chester Maydole/MPTVImages.com)

It may not have been a clear role for Steve McQueen at first, but most would agree that he was in his prime as Boston millionaire *Thomas Crown* in The Thomas Crown Affair. *A finely tailored three-piece suit and a Rolls-Royce coupe provided excellent props. (Photo Courtesy MPTVImages.com)*

Frank Bullitt, the essence of cool, was the cop that even the counter-culture youth of the day could root for. Although numerous high-profile offers came in afterward for more police roles, Steve turned them all down. (Photo Courtesy Mel Traxel/MPTVImages.com)

As part of its public debut, the original Bullitt *Mustang was displayed on the National Mall in Washington, D.C. (Photo Courtesy Historic Vehicle Association)*

"Hello, Engine. I'm Jake Holman." That's how Steve McQueen greets the engine of the US Navy ship, the San Pablo, *in* The Sand Pebbles. *(Photo Courtesy MPTVImages.com)*

While on location in The Philippines shooting **The Sand Pebbles**, McQueen had a 1966 Suzuki T20 race bike to rip around the streets. Because of the massive studio expenditure and publicity brought to the area, local police were instructed not to pull him over. (Photo Courtesy Ted Allen/MPTVImages.com).

Left: Here, McQueen is looking to make a fast getaway on his Triumph motorcycle during the filming of **Bullitt**. That's his Clark Cortez motor home behind him. He was one of the first stars to own his trailer and take it with him from set to set. (Photo Courtesy Mel Traxel/MPTVImages.com)

It must have been a good session of filming Le Mans *judging by the smile on Steve's face as he exits the Gulf Porsche 917. (Photo Courtesy Mel Traxel/ MPTVImages.com)*

Today's trophy trucks are million-dollar marvels that run the Baja 1000 with helicopter support. Back when Steve McQueen ran it in 1969, this buggy, named the Baja Boot *was the latest and greatest in off-road racing tech. (Todd Zuercher Photo)*

Here, Steve is playing around with his Rickman Metisse for a magazine pho-toshoot. The bespoke Metisse was the ultimate desert motorcycle of the day. (Photo Courtesy Gunther/MPTVImages.com)

Both Steve and Ali MacGraw, his second wife, were clearly style icons of t◌ mid-1970s. (Photo Courtesy Gary Lewis/MPTVImages.co◌

The quintessential Steve McQueen on the set of Le Mans in France, 1971. He's wearing his Tag Heuer Monaco watch and, although he's in front of the Gulf Porsche pits, you can see the Ferrari 512 behind him. (Photo Courtesy Mel Traxel/MPTVImages.com)

Here is Steve McQueen as Henri Charrière in Papillon *alongside costar Dustin Hoffman as Louis Dega. (Photo Courtesy MPTVImages.com)*

Steve has his Husqvarna loaded up and is ready for a day of filming On Any Sunday. *(Photo Courtesy Chester Maydole.MPTVImages.com)*

On the starting line of what appears to be the 1970 Lake Elsinore race for the filming of On Any Sunday, *Steve* is astride his trusty Husqvarna, one of two featured in the film. Notice that his helmet says "McQueen" on the side. That's just so you can pick him out for the film, otherwise he raced under the pseudonym Harvey Mushman. (Photo Courtesy Chester Maydole/ MPTVImages.com)

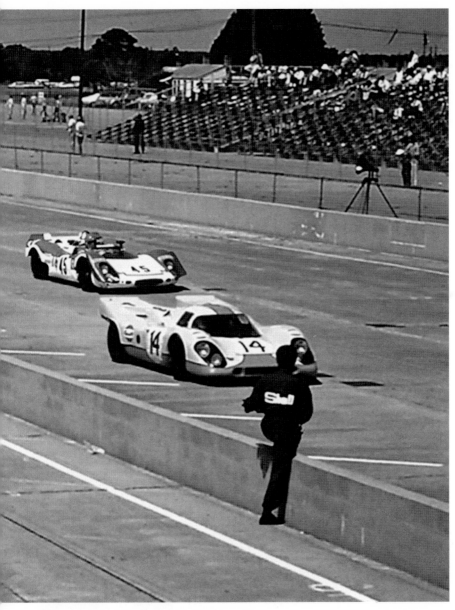

Steve chases the bigger Gulf Porsche 917s in his open-cockpit, unsponsored 908. (Photo Courtesy Louis Galanos)

Solar Productions owned the Porsche 908 that Steve used to prepare himself for filming **Le Mans**. His first big race in it was in 1970 at Sebring where he drove alongside Peter Revson. (Photo Courtesy Louis Galanos)

Steve broke his foot in six places in a motorcycle race just weeks before he planned to run the 1970 12 Hours of Sebring. Race officials finally allowed him to race after he covered his cast with fire-retardant material. (Photo Courtesy Don Bok)

Steve and Neile McQueen are shown before the start of the 1970 12 Hours of Sebring. This was one of the last times Neile saw him race as their marriage ended the following year during the filming of Le Mans. *Both publicly blamed the dangers of racing as a cause of the split. (Photo Courtesy Don Bok)*

He may not have been the top driver to compete at Sebring in 1970, but he was definitely one of the most popular with the press and public. Mario Andretti stated after he won the race that with all the press there, he'd never be able to live down losing to an actor. (Photo Courtesy Don Bok)

Since both Steve and Peter Revson drove the number 48 Porsche 908 at Sebring, how can one tell which driver is which? It's easy: Steve wore an open-face helmet and Revson wore a full-face helmet with visor. This shot shows Revson. (Photo Courtesy Don Bok)

Steve speaks with a journalist during practice rounds at the 1970 12 Hours of Sebring. Obviously, he didn't sport his famous Heuer Monaco watch until production on Le Mans began the following year. (Photo Courtesy Louis Galanos)

Here, Steve pilots the number 48 Porsche 908 in his open-face helmet. It's an interesting choice of protective gear considering how many millions of dollars he made with his face. (Photo Courtesy Don Bok)

Just like race drivers today, Steve enjoys a Coke with the crew. Notice the duct tape around his left leg that secured his fire-retardant cast and protective clothing. (Photo Courtesy Louis Galanos)

Earlier in the race, Mario Andretti in his number-19 factory Ferrari 512S passes Steve's teammate Peter Revson in the smaller-displacement number-48 Porsche 908. The number 19 Ferrari retired later in the race with mechanical issues and Andretti moved over to the race-leading number-21 Ferrari 512S and piloted that car to victory, once again passing the number-48 Porsche and Peter Revson with only laps to spare. (Photo Courtesy Louis Galanos)

Steve goes over strategy with team manager Andrew Ferguson after a practice session. Ferguson would later lead the charge with the 908 as a camera car during the 1970 running of Le Mans as well. (Photo Courtesy Louis Galanos)

One of the few times Steve and Barbara were seen in public was at the premier for Tom Horn *in Los Angeles. Steve was very much affected by his mesothelioma at this point, but he put on a happy face for the crowd and reporters. ((Photo Courtesy Gunther/MPTVImages.com)*

Legendary painter and customizer Von Dutch owned this 1931 Brough Superior SS80 before selling it to Steve McQueen for his collection. (Photo Courtesy Tyler Greenblatt)

This special World War I–era Harley-Davidson pigeon carrier motorcycle had been separated for many years after its use overseas. The motorcycle found its way into McQueen's collection while the pigeon carrier eventually found its way to Wheels Through Time museum in Maggie Valley, North Carolina. (Photo Courtesy Tyler Greenblatt)

The latest iteration of the Bullitt Mustang with 480 hp and a 163-mph top speed would surely have impressed Steve McQueen, even though he'd likely struggle with the 12-inch dashboard touchscreen. (Photo Courtesy Ford Motor Company)

Steve sits astride his Husqvarna 400 Cross before filming the Elsinore scene for On Any Sunday. *Wearing proper safety gear was important to him, and in 1971, this was it! (Photo Courtesy Chester Maydole/MPTVImages.com)*

It may not be the typical high-performance or beautiful motorcycle that Steve McQueen normally owned and rode, but he did put quite a few miles on this 1947 Indian Chief chopper nicknamed "The Blob." It is currently on display at the National Motorcycle Museum in Anamosa, Iowa, alongside a number of collectible Steve McQueen items. (Photo Courtesy Bryan Harley)

488. Upon leaving New York, he simply left the rental car in the hotel's parking lot and flew back to Los Angeles. Three months later, an angry Richard Zanuck, president of 20th Century Fox, discovered the car was still being paid for by the company and had it returned.

489. In the past, high-speed driving scenes had been faked by speeding up the film to make the cars look as if they were going fast rather than actually driving fast. Everyone knew that approach wouldn't work for the *Bullitt* chase, so it was decided that stuntmen would pilot the cars at actual chase speeds. The fastest speed attained by the cars in the chase sequence was 124 mph!

490. Yet again, a studio's insurance company prevented McQueen from doing any of the dangerous stunts in *Bullitt*, and that task fell to friend and stuntman Bud Ekins. It wasn't an easy sell to McQueen, who reportedly fought for four days to be allowed to do his own stunts. Having crashed the Mustang three times already didn't convince Steve, so director Peter Yates gave McQueen a false start time, and by the time he showed up on the set, Ekins had already completed the riskier shots.

491. In scenes where the car's rearview mirror is tilted up or not visible, that's Ekins driving. In the close-up detail shots where the mirror sits as it should, it's McQueen.

492. On his first day on the job, 12-year-old Mitch Vogel received a driving lesson from Steve McQueen in the yellow Winton Flyer. The day started with a publicity shoot at the CBS studio of Steve and Mitch with the car. Steve began driving the car around so that the press could take some action shots, but then he stopped and gave Mitch the wheel. His character had to drive the car in the movie, so why not learn how right away? Throughout the film, Steve took on a father-figure role toward the young actor, looking out for him when no one else was there to do it.

493. Von Dutch built the 1904 Winton Flyer in *The Reivers* from scratch with a three-month deadline and a $10,000 paycheck. Although the three months was tight, Von Dutch reportedly didn't get started on the car until he had only two weeks left to go. At that point he worked nearly 24-hour days, sometimes even 24 hours at a time, to finish the car in his backyard. Von Dutch was also hired to serve as an on-location mechanic for the film and played a blacksmith.

494. The 1967 Ferrari 275 GTS/4 NART Spyder (chassis number 09437) driven by Faye Dunaway's character in *The Thomas Crown Affair* was the first such convertible built by the North American Racing Team shop. The 275 GTB was never offered from the Ferrari factory in a convertible version, so to target his American customers, North American importer Luigi Chinetti, at the behest of his son, decided to build them himself.

495. Chassis number 09437 is one of two aluminum-bodied NART Spyders and the only one known to have ever been raced. It sold for nearly $4 million at auction in Pebble Beach in 2005.

496. The 1970 Porsche 911S used in the filming of *Le Mans* was delivered new to Steve on set. Interestingly, he owned a nearly identical 1969 911S at the time but opted not to use it for filming. Unlike his own car, the 1970 was fully loaded with factory air conditioning, yellow fog lamps, Blaupunkt stereo, and leather upholstery.

497. After filming, the Le Mans 911 returned to Los Angeles with McQueen, where he subsequently sold it in January 1971. The car sold for $1,375,000 in 2011 to its fifth and current owner.

498. Many people think that the TC 100 and TC 300 Massachusetts license plates used on Thomas Crown's Rolls-Royce and dune buggy were the result of creative license to add to the character. Actually, the state of Massachusetts had approved personalized vanity plates in 1966, just a year before filming began. Residents could create their own plate identification containing two to six characters. Massachusetts was one of the early adopters of the vanity plate concept, not surprising because it was also the first state to issue metal license plates to motor vehicles. Interestingly, the movie never shows a vehicle with TC 200.

499. That hot little dune buggy that Thomas Crown drives around the beach isn't just any run-of-the-mill Volkswagen-powered Manx. The "TC 300" buggy used in the film rocked a 140-hp, horizontally-opposed, air-cooled, six-cylinder out of a Chevrolet Corvair. Bruce Meyers' original purpose for his Manx concept was to create something that would provide a lot of inexpensive fun. A stock flat-four Volkswagen engine out of an old Beetle usually put out between 40 and 75 horses, maybe up to 100 if it was tuned properly. Either way, the raw torque of an air-cooled six and its spry 140 hp meant that Thomas Crown's dune buggy could keep pace with some of the finest sports cars of the day. It currently resides in Hawaii.

500. No stunt doubles were used during the dune buggy scenes in *The Thomas Crown Affair*. Yes, that means that in the scene where McQueen flings the vehicle off a dune and it takes a brute landing in the front, that's actually him and Faye Dunaway in it. Since the open-air vehicle made the passengers highly visible, it made using stunt doubles impossible without being obvious. According to Steve, his costar was "a trooper." After the big jump scene, he remembered, "I looked over and Faye was all bug-eyed; the back of the floorboard was scratched raw from her heels diggin' in."

501. Ironically, that small jump may be the only one of his career in which he was actually behind the wheel. His famous jumps in *The Great Escape* and *Bullitt* were handled by stuntman Bud Ekins.

502. While piloting the Meyers Manx dune buggy on the set of *The Thomas Crown Affair*, McQueen experienced a control system failure that left the steering wheel locked straight and the throttle jammed. Unable to do anything, the dune buggy sped into the ocean with him and Faye Dunaway aboard. In the film, the scene cuts out before the vehicle actually hits the water. After the incident, McQueen said, "Faye came out of it soaked and smiling." The engine had to be rebuilt to eliminate all of the damaging saltwater.

503. Steve knew that no pretty, bone-stock Mustang would suffice as Frank Bullitt's car, so a number of modifications were made to the two donor cars. The suspension and chassis were beefed up with Koni shocks and extra frame supports. The stock transverse muffler was removed to make the car sound even meaner on film. In a surprising move that auto manufacturers would likely not allow today, the badging was removed as was the famous pony in the middle of the grill. Most of the chrome was painted black or body color and the wheels were swapped for a set of American Racing Torq-Thrust mags.

504. The steering wheel used in the *Bullitt* Mustang is from a 1967 Shelby GT that famed upholsterer Tony Nancy wrapped in black leather.

505. A car losing its hubcaps during hard cornering is one of the hallmarks of classic chase scenes that, for the most part, is gone today. Basically, if a car today has hubcaps, chances are no one wants to see it in a chase scene. The producers of *Bullitt* wanted the drama of flying hubcaps; the only problem was that the Dodge Charger R/T used in the film would have come with mag or alloy wheels. For the movie, the stock wheels were replaced with steel wheels, hubcaps, and whitewall tires for the effect. Eight hubcaps are seen flying off the Dodge Challenger throughout the chase sequence with the right front hubcap coming off four times from start to finish!

506. In the *Bullitt* chase scene, the corner of Larkin and Chestnut streets provided some difficulty for the drivers. For those without a map of San Francisco built into their brains, it's the turn where McQueen (actually doing the driving) overshoots the turn and has to reverse the Mustang to correct. He then burns out the left tire in an effort to catch back up to the big-block Dodge. That same corner provided some grief for the Charger as well, although it's not quite so noticeable in the film. Stunt driver Bill Hickman took that same turn too wide and took out a camera!

507. Did you know that in the *Bullitt* scene where the motorcycle rider goes down in front of the Mustang, it's Bud Ekins sliding across the pavement? It was his idea to dangerously crash the BSA although Steve urged him not to. He told his friend, "You're liable to get kissed off, and your wife'll never forgive me." McQueen had to spin the Mustang sideways in order to miss him sliding across the pavement, which led to him spinning the car around twice and going off the road, nearly losing the chase. The idea for the motorcycle stunt came the same day it was filmed, with Ekins asking a friend with a motorcycle shop to send over a BSA 750 and a set of leathers.

508. Von Dutch's Winton Flyer creation looked right at home in 1968's *The Reivers*. What wasn't necessarily at home was the modern British Motors Corporation four-cylinder engine putting out about 65 hp when the original was only good for about 18. Because the drivetrain was never seen in the film, Von Dutch was able to take some creative license in that department, and because McQueen would be driving it, the extra power would come in handy. In truth, the modern drivetrain allowed the brass-era vehicle to be beat on like any other movie car, providing the most realistic experience for the moviegoer. The crank-to-start scenes and engine sounds were faked for the film; an electric starter and high-performance engine hum would have sounded awkward.

509. For the November 1966 issue of *Popular Science*, Steve McQueen lived out every motorcyclist's fantasy when he had the opportunity to test a handful of new off-road models. He tested a BSA Hornet, Norton-Matisse, Triumph Bonneville, Honda, Greeves, and Montessa. Of course, his favorite was the Triumph, but he admitted that Honda had developed an excellent scrambler. In just a few years, he was riding Hondas regularly as their machines became even better developed.

510. When it came to the high-speed chase scenes in *Bullitt*, the Mustang GT and Dodge Charger were plenty capable of performing at the speeds necessary to make viewers' hearts race. However, to film cars racing along at more than 100 mph, the crew needed a camera car that could not only keep up but also maneuver around them as needed. With that need in mind, a crewmember was sent to buy a brand-new convertible Corvette, which was stripped of its fiberglass body to make mounting cameras to the frame and birdcage easier. Metal panels were fabricated around the mounting points to act as fenders and protection for the occupants. The Corvette camera car's whereabouts are unknown today.

511. At the end of *Bullitt*, when Frank Bullit chases the killer on foot across the airport tarmac as planes take off and land all around them was shot in real time, and with Bullit nearly getting taken out by some landing gear! McQueen insisted on doing the scrupulously timed stunt himself so that the whole thing could be done in a single take. He was given the go-ahead to take off running at the precise moment and at the precise speed so that the Pan Am Boeing 707 would just miss him with both the landing gear and the jet wash that followed. The plane's wing even came within two feet of the film crew.

512. After the airport runway stunt, a reporter asked Steve why they didn't use a dummy (stuntman) for the shot, to which he replied, "They did!"

513. The most expensive movie prop to date was the 1920s-era gunboat built specifically for *The Sand Pebbles* to the tune of $250,000. The *San Pablo* arrived on the scene a couple of weeks late because the Keelung River was at low tide when shooting was initially planned. Steve and stuntman Loren Janes even enjoyed a special shipment of California Jam on board the ship, hidden from the rest of the crew.

514. The ship used in *The Sand Pebbles*, the *San Pueblo*, was a recreation of a Spanish ship seized by the United States in the

Spanish-American war and was recommissioned as the USS *Villa-lobos*. It was actually used by the Navy in the Far East. The movie ship was built in Taiwan, and although it was for the most part operational, it actually couldn't move. A host of movie equipment was mounted to the hull that included lights and camera rigs, plus it had to remain steady so as not to sicken the cast and crew while swaying back and forth. A real seaworthy vessel would have made shooting much more difficult, and not any more realistic.

515. The massive steam engine that McQueen's character, Jake Hol-men, works on and talks to in *The Sand Pebbles* was actually located on a sound stage in California, with the rest of the engine room being built around it. So what powered the *San Pueblo*? The ship built for the movie used diesel engines, which give off barely any exhaust smoke compared to a coal-fired steam engine. To simulate the appearance of a coal-burning smoke stack, the movie ship was built with a burn room at the base of the smoke stack where the crew burned old tires and other waste to create realistic billowing black smoke. The engine from the sound stage is on display aboard the USS *Lane Victory*, a World War II ship stationed in Los Angeles.

516. In *The Thomas Crown Affair*, McQueen's character, Thomas Crown, sneaks out of his house to avoid detection, knocks out the detective on duty, and sends him in his car rolling into a tree doused in booze. The accident appears worse than it is; like most front-end crashes, the radiator is punctured and steam comes billowing out from under the hood. The only problem is that the car had been idle for several hours at night when it's cooler, making it extremely unlikely that the coolant would be anywhere near hot enough to create steam.

517. As you might imagine, the hill-jumping chase scene in *Bullitt* did a real number on the cars involved. Even with additional chassis bracing and suspension upgrades, the cars needed serious repairs after the shoot. The Mustang lost both door handles and broke the front shocks and passenger-side steering armature. After the final shooting scene, the entire door fell right off the hinges as

Bud Ekins stepped out! None of the damage was surprising considering that to nail the 30-foot jumps Ekins had to drive down the hill at 60 mph, bottoming the car across the flat intersection, and launch it off the next hill. Any minor mistake could have sent the car barrel-rolling down the entire hill.

518. Members of the *Le Mans* production crew formed a special club called The Le Mans Daredevil Driving and Beer Drinking Society because so many of them had crashed their personal and/or movie vehicles during the movie's filming. Membership into the society could only be attained by crashing a vehicle, which was fairly easy to do with the entire Le Mans circuit available to the crew at all times. The "beer drinking" aspect of the club likely helps explain why there were so many accidents.

519. The idea for jumping the Mustang and Charger down San Francisco's hills in *Bullitt* was actually McQueen's idea. He and Don Gordon were riding their motorcycles around the city in the middle of the night when Steve took off, hit one of the intersections at speed, and launched spectacularly in the air. Immediately after nailing the jump, Steve stopped and thought how cool it would be if they could get a car to do that. Later that morning, he worked with Bud Ekins and the crew to develop his car-jumping vision into a reality and making Bullitt's car chase one of the most exciting of all time.

520. During one scene in *The Thomas Crown Affair*, Crown's Rolls-Royce had to be placed on a flatbed trailer so that Steve could concentrate on his dialogue with Faye Dunaway without having to worry about also driving the car. A behind-the-scenes camera filmed the entire scene, but viewers of the film couldn't tell the difference. Steve was clearly shown pretending to drive the Rolls-Royce while it was sitting on a flatbed. When he saw the footage that went public, he was furious, thinking that it affected his image as a driver.

521. Throughout the filming of *The Sand Pebbles*, Dick Crenna (the captain) was given personal use of the ship's captain's cabin. He and McQueen hit it off immediately after they spent five hours one day early on talking about their roles. Yet Crenna still felt awkward about having his own quarters and the star of the movie having to be with the rest of the crew. He allowed Richard Attenborough to share the quarters with him until Steve showed up on set with Neile's homemade cinnamon bread and told Crenna that if he included him in sharing the captain's quarters Neile would make him cinnamon bread every day.

522. The glider that McQueen flies in *The Thomas Crown Affair* is a Schweizer SGS 1-23H-15. The one used in the film was owned by a private aviator in New York until 2013 when he crashed it in Georgia.

523. During the chase sequences in *Bullitt*, McQueen purposely keeps his face as close as possible to the window so that viewers can see that it's actually him driving the car and not a stunt double.

524. The *Bullitt* chase scene lasts 10 minutes and 53 seconds.

525. The original plan for the *Bullitt* chase scene called for a powerful musical score to accompany it. After seeing the footage and hearing the raw soundtrack, composer Lalo Schifrin believed that all the real sounds of the chase were so good that it didn't need any music. Therefore, there is no music for the entire chase scene.

526. In the opening credit scenes of *Bullitt* when an extra is driving out of the garage, Steve's green Jaguar XKSS is visible sitting in the parking garage.

527. Like many race car drivers who like to chew gum while they drive, Steve chews gum during the *Bullitt* chase scene. In the close-up shots of him driving you can see him chewing.

528. After the filming of *Bullitt* was complete, the primary Mustang was refurbished on behalf of Warner Brothers and sold to police detective Frank Marranca of New Jersey along with a letter from Ford authenticating the vehicle has having been originally sold to Solar Productions for use in *Bullitt*.

AUTOMOBILE COLLECTION

529. One of the most historically important cars owned by Steve McQueen was a 1966 Corvette that was specially prepared for him to review in an article in the August 1966 issue of *Sports Illustrated*. Unlike the vast majority of vehicles he owned over the years that are preserved with their Steve McQueen provenance, the Corvette disappeared after he sold it in the late 1960s. Thanks to the efforts of Corvette experts Franz Estereicher and Kevin Mackay, the car was finally discovered in 2016 for sale on eBay, and quickly purchased by Estericher.

530. To confirm the car's true identity, Kevin Mackay flew to Seattle to inspect it in person. Based on what he could see in photographs, he knew that the car needed to have several rare options, including a saddle vinyl interior, Milano Maroon paint, sidepipes, headrests, and shoulder belts. The car checked all the boxes, making it a statistical likelihood that this was the missing McQueen Corvette. Mackay and Estereicher knew that for it to be the right car, it would have been delivered to a Southern California Chevrolet dealership.

531. The all-important National Corvette Restorers Society (NCRS) shipping and data report revealed that not to be the case. In fact, the Corvette was shipped directly to GM Engineering to be outfitted with experimental high-performance components, since it was to be tested against other sports cars on the track. This was the only Corvette shipped to Engineering in the timeframe of the article, and letters between Steve McQueen and Zora Arkus-Duntov confirm that's where the car in the article was originally sent.

532. Can you imagine Steve McQueen driving a Mini Cooper? It's true! He purchased a new Austin Mini Cooper S in 1967 and immediately sent it to Lee Brown for customization. Brown repainted the green and white car medium brown metallic with a beige top because Steve preferred subtle colors for his cars. Brown added a wood dash and, at McQueen's unusual request, a single fog light on the right side of the bumper. Tony Nancy was hired to redo the interior in a light brown vinyl. McQueen kept it for a few years before selling it, but the Mini's story doesn't end there.

533. The current owner of the Mini Cooper S, Lee Brown, saw an ad for the car in the *Los Angeles Times* in 1990, recognized it, and purchased it for $10,000.

534. A Mulholland Drive resident received an interesting visit one night when Steve McQueen knocked on his door. McQueen had been out driving his Mini Cooper when he pulled over to relieve himself. Apparently, he had left the car in neutral and it rolled away, smashing into another car. McQueen offered to pay for the damage, but the car's owner insisted he didn't want any money, he just wanted to talk to the actor for a little while. Steve didn't get out of the man's house until 6 a.m. when he drove the Mini to Lee Brown's shop to get it fixed.

535. Steve McQueen must have liked *The Thomas Crown Affair* Ferrari quite a bit, as he went on to buy his own, taking delivery in the spring of 1967. McQueen's 275 GTS/4 NART Spyder, chassis number 10453, is 1 of 10 produced and 1 of the 8 that used steel bodywork. Immediately, he commissioned Lee Brown to repaint the car a different shade of blue and do some custom work. He removed the bumpers, added some race-style components, a built-in radio (since the car didn't come with one), and a Frenched-in power antenna. Of course, Tony Nancy lent his efforts to the leatherwork.

536. Steve picked up his newly-customized NART Spyder on a Thursday and wrecked it over the weekend through no fault of his own when he was sandwiched at a red light by a truck. The car was destroyed and had to be rebuilt, this time by Junior Conway, who added a larger rear spoiler and changed the shade of blue. By the time repairs were complete, Steve had other cars, including newer Ferraris that he was enjoying, so he sold the car in 1971. The car currently resides in New York.

537. McQueen's Jeep CJ was known as "Super Jeep" and built by Con-Ferr in Burbank, California, the same firm that built the Corvair-powered dune buggy in *The Thomas Crown Affair*. Steve dropped off a base Universal Jeep and had the company completely tear it down and rebuild it with the latest off-road technology, with speed, durability, and safety all top priorities. Extra welds and bracing were added throughout the frame and dual Koni shocks were fitted to all four wheels, with the rear wheels each receiving a dual leaf-spring setup. Two 15-gallon fuel tanks were stuffed behind the taillights and a 30-gallon tank sat under the rear deck.

538. The 350-ci Chevy engine under the hood, tuned to an estimated 400 hp by some accounts, would need all the fuel it could get. "Super Jeep" was featured in *Rod & Custom* magazine after Von Dutch did the pinstriping on the off-roader. It was later sold to Sonny Bono, but its current whereabouts are now unknown.

539. Although Steve's 1969 Porsche 911S was the hot ticket when he ordered it in November 1968, Neile was actually driving an even rarer 1968 Porsche 911L. What made the car special was that it was one of 450 produced with Porsche's new Sportmatic transmission. It may sound like it, but it wasn't actually an automatic transmission. The driver still had to shift gears, but without a manual clutch. Considering that Neile had crashed her Corvette a decade before, this was probably the perfect car for her to use around town.

540. When the McQueen family went to the local drive-in theater, do you imagine them taking a station wagon? Probably not. Instead, according to Chad McQueen in *McQueen's Machines* by Matt Stone, when his family went to the theater it was in Steve's Army surplus half-track truck. The truck sported traditional wheels on the front but had a tank tread driving it from the rear. Steve had the seats replaced with a set from Solar Engineering and Von Dutch paint pinstripes right over the olive drab camouflage paint.

541. As usual, Steve McQueen was given a vehicle of his choice to use during the filming of *The Sand Pebbles*, which occurred in late 1965 and mostly in 1966. In the mid-1960s, Japanese cars hadn't quite found their groove with enthusiasts, but the racing motorcycles sure had. Fox brought in a new Suzuki T20 prepped for Grand Prix racing for him to use in his free time. The blue and silver motorcycle had a complete race fairing and no headlight. Stories abound that he used to race Army officers stationed in Taiwan from bar to bar with the loser having to buy the next round.

542. During the filming of *The Sand Pebbles*, Taiwanese police were ordered never to pull Steve over, no matter what vehicle he was driving or how fast and recklessly he was driving it.

543. Before shooting the chase sequences in *Bullitt*, McQueen received a letter from Warner Brothers forbidding him to ride a motorcycle until after the film was completed. The letter stated that safe transportation would be provided by the studio. Rather than sign the attached agreement form, McQueen "scrawled something obscene across it and mailed it back." Not only did he recognize that the studio had no legal authority to keep him off a motorcycle, but he found it "incredibly stupid" that he could drive a Mustang over 100 mph through the city but not ride his motorcycle at relatively legal limits.

544. For her birthday in 1966, Steve bought Neile a green Excalibur S3 Roadster. The family presented the car to her with a green bow across the grille while a Mexican mariachi band played "Happy Birthday." Excalibur only built around 30 cars that year, with the Milwaukee-based firm having only first displayed a prototype in 1964. The fast sports car was especially meaningful to Neile because until this point (after wrecking the couple's Corvette in the early days of their relationship), Steve had relegated her to large cars such as Cadillacs, Lincolns, and Fords. Being handed the keys to a sports car again was the ultimate compliment!

545. Did you know that Steve McQueen had initiated talks regarding creating his own motorcycle brand? In 1967, through his Solar Plastics and Engineering company, Steve began negotiating with Montgomery Ward about selling and marketing a motorcycle entirely of his own design. Montgomery Ward was an all-in-one department store that competed with Sears & Roebuck. At the time, Sears marketed motorcycles under the Allstate name. Montgomery Ward eventually built motorcycles using the name Ward and basing them primarily on Benellis.

546. Steve's marketing of a motorcycle would have been way ahead of its time in the sense that a line of men's lifestyle clothes was set to follow the motorcycle's launch. Without a doubt the clothing sales, with McQueen's name behind them, would have far outdone the motorcycles.

547. Steve McQueen, through his Solar enterprises, and John DeLorean, head of GM's Chevrolet division, worked out a deal that would supply Steve with a variety of Chevrolet models in exchange for him driving, racing, and generally being seen in them. Originally, DeLorean wanted Steve to be the company's spokesperson, but Steve declined. A fleet of vehicles was given to Solar for use by the production company as personnel and film vehicles.

548. As he usually did, McQueen finagled a special vehicle for himself out of the deal with Chevrolet. He asked that a brown pickup truck be built at the factory especially for him. An 18-year-old Solar gofer, Mario Iscovich, was sent to Michigan to pick up the truck and drive it home. When Mario arrived, Steve was upset that the nearly 2,300-mile drive had taken him three days instead of two to complete. The whereabouts of this truck are currently unknown, but it's a rare and likely valuable truck, having been a COPO build for Steve McQueen. You can bet it's out there somewhere tricked out with all the bells and whistles you could order in 1969, and maybe some you couldn't.

549. In 1969, McQueen bought a Clark Cortez motorhome for use on film sets and for vacationing with his family. He drove it, with his family onboard, to the Playboy Club in Phoenix one night for dinner. When directed to the back of the parking lot he decided to drive right up the front steps of the club. This is yet another Steve McQueen-owned vehicle the whereabouts of which are unknown today. It may not be one of the most valuable of his vehicles, but the scratch marks on the frame would give the owner a great story to tell at campsites.

550. One of Steve's few good run-ins with law enforcement occurred when he was pulled over for speeding in his Ferrari in Brentwood. The officer who pulled him over was about to hand him a ticket when he realized that it was Steve McQueen. Rather than give him yet another speeding ticket that he would simply pay and continue speeding anyway, the officer told him to simply wait until he was out of sight, then Steve could open the car up again.

RACING

551. The August 1966 issue of *Sports Illustrated* featured an article written by Steve McQueen in which he tested eight of the latest and greatest sports cars and grand tourers from around the world at Riverside International Raceway in Riverside, California. Although he had an agreement with his studio that he wouldn't race anymore, he bent the rules a little bit by going out for a glorified track day. He turned laps around Riverside in a Mercedes 230SL, Cobra 427, Aston Martin DB6, Porsche 911, Alfa Romeo Duetto Spider, Jaguar E-Type, Ferrari 275 GTS, and 427 Corvette.

552. The Corvette McQueen tested for the *Sports Illustrated* article was hardly your run-of-the-mill showroom big-block. The Milano Maroon 1966 coupe was actually sent from the assembly line to GM Engineering where Zora Arkus-Duntov equipped it with the Heavy Duty L88 racing package that featured a 560-plus-hp 427-ci engine. Corvette fans will note that the L88 package wasn't officially available until 1967, making the McQueen Corvette one of only 13 L88 development cars. In his article, he wrote: "Other than the Ferrari, it was the best car I drove at Riverside. And let's face it, it went out the door at $5,500 instead of $14,000. . . No question, it's a brute, a terribly quick car. It must be one of the fastest production cars you can buy for that kind of money." The only catch was that it wasn't exactly a "production" car.

553. McQueen liked the Corvette so much that he convinced Zora Arkus-Duntov to let him keep the car for "a while" with the experimental components, including the heads, tires, and wheels. It remained in this state until March 1967 at which time the experimental components were removed and the car was officially sold to him as a stock 427/425 Corvette. Because the Corvette was meant for the track, it was also optioned with headrests, shoulder harnesses, and a side-pipe exhaust system. The Saddle vinyl interior offset the Milano Maroon paint beautifully; GM hoped to entice buyers looking for style as well as performance.

554. Young Chad McQueen entered his first car race while in France at the two-hour Mini Le Mans kart race. Chad raced a mini Ferrari and was on the tail of the lead racer in a mini GT40 when he bumped him coming out of a corner, sending him into the hay bales. After that, it was Chad's race to win. Not only does he still have the trophy, but he remembers how happy and proud his father was of him.

555. Not all of Steve McQueen's racing was done on the track. He and photographer William Claxton used to race to lunch stops, Steve in his Ferrari Lusso and Claxton in his Porsche 356 SC. At one point during the spirited on-road dual, McQueen took off, leaving Claxton in the dust. Later, Claxton caught up to Steve, who was parked on the side of the road pretending to be bored with waiting.

556. McQueen used his Chevy V-8-powered Jeep to pre-run the 1969 Baja 1000's 832-mile course in October 1969. The Jeep was fast, but it was hardly as smooth as the *Baja Boot* that he ended up competing in. Nowadays, Baja pre-runners are nearly as advanced and complex as the actual race trucks that compete.

557. Although Ferrari's NART Spyder was essentially just a convertible version of the venerable 275 GTB, only one of the ten was ever used for racing purposes and it just happens to be the one driven by Faye Dunaway's character in *The Thomas Crown Affair*. The first Spyder built used an aluminum alloy body, which made it the perfect example for Luigi Chinetti to enter it in the 1967 Sebring 12-Hour. Not only was the car made famous by being driven by a woman on film, but it was campaigned by an all-female driving team that consisted of Denise McCluggage and Pinkie Rollo.

558. Herbert Linge and Jonathon Williams piloted the Solar Productions Porsche 908 at Le Mans that year primarily for the purpose of filming the race, and especially Steve in the Porsche 917. The car was entered and prepped to house several cameras to capture footage that at the time would have been impossible to get otherwise. Linge and Williams would have finished in an impressive ninth place had they completed enough laps. Only seven cars completed the required mileage that year, and it's believed that the Solar team only fell short because of its extended pit stops to swap in cameras with fresh film and careful driving to film the entire race and leave the car in good shape for filming afterward.

559. McQueen once said that if he couldn't handle driving the Porsche 908, there was no point in making *Le Mans*. It turned out that he could handle it, and well, and after two excellent showings in the United States his intentions were to fulfill his lifelong dream and race in *Le Mans*. Solar Productions purchased a new Porsche 917 for him to run along with friend Jackie Stewart under the banner of the factory-backed Gulf-Wyer team.

560. Cinema Center wouldn't allow the star of the film to compete in one of the most dangerous auto races just days before filming was set to begin. Jo Siffert and Brian Redman piloted the car but, as with the other two Gulf-Wyer Porsches, they were forced out of the race with mechanical issues.

561. Have you ever heard of a remote-controlled race car? The idea in today's world of drones and driverless cars isn't all that far-fetched, but in 1970 it was downright revolutionary. To simulate a fatal, fiery crash in the filming of *Le Mans* without hurting a driver, crews had to make two of the Lola-based race cars remote controlled. A system was devised that used electric servo motors for the controls and a chain-and-sprocket system around the steering column to operate the car. An operator sat in a rig set up with the necessary controls, pedals, and steering wheel that triggered an identical operation in the car.

562. To film the high-speed scenes in *Le Mans*, the crew took what was then an obsolete Ford GT40 race car, cut off the top, and turned it into a camera car. Two full-size cameras were mounted in the nose of the car while a rear camera sat on a rotating deck in the rear. The rare race car also housed a passenger seat and harness so that a cameraman could directly control a fourth camera from the car's passenger-side door. The GT40 made a couple of pre-race runs to record the action on pit lane before the actual race and then was heavily relied on for filming the movie.

563. Fellow actor and friend James Garner had also become a race driver to be reckoned with by the late 1960s. After the success of his racing epic, *Grand Prix*, he became involved in off-road racing, just as Steve McQueen had. The two competed not only on the silver screen in the *Grand Prix* versus *Le Mans* battle, but in the off-road world in the Baja 1000 and in the Stardust 7-11.

564. Steve McQueen first competed in the famed Baja 1000 in 1969, which was only the race's third time being officially held. The 832-mile course ran from Ensenada to La Paz, Mexico, essentially running the length of the Baja Peninsula. McQueen and co-driver Harold Daigh competed against nearly 250 other vehicles in a variety of classes. Their vehicle of choice was the Solar Plastics Engineering/Hurst Baja Boot that McQueen said could get "airborne for 50 to 70 feet over road dips . . . Even in bad, choppy sections it'll do 60 or so." Unfortunately, a leaky cooling system caused problems early on in the race, and before even a third of it was run, the transmission failed, forcing them out of the race entirely.

565. The high-performance Baja Boot was designed for high-speed desert racing and would have been severely overrated for short track use, a new version of off-road racing that was the pre-curser to stadium racing. For these specialized races, McQueen bought a long-wheelbase Jeepster powered by a hopped-up Chevrolet engine not all that dissimilar from the one in his CJ. He actually just kind of fell into competing at Ascot. He simply took Chad there one night to watch the races and turned a lap in a friend's racer after it was over. As you might imagine, Steve McQueen can't just do a lap for fun, and it took less than a day for the rumor mill to say that he would be racing on the dirt track soon enough. Steve didn't need much convincing to make the rumors a reality, and he ended up racing several times there in the summer of 1969. And yes, he won.

566. Steve raced Solar Productions' new Porsche 908 for the first time at Holtville Raceway in February 1970, just a month before Sebring. The 350-hp 1,400-pound race car was easily the best on the track that day, allowing McQueen to lap the entire field and set a course lap record in the process.

567. McQueen's Sebring dreams almost came to a disastrous end just a few weeks before the big race when he campaigned the 908 Porsche at Riverside the weekend after Holtville. He won his preliminary race on Saturday but was forced out of Sunday's main event when the car's gearbox exploded. The 908 was equipped with tall Le Mans gears to satisfy the high-speed needs of the French course's famed Mulsanne Straight. He had just run the straight next to pit row and entered Turn One at about 150 mph when "the whole gearbox exploded under me!" The car entered a severe spin, but luckily, didn't crash.

568. The final "practice" race before McQueen took his Porsche 908 to Sebring was the Winter Sprint at the Phoenix International Raceway held on March 1, 1970. The 17-lap race was actually a charity event benefitting the Arizona Boy's Ranch. That didn't mean that McQueen took it easy. He started the race in pole position and not only won, but set yet another lap record. Following the Phoenix race, he was leading in points for the SCCA Southern Pacific region Class A Sports Car Championship. Had he continued on, it's likely that he'd have won the amateur title that year.

569. In a 1966 *Sports Illustrated* article, Steve reviewed a handful of off-road bikes. Although those he rode were the top models of the day, he made it clear that in his opinion, none were as good as the custom-built machine that he rode. As he put it, "I prefer the big four-stroke engine but on a light bike."

570. The bike that he describes is his Rickman-Matisse/Triumph, which took a 650-cc Triumph engine and popped it into a lightweight Rickman-Matisse frame. Long-travel Ceriani forks and lack of excess wiring, brackets, and controls made it a strictly off-road motorcycle. At the time, nearly every motorcycle built for off-road use still came with all the street-legal trimmings; most people wanted to ride to and from their favorite trails.

571. McQueen's Jeepster Commando, built exclusively for the purpose of racing at Ascot, was the ultimate dirt-track racer of its day. The Commando sported a longer wheelbase than a CJ and planted its weight lower to the ground. McQueen's had a foam-padded roll cage, completely protecting the driver and passenger, and tooled-leather bucket seats with harnesses. A full-race suspension and severely lightened chassis allowed it to take the jumps and logs with ease while still being quick in the turns and straights.

572. Because dirt racers need a much higher power-to-weight ratio than road racers, Steve had TRACO Engineering build a 550-hp Chevy V-8 to power the beast. No other information exists about the engine, but for that kind of power output it was most likely a 427-ci big-block, either brought up to L-88 spec or having started life as an L-88. TRACO specialized in these high-performance factory engines, which most notably served in Corvette road racers from 1966 to 1969.

573. Steve McQueen first attended the famed 24 Hours of Le Mans race in 1969 while attending a tribute by the Royal Academy of Dramatic Arts. The event was just an excuse for Steve to go to France for the race. He brought a Solar Productions crew with him to film the race, and they ended up with more than 35,000 feet of footage with the goal of using it to promote a racing film to investors. He knew it would be difficult to convey the excitement and drama of the international race to investors, so the footage was compiled to show the potential of a racing film.

574. Throughout their many years of racing together, Steve McQueen only beat his friend Bud Ekins once, although the circumstances were a little suspect. Two years after retiring from racing, Ekins received a call from Steve inviting him for a little "go-round" at the Indian Dunes. According to Ekins, Steve had been out at the site every day practicing until he felt he was finally ready to take on the legendary off-road racer. He succeeded in his quest and bested the "rusty" Bud Ekins. Afterward they grabbed a beer and Steve couldn't put away that world-famous grin!

575. Unlike most racing drivers who inserted a wax ear plug into each ear before a race to reduce the sound of loud noises, McQueen only used one ear plug. By the time he started endurance racing, where the sound would actually have an effect, he was deaf in his left ear. Since he couldn't hear in it anyways, there was nothing left to protect! He did, however, protect his right ear to prevent himself going completely deaf.

576. One of McQueen's most revered and repeated movie lines of all time comes from *Le Mans*, "Racing is life. Everything else is just waiting," is actually a play on a famous quote that was said to Steve during production. Karl Wallenda, high wire artist of The Flying Wallendas once said of his craft: "Life is walking on the wire; the rest is waiting in the wings." The connotation has a near-perfect crossover to auto racing and Steve instructed writers to come up with something similar and add it to the script. After the movie's initial and gravely disappointing release, these eight simple words have managed to etch themselves permanently into racing and cinema culture.

577. *Le Mans'* original incarnation as *Day of the Champion* included racing at various European racetracks to give the viewer a feel of what endurance racing is like. As part of this, Steve and director John Sturges had Stirling Moss drive in the Nürburgring Grand Prix with a camera mounted to his racecar, which could be used as background footage. Sturges walked away with 27 reels of tape until the producers of *Grand Prix* took Sturges to court arguing that his deal with the Auto Club of Germany was invalid. The contract held up in court, however, and as we now know, scenes from Nürburgring were not used in the final film.

578. As part of McQueen's deal with John DeLorean, Chevrolet sent several Blazers to Solar Plastics & Engineering to have Solar racing seats installed as part of the race prep for the upcoming Baja 500. Although builder Vic Hickey was best known for building McQueen's Baja Boot and the Chevrolet C30 COPO off-road racer that Steve also eventually owned, he in large part developed the Blazer as well. Unfortunately, the Blazer struggled to compete against the nimbler Ford Bronco and these early test/race vehicles have gone unnoticed.

579. McQueen appeared for the third and final time on *The Ed Sullivan Show* in 1968, not to promote a film but to show off the racing products made by Solar Engineering. He did wheelies on a bike equipped with Solar accessories and then took Sullivan for a ride in a Solar off-road buggy. Of course, he also displayed and discussed Solar's hottest product, the safety seat, which was used by off-road racers all over the world.

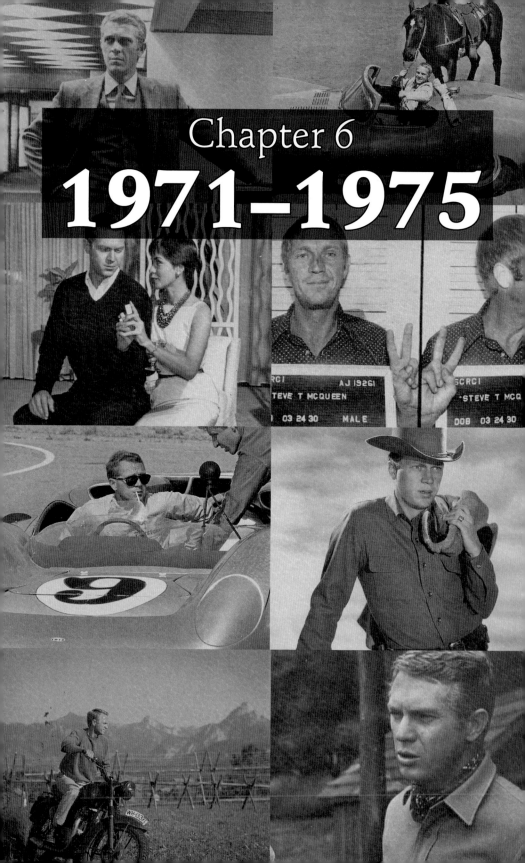

Chapter 6
1971–1975

PERSONAL LIFE

580. Two years after *Le Mans* was released, McQueen brought a lawsuit against four Japanese companies, Dentsu, Matsushita Industrial Company, Towa Company, and Yakult for using stills from the movie in their product advertising campaigns without his permission. The $1.6 million suit would have given him at least some earnings from the film, but the courts kept delaying the case. In 1978, Steve even flew to Japan to appear in court and testify against the companies, but the firms were successful in continuing to push back the suit. Three days after his death in 1980, a Japanese judge ruled in favor of the companies.

581. After announcing a separation during the filming of *Le Mans*, Neile filed for divorce on June 1, 1971, in Los Angeles. When the couple returned from France, they tried one last time to make the marriage work by living in separate houses and going on dates several times a week, essentially getting back to basics. After a particularly bad fight one night, they realized that the marriage wouldn't work, exchanged "I love you's," and the following day Neile went to the Superior Court of California. Steve and Neile were married for 15 years.

582. Following the disastrous *Le Mans* chapter of his life, McQueen decided to embark on a simpler life that more closely resembled his early years than his time in Hollywood. After being hit with a $2 million bill for back taxes, he got rid of his Solar empire and the army of staff that supported the operations. He said, "I was working 16 hours a day... And I was not very happy."

583. With Solar Productions behind him, Steve joined the newly formed First Artists Production Company, which already sported names such as Paul Newman and Barbara Streisand. First Artists provided greater creative control over filmmaking by partnering with studios rather than being hired by them. Actors gave up the traditional big paycheck at the beginning in exchange for profit points, usually about 10 percent. McQueen had to commit to three films for First Artists, which would put up a third of the initial financing for a film. The concept made sense on paper, but McQueen considered it another pressure-cooker situation as he had experienced before.

584. McQueen dated Barbara Leigh, whom he met when she auditioned for the role of Charmagne in *Junior Bonner*. Leigh was already publically dating MGM President Jim Aubrey while privately seeing Elvis Presley. She was originally passed up for the *Junior Bonner* part, but when actress Tiffany Bolling had to cancel on the production, Leigh was called to take her place. Elvis and McQueen knew about each other and had a bit of a jealous rivalry over Barbara. Elvis would ask her, "How's that motorcycle hick?" and Steve would ask, "How's that guitar hick?"

585. In the middle of their off-screen romance, Ali MacGraw's husband Robert Evans arranged for her to fly back to California for a two-week spa visit. Sam Peckinpah assigned Bobby Visciglia to escort her, with the understanding that Steve McQueen be kept off the flight and away from Ali. Well, Steve managed to learn their plans and sneaked on the plane with a coach ticket and a disguise. After the plane reached cruising altitude, he calmly walked up to the first class section where Ali and Bobby were enjoying a glass of wine, tapped Bobby on the shoulder, and told him his services were no longer needed. What was Bobby going to do? He gave up his seat to Steve and took the seat in coach.

586. Steve outsmarted Robert Evans again when he and Ali were on vacation in Palm Springs, where Steve owned a home. Friend Katy Haber secretly delivered a message to Ali that Steve wanted to see her. Because Steve McQueen tended to drive cars that stood out in a crowd, he traded cars with Haber for the secret rendezvous with Ali. Steve gave Katy the keys to his Porsche 911 while he drove around in a blue Ford Pinto.

587. On June 27, 1972, McQueen was arrested in Anchorage, Alaska, on the charge of reckless driving, to which he pleaded innocent. Although he and the vehicle's passengers had been drinking, likely well past the legal limit, there was no charge related to driving under the influence, although that's usually how the story is told. He posted a $250 bail and requested that the trial be moved to Fairbanks, since the press coverage in Anchorage had understandably been immense. A judge agreed to the location change, but Steve failed to return to Alaska, forfeiting his bail. Since the charge technically amounted to a traffic violation, Alaskan police decided not to go through the effort of having him extradited.

588. After Steve threatened to change Ali's son Joshua's last name from Evans to McQueen, Robert Evans paid $150,000 to Sidney Korshak, his godfather and famed mafia attorney and fixer to find leverage against Steve. Korshak was able to quickly deliver a 12-inch-thick dossier with evidence damning enough to scare Steve into backing off. To this day, everyone involved has kept silent on the contents of the "career-ending" file.

589. In the summer of 1972, Steve and Chad began taking lessons with Chuck Norris at his Sherman Oaks karate studio. They had been taking lessons from Bruce Lee after Chad got into a fight at school, but Lee had stopped teaching to pursue a successful film career. He told Steve before leaving, "If you ever want to take karate lessons, Norris is the best." Soon, Chuck Norris' film career began to take off, and his best understudy, Pat E. Johnson, took over and ended up becoming one of Steve's best friends.

590. While Ali dealt with her divorce and custody of Joshua, she and McQueen decided that they wouldn't live together, technically. Instead, they each rented a house in Coldwater Canyon separated by a large field that was still an easy walk. This arrangement might have actually been perfect for them, since anytime they fought, which was often, they could simply retreat across the field back home. Ali said they regularly ran into each other in the field after such an argument on their way to see the other.

591. While walking along the beach in Malibu, the McQueen family dog, named Junior, bit Governor (and future President) Ronald Reagan on the butt, much to the dismay of his security team who scrambled after the dog. Steve had found Junior, a shepard-collie mix named after Junior Bonner, in the desert. Although the McQueens never had a problem with the dog biting one of them, he often bit others.

592. Steve McQueen was originally offered the 1974 Golden Globe for Best Actor for *Papillon*, but to receive the award he had to guarantee that he would be present to accept it. Steve flat out refused to be there in person, but did offer to issue a statement about the award. The Golden Globe committee stuck to their guns and gave the award to Al Pacino for *Serpico*.

593. Steve McQueen married Ali MacGraw on July 12, 1973, in Cheyenne, Wyoming, in the city's Holiday Park. Steve, Ali, Terry, Chad, and Joshua rented a blue Cadillac and stayed at the Holiday Inn upon arrival. Justice of the Peace Arthur Garfield was playing a round of golf when he received an urgent phone call saying that the famous actors would like to get married right away.

594. The wedding was as low-key as they come, with the only photography coming by way of a Kodak camera that they had purchased at a local store. Arthur Garfield also acted as the wedding photographer to snap the whole family together.

595. McQueen served as a pallbearer at Bruce Lee's funeral along with James Coburn and Chuck Norris. Coburn delivered the eulogy at Lee's Seattle funeral; a funeral was held in Hong Kong as well.

596. It's difficult to discern in his films, but Steve McQueen struggled with Ss and Zs in words. The reason this isn't obvious is because he worked with his screenwriters to remove or replace words that he didn't feel comfortable saying. When it came to protecting his image, no one was better than McQueen.

597. Steve's final public appearance for the following six years was in 1973 at a fundraiser for actor James Stacy who had been hit on his motorcycle by a drunk driver. His girlfriend was killed instantly in the accident and doctors had to amputate an arm and a leg to save James. At the event, attended by many A-list celebrities, Stacy took advantage and asked McQueen if he would help him get back in the ocean for the first time since the accident. Steve agreed, and invited Stacy to Malibu where he taught him how to body surf.

598. The 1973 Rolling Stones song, "Star, Star" uses a line about Ali MacGraw and Steve McQueen in the lyrics, which are decidedly raunchy and not printed here. The Stones had to get permission from McQueen to use his name in the song. No word on how Ali felt about it. Mick Jagger repaid this favor years later when Steve surprised his third wife, Barbara Minty, with Rolling Stones tickets and backstage passes.

599. After taking a step back from movies and public life, McQueen let his hair and beard grow out and rendered himself undistinguishable. To get around Hollywood, he'd dress up as a construction worker with hat, tool belt, and boots and go visit friends without anybody noticing him.

600. One of Steve's favorite pastimes was working in a bar called Old Place in the Agoura Hills neighborhood. The bar was frequented by bikers, surfers, ranchers, actors, and locals who'd be served by Steve McQueen for hours and not even know it!

601. Katharine Hepburn came calling to the McQueen residence for a meeting one day to try to talk Steve into working with her on a film called *Grace Quigley*. Right before she arrived, Steve rode off on his motorcycle and left Ali to entertain Katharine Hepburn. She was hungry, so Ali heated some canned soup for her. When Steve finally returned, Hepburn complained that his wife had made her bad soup.

602. Ali fit in perfectly with Steve and his children, Terry and Chad, early in their relationship. She was just what each of them needed in both a spouse and a stepmother at that time in their lives. Terry was a young teenager who could look up to Ali's fashion sense, and the younger Chad enjoyed her general warmth and honesty.

603. Steve kept up with his fitness regimen during the filming of *Le Mans* by having his personal home gym transported to the French countryside. The studio was dismayed at the massive expense of flying heavy equipment halfway around the world. When asked why the gym in the rented chateau wasn't working for him, Steve responded, "It doesn't feel right." McQueen also had his favorite oatmeal cookies flown in regularly from Los Angeles because he didn't like any of the ones available to him in France.

604. It has been a common theme in Steve McQueen's life that he adored children and enjoyed spending time with them. Once he and Ali broke up, he continued to play an important role in her son Joshua's life. The boy grew up with Steve as a father figure, and he wasn't about to let him down. Even after the divorce, Joshua walked to the McQueen house several times per week and the two of them spent quality time together.

605. One of Steve's most prized personal possessions was a folding knife customized by Von Dutch. The 4-inch-bladed knife with wooden handle has an eagle claw and head engraved into the bronze end pieces with wings engraved into the wood. The best part of the piece is the writing scrawled into the backbone: "TO STEVE FROM DUTCH."

606. McQueen frequently gave the knife to his third wife, Barbara, but then would take it back, until one day he let her keep it permanently. Would you believe that this knife sold at auction in 2006 for $38,025?

607. In 1975 Von Dutch hand fabricated a pair of .45-caliber black-powder pistols for him and his friend Steve McQueen. The intricately-crafted firearms had their own perfectly matched and handcrafted display cases with all the necessary accessories. Von Dutch kept the right-handed version for himself and gave the left-handed version to McQueen. The right-handed pistol sold at a Bonhams auction in 2007 for $14,040.

608. Playing the role of Henri Charrière in *Papillon* opened Steve's eyes to the plight of prisoners in his own country who perhaps didn't deserve to be behind bars. He began writing to young people in prison whom he felt he could rehabilitate. He discovered a church that allowed people to be secret pen pals with such inmates to give them an outlet to communicate with someone on their side. Whenever a pen pal of his was freed, he'd send them some money and, if possible, secretly help them find work.

MOVIE FACTS

609. The 12-gauge pump-action shotgun used in *The Getaway* was originally purchased a couple of years earlier for protection of the Solar Productions office in Studio City. Solar's Corporate Vice President Bill Maher purchased the High Standard Riot 18-7 model K-120 while Steve and the rest of the Solar crew was in France shooting *Le Mans* and he manned the office by himself. Steve noticed the gun before *The Getaway* started filming and thought it would be perfect for his character.

610. After using it for the film, Steve returned it to Bill Maher, who never had to use it afterward. The shotgun was sold at the 2008 Bonhams auction for $22,800 with Steve McQueen believed to have been the only person ever to have fired it.

611. Following the green light given to *Le Mans*, producer Robert Relyea wanted to hire a young Steven Spielberg in what would have been his first feature film. Steve McQueen was on board with Spielberg after meeting him, but it was Cinema Center that turned him down because he was too young. George Lucas was Relyea's second choice, but was turned down as well due to his age and lack of experience.

612. At the 1969 running of Le Mans, director John Sturges shot more than 35,000 feet worth of film, which should have been a major head start for the movie; however, the film was deemed unusable. The Gulf Porsche car that McQueen would be driving in the movie crashed early in the race, providing very little footage.

613. The course was given an update in 1970, as was the styling of many of the race cars. Even a new grandstand was added. Those differences made it too difficult to match the tiny handful of shots from 1969 to the actual film production in 1970.

614. Many people don't know that Solar Productions also produced films that didn't feature Steve McQueen. One of the early attempts was *Adam at 6 A.M.*, which was the company's second film. Jim Morrison, lead singer of The Doors, lobbied for the lead role, even cutting his hair and shaving his beard to make a good impression for Steve McQueen, despite his drug and alcohol addiction. Michael Douglas ended up scoring the role, his second lead in a feature, after Morrison was passed up for the part.

615. McQueen was driving a few crewmembers from his chateau to their hotel near the Le Mans track in the middle of a rainy night when he took a turn too fast in the Peugeot, launching off a cement bunker and crashing into some trees. He and a female actor flew through the windshield and landed unconscious on the hood; the backseat passengers broke an arm and cracked a couple of ribs. After coming to, he thought that he had killed his female passenger, but she turned out to be okay.

616. Derek Bell and Jo Siffert were doing some hot laps for footage when they came around a bend at Le Mans and saw a man lying in the middle of the track with a camera. He was positioned just out of their race line, but Bell went back to the pits and announced to director John Sturges that there was "some nutcase" on the track filming. Sturges hailed McQueen on the radio to come see him, likely to get chewed out for risking a cameraman's life. When Steve showed up, Sturges angrily asked who he had put on the track. It turned out that Steve had grabbed a camera, and it had been *him* on the track shooting as the race cars whizzed just feet from his face at 160 mph.

617. Everyone involved with *Le Mans*, including Steve, knew that the film wouldn't amount to much financially or critically. Steve even called former director John Sturges to apologize for his behavior and admit that he was wrong about the movie needing a character-driven script. Even so, nothing stopped Cinema Center from putting $2 million into advertising that included a 22-page booklet for the media explaining the film. For the public, the studio put together a 48-page booklet that cost $1 and a free four-page publication.

618. *Le Mans* premiered in Indianapolis, the epicenter of racing in the United States, in June 1971 to harsh critiques and a seemingly vanished Steve McQueen. Even at the time, critics admitted that the film would play well with race fans who would appreciate the long, drawn-out driving scenes but bore regular moviegoers who want a character-driven story. Kathleen Carroll of the *New York Daily News* hit it strikingly close to home: "*Le Mans* is an excuse for Steve McQueen to indulge his passion for auto racing." Even McQueen's friend Stirling Moss called it "a very bad film."

619. Steve gave up everything to make *Le Mans*. He lost his wife, company, friends, business partners, and his deal with Cinema Center. In the end, the film only made about $7 million at the box office, and McQueen didn't make a dime off his dream project because he had given up his salary and profit points to save the film from being canceled.

620. *On Any Sunday* has become known as one of the greatest, if not the greatest, motorcycle film of all time. When the documentary was released in July 1971, it took the complete opposite trajectory of *Le Mans*, becoming the surprise hit of the year and grossing $24 million globally and much more since then. This big win in a motoring passion project helped Steve's spirits tremendously in what was otherwise an extremely difficult year, both personally and professionally.

621. The big bar fight scene in *Junior Bonner* was actually fueled by real alcohol, courtesy of director Sam Peckinpah. Peckinpah replaced the bartender and started pouring drinks for the actors to get everyone loose in order to make a more realistic fight scene; the booze in the glasses was real in the movie. After a few takes, the cast was drunk and was able to do the scene perfectly.

622. For the bull-riding rodeo scenes in *Junior Bonner*, McQueen wanted to do all the stunt scenes himself. Director Sam Peckinpah compromised and let him do the horse riding scenes, but for the bull-riding close-ups, he had to ride a mechanical bull. Even if Peckinpah had been okay with it, the insurance company never would have allowed the star actor to ride a real bull. Pro rider Frank Kelly was called in to do the actual bull-riding scenes on "the meanest bull west of the Mississippi" named Sunshine.

623. In desperate need of money to cover his tax bill and pending divorce, McQueen agreed to let agent Freddie Fields book a Honda commercial to be shown only in Japan. Honda paid Steve $1 million to ride a CR 250m Elsinore around the Southern California hillside and relay the importance of safe motorcycle practices. In the 30-second ad he says, "This is what I do to relax. I ride fast. I ride fast in the dirt with the right safety equipment. When you're riding in the street, be safety-minded. Please don't ride too fast."

624. For the prison scenes in *The Getaway*, director Sam Peckinpah used real prisoners instead of extras. Fifty-two inmates at the Texas State Penitentiary signed releases to appear in the film. Real prisoners were used in the shower scene as well, although McQueen later found out that they were from the "homosexual unit," since it was believed that they'd be less likely to try to take him as a hostage or hurt him.

625. In the chain gang scene where the prisoners, all dressed in white, are hoeing the fields, McQueen almost found himself mauled to death by guard dogs. Everything in the film was real, and that included the guards on horseback and the guard dogs, who were trained to attack anyone wearing white who made a sudden move away from the rest of the group. On one occasion, Peckinpah yelled "Cut!" and Steve instinctively dropped his hoe and began walking toward the crew to discuss the scene, which he was warned not to do. The dogs instantaneously leapt forward and charged at him, but luckily the guards sprung into action quickly and were able to control them.

626. Ali's ex-husband Robert Evans got the last laugh in 1972 when a film that he produced, *The Godfather*, quadrupled the box office take of *The Getaway*, earning $144 million versus $36 million. *The Godfather* is officially credited with having the highest earnings in 1972 (*The Getaway* came in seventh).

627. Although Steve and Ali went to France on what was supposed to be a promotional tour of *The Getaway*, when they arrived Steve said that he would do only one interview with one news outlet. The on-site rep chose the magazine *Paris Match* and worked out a deal for cover treatment to make the biggest splash with the one interview. When the photographer arrived to photograph the couple, Steve informed him that he could only shoot them in black-and-white. The unusual request lost them the cover and relegated the story to just one column in the back with a 2-inch black-and-white photo.

628. McQueen's earnings for 1973's *Papillon* was his biggest yet, having started with a $2-million salary plus a cut of the earnings. All told, after the film's initial box office run, he had pocketed $6.7 million, with more to come in the years that followed.

629. Unlike most films, where scenes are shot in order of convenience, *Papillon* was shot in sequence from beginning to end. The primary catalyst behind doing it this way was that the film was given a 10-month financing deadline to be entirely completed, but Dalton Trumbo's script was still in the works. There was no ending in place when shooting began for the film, and for much of the filming, Trumbo was only 10 pages ahead with his script. The side effects were all positive, however; chief among them were that McQueen and Dustin Hoffman, who met for the first time in real life, also met for the first time on camera. As they got to know each other off-screen, their characters become more comfortable with each other on-screen. The makeup department was the other primary recipient of the sequential shooting because they had to age the actors 12 years throughout the course of the film.

630. In the cigar-smoking scene in *Papillon* where McQueen accepts and puffs on a cigar being smoked by a leper to earn his trust, actor Anthony Zerbe had actually been chewing on that cigar all day. He handed Steve a "soggy stogie" just to test the actor's mettle, just like his character in the film. Would Steve accept the cigar and take a puff on that take, or would he call cut and ask for a clean replacement? Sure enough, he accepted the soggy stogie and continued with the scene. What viewers see in that scene is about as real as it can be, with Zerbe later commenting that it was "one of the most amazing reactions I have ever seen on the silver screen."

631. The budget became so tight during the filming of *Papillon* that producers decided to cut everyone's per-diem living allowances to try to make it work. When McQueen found out about this, he went on strike, refusing to work until the crew got paid. He had already received a sizeable salary, and at that point was wholeheartedly concerned with the crew's needs. He shut down the production for five days until every last crewmember was paid, leading to a $250,000 overrun.

632. Dustin Hoffman invited some friends and relatives to the set of *Papillon* to watch the filming, whom McQueen saw taking pictures and had immediately kicked out. Steve didn't like to have any extra people on the set and in potentially embarrassing scenes, requested that only the bare minimum crew be present. Whether he knew it or not, among the group of friends and family was Beatles member Paul McCartney and his wife Linda. After this fiasco, neither lead actor spoke to each other off-camera for the remainder of filming, communicating only through a go-between crewmember.

633. The inspiration behind *Papillion*, Henri "Papillion" Charrière visited the film set to share his stories with the cast and crew, although he later revealed that the memoir about his time at the French penal colony was only 75 percent true. Modern researchers believe it to be even less than that today, crediting Parisien Charles Brunnier as being the man Charrière's book was actually about.

634. Either way, the novelist died on July 29, 1973, shortly after he visited the set, and never had the chance to see the movie. The novel *Papillon* spent 21 weeks as the number-one bestseller in France where 1.5 million copies were sold. *Papillon* has been released in 239 editions and 21 languages.

635. Although it was only the fourth highest-earning film of 1973, *Papillon* was Allied Artists' most successful film ever. It grossed $56.2 million domestically and more than $100 million worldwide, proving that Steve McQueen was still a winner at the box office.

636. *The Towering Inferno* was the highest-earning film of Steve McQueen's career in terms of what he took home. He received a $1 million salary up front, plus ten percent of the gross profits, which brought his total income to $14.5 million after just the first year. The film earned three Academy Awards, two Golden Globes, and two BAFTAs (from the British Academy of Film and Television Arts) in addition to pulling $116 million domestically and around $230 million globally.

637. Originally, McQueen signed on to play the role of the architect in *The Towering Inferno*, which was played by Paul Newman.

Ernest Borgnine was set to play the fire chief; however, after reading the script, McQueen felt that the fire chief was the true main character of the film and that the architect's part was simply pasted together. Plus, the fire chief is the one who comes in toward the middle of the movie, saves the day, and delivers the final line.

638. The billing for *The Towering Inferno* proved to be difficult due to the notoriety of both Steve McQueen and Paul Newman. Newman had been in the business longer, but McQueen was the box office magician. Using the system originally developed for their potential partnership in *Butch Cassidy and the Sundance Kid*, they agreed that the name on the left would be low and the name on the right would be high. McQueen was given first choice, and he chose the left name since it would be read first.

639. McQueen prepared for *The Towering Inferno* by training as a firefighter with several Los Angeles fire officers, and he actually ended up helping put out a major fire. A huge fire erupted at the Samuel Goldwyn Studios on May 6, 1974, when two soundstages were ignited when a studio light sparked onto a polyfoam cave on the set of a children's show. While the pros were training Steve, the call came over the radio. The firefighters invited him to help, so he donned the equipment and went to battle the blaze with 250 of LA's Bravest. After the event, McQueen was awarded the title of Honorary Los Angeles Fire Fighter in a ceremony at City Hall.

640. In the post-production sound-editing phase of *The Getaway*, McQueen and director Sam Peckinpah had different ideas of how the firearms should sound. They repeatedly gave contradicting orders to the editor, who wasn't sure either of them was qualified. Peckinpah had low-end hearing issues while McQueen had high-end hearing issues and only one working ear. Sounds that came across perfectly for them individually actually sounded different to everyone else who'd be watching the movie!

641. Although *Papillon* took place on a tropical island prison off the coast of French Guiana, the actual filming took place in

Jamaica. There were 600 extras recruited for the movie, largely German-descended farmers living in Jamaica. Upon visiting the set, the real-life Henri Charrière found the reconstructed prison to be nearly identical to the one in which he had been interned.

642. *The Towering Inferno* was the first film to be a joint production between Warner Brothers and 20th Century Fox. Each studio had, unbeknownst to the other, paid several hundred thousand dollars for rights to stories involving high-rise fires at around the same time. When all parties involved realized what was happening, they knew it made little sense to come out with two similar big-budget blockbusters. It was director Irwin Allen that was able to pull it off, with both studios agreeing that if anyone could do it, it was the man responsible for the massive success known as *The Poseidon Adventure*.

643. McQueen wanted a project that would shoot in California only, and preferably in a studio in Hollywood because he was still recovering from *Papillon*. *The Towering Inferno* provided that needed respite and, in addition to the exterior scenes being shot on-location in San Francisco, a record 57 sets on 8 sound stages were built at the Fox studios. The Promenade Room alone cost $300,000 to build. In addition to the sets in Los Angeles, Fox also built a four-story section of building at the Fox Ranch for additional outdoor shooting. The elevator scene was shot there.

644. Because so many scenes involved a set being destroyed by the fire; what happened if for some reason the director needed to do a reshoot? The only answer was to essentially rebuild the set from the ground up. For every fire scene, a crew was standing by with paint, carpet, wall trimmings, furniture, and props and could bring a set back to life in 20 minutes.

645. More than 350,000 extras were brought in for the crowd scenes in *Le Mans*. The annual race is one of Europe's most popular sporting events, so to portray it accurately required showing the massive crowds in the grandstands, at the carnival, and overwhelming the French countryside.

646. In addition to the massive number of extras, all the signs and posts on the post-race streets were replaced with the actual signs used during the race. To further ensure authenticity, more than 20,000 props were brought in to cover every single detail.

647. After everything he put into it, and everything that he had lost because of it, Steve McQueen didn't even attend the Indianapolis premier of *Le Mans*. What kept him from attending the event just miles from his birthplace? Even though he liked the finished product, he knew he was wrong about the need for a solid storyline. After seeing the film for the first time, he apologized to Bob Rosen, Elga Anderson, and director Lee Katzin for his mistakes on set. It was a film that everyone, including McQueen himself, wanted to put behind them.

648. Steve got the idea for using a gold tooth in *Papillon* from Eli Wallach's character in *The Magnificent Seven*. Ever since he had seen Wallach's gold tooth prop, he had wanted one for himself in a movie. *Papillon* proved to be the perfect vessel for making that dream a reality, and it worked perfectly alongside Dustin Hoffman's thick wire glasses. It allowed each star to have a prop to help them stand out and be remembered.

649. Steve McQueen presented the award for Best Picture at the 1971 43rd Annual Academy Awards to Frank McCarthy for *Patton*.

650. *The Blob* was re-released globally after Steve's success with *The Towering Inferno*. McQueen fans who may not have been familiar with his early work were able to see it. It was, however, somewhat falsely marketed as a disaster movie just like *The Towering Inferno* and likely left some viewers scratching their heads.

651. In *Junior Bonner* the actors playing Steve McQueen's parents were only 12 years older than him in real life.

652. In *The Getaway*, when Steve McQueen slaps Ali MacGraw, the slap was actually unscripted, and Steve came up with it on the spot. Ali's shocked reaction looks like great acting, but in reality, she's actually shocked that her costar slapped her!

653. Steve didn't like the original score for *The Getaway* so at his insistence Jerry Fielding was replaced with Quincy Jones. Director Sam Peckinpah preferred Fielding's score and had worked with him many times before. After his firing, Peckinpah even took out a full-page ad thanking him for his work on the film.

654. The part in *The Getaway* when Steve shoots at and blows up the police car was his idea and not originally in the script. Holding up the two officers at gunpoint was, however, originally in the script.

655. McQueen had final say on the editing of *The Getaway*, which infuriated director Sam Peckinpah. Peckinpah said of the final edit that McQueen played it safe and chose all the "playboy shots of himself."

656. The handgun that Doc McCoy carries in *The Getaway* is a Colt M1911A1.

657. McQueen actually performed the cliff-jumping stunt in *Papillion* himself. He later said that it was one of the most exhilarating experiences of his life.

658. Steve was paid $750,000 more than his *Papillion* costar Dustin Hoffman even though the pair received equal billing.

659. Before finishing the on-set script for *Papillion*, writer Dalton Trumbo was found to have lung cancer and returned to California to pursue treatment. His son Christopher finished the script.

660. Throughout the filming of *The Towering Inferno*, McQueen was nervous that the fireman's helmet made him look too goofy to be taken seriously.

661. After a particularly difficult day of filming on *The Towering Inferno*, Steve McQueen and Paul Newman went back to one of their trailers to enjoy some fresh popcorn and beer. They ended up inviting a few of the special effects crewmembers back with them to show appreciation for the hard work they had done on the film.

662. Author Roderick Thorpe had a nightmare after watching *The Towering Inferno* that he was being chased around a skyscraper by gunmen. After that dream he woke up and began putting together his novel *Nothing Lasts Forever*, which was turned into another classic action-in-a-skyscraper film: *Die Hard*.

663. Much of the filming of *The Towering Inferno* required the use of models and miniatures, which was done at the 20th Century Fox ranch in the Santa Monica mountain range. Among the shots done there was one in which a radio-controlled helicopter rescued a Steve McQueen doll from a miniature glass elevator. At one point during that shoot a gust of wind forced the helicopter to crash to the ground on top of the Steve McQueen doll.

664. While setting up the final water deluge scene in *The Towering Inferno*, one of the hoses snapped under pressure and began snaking around, spraying water everywhere. Special effects crewmember Gary L. King jumped on the hose to try to prevent it from hitting all the expensive equipment while everyone else backed away. Another man jumped in to help him harness the hose before the water was finally shut off. A soaking-wet King turned to the equally soaked man next to him to thank him for the help, and when he did he discovered that man to be none other than Steve McQueen!

MOVIE AUTOMOBILE FACTS

665. Six race cars were purposely crashed during the filming of *Le Mans* to the tune of about $45,000 per car. Two of the crashed cars, the Porsche 917 and the Ferrari 512 (which was actually remote-controlled), were fakes built on older Lola T70s.

666. Costing almost as much, McQueen missed a shift and blew the engine on a Porsche 917, adding to the carnage.

667. Understandably, in addition to the planned crashes, the *Le Mans* production was rife with serious injuries. The worst one during filming occurred when David Piper's Porsche 917 hit a spot of oil on the track at high speed and tumbled end over end down the track. Piper suffered a triple compound fracture in his right leg, which also became infected, and doctors decided to amputate the leg below the knee. The end credits thanked him "for his sacrifice" and the film was dedicated to him.

668. During one racing scene in *Le Mans*, Derek Bell and Jo Siffert decided to have a little fun with McQueen when they had his car locked in place between their cars headed into an S-bend. During a real race, they would take the S-bend at about 160 mph, much faster than what the movie shoot called for. So, with McQueen stuck between them and about 3 feet to spare in the front and back, Bell stayed on the accelerator, hitting the curves at the full 160 mph. Siffert didn't back off either, forcing McQueen through the bends at full speed, something they knew he could handle, even if he wasn't ready for it. When they got out of the cars, McQueen was white and trembling while the pro drivers were laughing hysterically. It's doubtful that the insurance company would have found the joke funny.

669. Steve McQueen successfully used his superstar and, more important, his former marine status to secure permission to shoot a scene for *On Any Sunday* at Camp Pendleton Marine Corps Base. Director Bruce Brown thought that the dunes would make a perfect setting, but he couldn't get anywhere with his request. The day after mentioning the setback to McQueen, Brown was instructed to call a general to nail down the specifics.

670. McQueen destroyed yet another rental car on the set of *The Getaway* when he, with Ali as a passenger, purposely drove the station wagon into a deep water hole at the edge of a parking lot. The car submerged quickly, forcing Steve and Ali to escape out the back window with the help of several crewmembers.

671. While technically on a publicity tour in France for the release of *The Getaway*, McQueen drove his Mercedes right at a photographer (who had been tipped off to the McQueens' whereabouts by someone on the hotel staff) and ended up hitting him! It's doubtful that he actually meant to hit the photographer, but the man was unable to get out of the way of the speeding car in time. Steve stopped the car to ask if he was okay, and when the photographer said yes and asked for a picture, he went off on him and drove away with Ali. A First Artists rep stayed behind to deal with the mess.

672. It certainly doesn't look like it in the movie, aptly called *The Getaway*, but Ali didn't know how to drive a car when filming began. Undoubtedly, this added some difficulties to the shooting as her role in the film was as a getaway driver. She couldn't shoot a gun, either, before filming began. If only one of her costars could have helped her with those issues. . . .

673. During the filming of the last scene of *On Any Sunday*, where Steve McQueen, Mert Lawwill, and Malcolm Smith are simply having fun riding and goofing off on the beach, Lawwill is riding a Greeves 360 Challenger off-road motorcycle. However, because of his contract with Harley-Davidson as a factory racer, he put XLR 900 decals on the gas tank so it resembled a Harley. Although the single-cylinder Greeves is obviously not a V-twin, it was definitely the better choice for the sandy scene.

674. One of the most memorable scenes in *On Any Sunday* was of the rider who became lost in the desert and accidentally burned up his motorcycle trying to make a signal fire. It takes a second to realize that it's a set-up scene meant to add a little humor to the documentary. The bike used in the scene was a Husqvarna owned by Malcolm Smith that had a blown engine. It looked just like a bike that would have raced that day in the desert, but with the blown engine, it wasn't worth much.

675. Contrary to what you may think, the bike wasn't a write-off after the shoot. Malcolm Smith repainted it, rebuilt the engine, replaced the cables, threw on a new seat and tires, and sold it! It's possible that if it wasn't destroyed in the years following, that bike is sitting in someone's garage or barn today.

676. Steve protested to director Sam Peckinpah about Ali being the getaway driver in *The Getaway*, saying that he gets nervous in a car with an amateur driver, especially considering some of the driving stunts Ali would have to do. Steve even asked if the scene could be switched to let him do the driving and Ali do the shooting. Peckinpah rejected the idea, and Steve was in a nervous sweat throughout the driving scene.

677. While scouting locations in France for *Le Mans*, McQueen and producer Robert Relyea stumbled upon a carnival in the town of Richelieu. There wasn't a theater anywhere around, and no one there knew who Steve McQueen was. They went to the carnival and paid off the bumper car operator to let them use the attraction for the rest of the night. After grabbing six unknown Frenchmen off the street, they drove bumper cars into one another for six hours until the next morning. According to Relyea, he had never seen Steve happier than when he was letting loose on those bumper cars!

678. The motorcycle that McQueen rides in *On Any Sunday*, and the off-road vehicle most closely associated to him, is the Husqvarna 400 Cross. It also happens to be the motorcycle on which McQueen was photographed shirtless on the cover of *Sports Illustrated* magazine. Steve bought the actual movie bike, serial number MH-1341, new through Solar Productions in February 1970, and he owned a total of five Husky 400s throughout his life.

679. The exact movie bike can be easily deciphered thanks to a letter from director Bruce Brown to US Marine Corps Camp Pendleton's Public Affairs Office regarding the vehicles to be used in the beach riding scene that took place on the base. The letter clearly identifies each rider with his motorcycle make and serial number, thereby forever linking Steve McQueen to this particular motorcycle. As one of the most historically important vehicles owned by the actor, although he'd likely prefer the term racer, this bike sold at a Bonhams auction in 2018 for $230,500.

680. Steve McQueen did ride other motorcycles in *On Any Sunday*, with his custom 1963 Triumph Bonneville Desert Sled being one of the more famous ones. Although he grew up riding Indians, he discovered Triumphs in the early 1960s after strolling into local Southern California dealer Bud Ekins' shop. There, he noticed Ekins wrenching on a tall, barebones bike built exclusively for off-road riding, and he knew he had to have one.

681. The 1963 Triumph Bonneville used in *On Any Sunday* was built by Bud Ekins and painted classic Steve McQueen green by none other than Von Dutch. It was sold to Solar Productions in 1971 when it became a "business expense." This particular Triumph sold for $103,500 at Bonhams in 2016.

682. Due to the massive size of the set on *Le Mans*, which was essentially the entire racetrack and town, Kawasaki provided six G31M Centurians to be used by the crew for getting around.

683. Steve loved the lightweight two-stroke, which produced 18.5 hp out of a 100-cc engine, and he had one shipped back to the United States once filming was complete. The factory green paint didn't suit him, however, and he asked friend Von Dutch to give it a unique flavor. Von Dutch changed the paint to orange and painted "RINGADINGDOO!" on the sides of the gas tank in reference to the noise a small-displacement two-stroke would make.

684. Later in life, Steve used it as easy transportation around the Santa Paula airport. *Ringadingdoo* sold at Bonhams in 2007 for $55,575 and is considered just as much an icon of Von Dutch as Steve McQueen.

685. After the filming of *Le Mans*, the Gulf Porsche 917 driven by Steve was sold to a private race team to continue competing. It was driven by Reinhold Jost and Willi Kauhsen before being sold to Brian Redman, who participated in filming *Le Mans*.

686. Did you know that the 917 Porsche Steve McQueen drove in *Le Mans* won the overall victory at Le Mans in 1970? It was entered by the factory Porsche team in a red with white stripes livery and driven by Richard Attwood and Hans Herrmann. This was the first time that a Porsche won.

687. Richard Attwood went on to buy the Porsche 917 from Brian Redman, painted it in his winning colors of red with white stripes, and attended vintage racing events and shows with it. He was the last owner to race the car.

688. Richard Atwood sold the *Le Mans* Porsche 917 in 1974 after returning it to its original Gulf livery at RM Auctions during Monterey Historics weekend for less than $1 million. It was purchased by *Los Angeles Times* publisher Otis Chandler who kept it in his collection until 2001 when he sold it to collector Bruce McCaw.

689. In *The Getaway*, Steve McQueen and Ali MacGraw drive past an orange Volkswagen Beetle as they're fleeing from a bank heist. Did you get a close look at who was driving the Volkswagen among all the chaos? It's none other than Steve McQueen's good friend James Garner who happened to be in town visiting the shoot. While he was on the set, stunt coordinator Carey Loftin asked if he would like to do some stunt driving.

690. The engine sounds heard while Steve is tied up on the ship in *Papillon* are from the same soundtrack as *The Sand Pebbles*. Because the ships were from the same era, the engine sounds were a perfect match.

691. McQueen performed the stunt in *The Towering Inferno* where he jumps off the helicopter onto the top of the burning building. Director Irwin Allen didn't like the idea of his star doing something so dangerous, but Steve insisted on doing it.

692. The first fire trucks on the scene in *The Towering Inferno* are open-cab American LaFrance rigs. Initially they have the correct San Francisco Fire Department logo for 1974, but when they arrive on scene they have an earlier logo that hadn't been in use since 1970.

693. In 1974, Frank Marranca took out a classified ad in *Road & Track* magazine listing his "Bullett" Mustang for sale. Robert Kiernan purchased it for $6,000.

AUTOMOBILE COLLECTION

694. The McQueen family essentially moved to France for the filming of *Le Mans*, and Steve set himself up splendidly. The McQueens rented Chateau de Launay, a 30-room castle.

695. The real perks sat in the garage. Several high-performance Porsches, a Ferrari 512, an Alpha Romeo Tipo 33, a Ford GT40, and a few other race cars were all at his personal disposal throughout filming.

696. Bruce Brown invited McQueen on a guys' trip to Alaska in June 1972 to help get his mind off Ali and everything that was going on. Brown's friend, Hayes, a hunting and fishing guide, owned a front-wheel-drive Oldsmobile Toronado, one of the first cars to be so equipped. Between that and a new set of Firestone tires, which at the time used the slogan, "You can't break loose from their grip," the car was perfect for Alaska. After Hayes took the crew on a wild ride through Anchorage showing off the car, McQueen hopped behind the wheel to see what he could do. He quickly found a State Trooper in his rearview mirror and tried to ditch him by running red lights and stop signs. He failed to outrun the law, but he did get the Toronado's tires to break loose.

697. Bruce Lee purchased his first Porsche and, of course, wanted to show it off to his friend Steve McQueen. Steve asked to drive it, to see how it handled, to which Bruce said okay. He probably should have seen it coming, but before he knew it, McQueen had the Porsche up to 100 mph on Mulholland Drive, ripping it as fast as he could down the winding mountain road. Bruce Lee was as scared as can be and starting yelling for his friend to slow down. In response, Steve said, "I'm going to drive the car as fast as I can until you calm down."

698. Steve celebrated Ali's 37th birthday when he rode his motorcycle into The Bistro, a restaurant in Beverly Hills where she was having dinner with friends, carrying a birthday cake. Ali had insisted that he come to the dinner, although weaving around tables revving his engine probably wasn't what she had in mind. Reportedly, everyone at her table jumped up to take cover except for Ali, who remained seated, fuming at her husband. Steve had set up everything with the restaurant's owner ahead of time, who was in on the stunt, and handed him an envelope full of cash as he rode out of the restaurant.

699. In 1974, 15 years after he sold it, McQueen bought his old 1958 Porsche Speedster 1600 Super back from then-owner Bruce Meyer. Meyer had purchased it in 1965 for $1,500 to use as his everyday transportation. The seller told him that the car used to be Steve McQueen's, which added a cool factor, but it didn't do anything for the value at the time.

700. Steve heard that someone was driving around in a car they claimed to have been his. He found out who the owner was and called him to see if he could look at the car. Upon meeting, Steve checked under the carpet to see if the bolt holes for a roll bar were there, and he noticed his Garner Reynolds racing recap tire in the trunk. It took a couple of months of calling every week to finally convince Meyer to sell it, but he finally did.

701. One of Steve's favorite and most-used cars was his 1972 Mercedes-Benz 300 SEL 6.3 sedan. Mercedes transplanted its powerful fuel-injected 300-hp V-8 serving in the 600 Pullman limousine into the smaller sedan and adjusted the tuning for better performance. McQueen's SEL was actually a European-spec car, which had higher compression than its American counterparts. Air suspension, disc brakes, power-operated Webasto sliding steel roof, and hand-cut wood trim made for a comfortable 5.5-second sprint from 0 to 60 mph.

702. He originally purchased the SEL after driving on the Autobahn at 130 mph in a Porsche 911S and watching an older gentleman smoking a pipe blow by him in the utmost of leisure. The car sold at auction in 2007 for $45,100 and as of this writing, is listed for sale by a San Francisco dealer for $369,995.

703. An endless supply of money, time, and passion are what it takes to build a motorcycle collection like Steve McQueen's. Unlike most people, he didn't need to sell one bike to buy another, so his collection simply grew. On some occasions, he would give a motorcycle to a friend or employee as a reward for above and beyond work or as returning a favor.

704. Although he had access to a myriad of the finest cars on the planet during the filming of *Le Mans*, Steve, as always, needed a hot motorcycle for getting around. He shipped his Norton Commando to the set in France where he primarily used it to get to different locations on the racetrack and for enjoyment in the countryside.

705. Steve also used his Norton Commando to give other actors and actresses rides to their next shooting location while on the set of *Le Mans*.

706. In September 1975, Steve McQueen sent a letter to *Cycle News* regarding the burgeoning motorcycle safety laws. Cars had been the subject of many government regulations over the previous several years, and now the safety net was turned on motorcycles. Like most motorcyclists to this day, McQueen's belief was that safety should remain in the hands of the individual rider and on a state-by-state basis. He often wore proper safety equipment when riding, and believed in its use in part to increase the respect of the motorcycling population.

707. Ali MacGraw told one magazine journalist in 1975 that Steve's career break after *The Towering Inferno* was "Steve's farm truck period." At any given time there were half a dozen classic trucks parked on the street outside their Trancas home, often leading to arguments with the neighbors over parking space.

708. Speaking about his entire collection of trucks, most of which were at various other locations, Ali once said, "If you parked them in a line, bumper to bumper, Steve's trucks would stretch from here to South Dakota."

709. Before an important meeting with *An Enemy of the People* director George Schaefer, McQueen stopped at an automotive swap meet and found a pair of headlights that he had been looking for. When he got to the meeting with Schaefer, not only was he happy about the headlights, but he was thrilled that he was able to walk around and enjoy the swap meet with no one recognizing him! The overweight, long-haired, bearded man strolling the swap meet blended right into the crowd because there were so few public appearances that gave away Steve's new look.

710. Right before filming the final water deluge scene in the promenade room for *The Towering Inferno,* Steve made the announcement to the cast that if anything were to happen to him, his wife Ali could have his pickup truck.

RACING

711. Steve McQueen was never one to let a good gearhead opportunity to pass him by, and he took full advantage of the upcoming *Le Mans* film by having Solar purchase a Porsche 908 Spyder. This was the most advanced race car he had yet purchased, and he wanted to practice driving at a high level so as to do all his own driving for *Le Mans*. He once remarked, "If I can't cut it in the

908, then there's no point in making the film." He went on to enter the Porsche in several races before taking it to Le Mans, all on the studio's dime, as movie research.

712. A few weeks before the 1970 running of the 12 Hours of Sebring race, McQueen competed in the famed Lake Elsinore off-road motorcycle race in Elsinore, California. Of course, he rode his 405-cc Husqvarna in the 500-rider field. He was running in the top ten when he hit a dip in the road, launched in the air, and crashed into the crowd. He was the only one injured, breaking his foot in six places. The Husky was fine, however, allowing Steve to hop back on and finish the race, preserving his top-ten position.

713. McQueen competed in the biggest race of his life, the 1970 12 Hours of Sebring, with his broken left foot still in a cast. He had to get special permission from race officials, who made him wear fireproof socks and a hard boot over the cast. The boot made clutching difficult as it kept sliding off the pedal, so he glued a piece of sandpaper to the bottom, which kept his foot on the pedal for the race.

714. He was awarded the Hayden Williams Memorial Sportsman-ship Award for racing on the broken foot.

715. Only one driver beat Steve McQueen's team at the 1970 Sebring, and he had a 5-liter 12-cylinder engine compared to the Porsche's 3-liter, 8-cylinder engine. That driver was Mario Andretti, who had to drive the race of his life and only won by 23.8 seconds.

716. The McQueen/Peter Revson team still won their class and took a very respectable second place overall, which was a seri-ous feat for a smaller-displacement car. Fans watching the race saw the amateur actor/businessman team as the real winners of the day, with McQueen standing on the car delivering the peace sign at the end, cementing his legacy.

717. Although Sebring was the biggest race McQueen competed in, his primary goal was to compete in the 24 Hours of Le Mans the following month. He had set up a ride co-driving a Porsche 917 with his friend Jackie Stewart, with footage of the actual race to be used in the film. As had happened before, the insurance company stepped in and prevented him from participating in the race.

718. Solar Productions hired 45 of the day's finest race drivers for the filming of *Le Mans*. McQueen's favorite part of filming the picture, besides his driving sequences, was likely palling around with the drivers. As a world-class driver himself, he shared a mutual respect and understanding with them. Richard Atwood, Derek Bell, Vic Elford, Jacky Ickx, David Piper, and Jo Siffert were among the pro drivers that took part in the film.

719. Because of insurance requirements, Steve had not been able to enter the 24 Hours of Le Mans and share in the competition and camaraderie with the other drivers. With that being the case, he apparently created his own Le Mans to enjoy.

720. To promote their involvement in Le Mans and to score some Steve McQueen sales juice, Gulf Oil printed around eight million posters to be given away at its gas stations. The free gift was available at 30,000 individual stations and featured a large headshot of McQueen in his racing gear and the gorgeous Gulf Porsche 917 race car from the film. The only words on the poster are "Le Mans," and the poster is copyrighted by Cinema Center. These are still readily available today, making it a wonderful piece of Steve McQueen history that anyone can afford.

721. The August 23, 1971, issue of *Sports Illustrated* featured a shirtless Steve McQueen popping a wheelie on his Husqvarna Cross 400 dirt bike on the cover. The article, titled "Harvey on the Lam," in a nod to McQueen's racing pseudonym Harvey Mushman, follows the actor's motorized exploits on four wheels and two, street and dirt. McQueen's own comments and stories about his racing history are among the few examples available.

722. Steve McQueen saved Mert Lawwill's racing career in 1971 when the flat-track champion was in a riding accident and severely damaged his hand. The first doctor he saw told him that he had to permanently fuse the knuckles together, relegating the hand useless. When McQueen heard this, he took Lawwill to Los Angeles specialist Dr. Robert Stark who performed five successful operations using seven pins to give Lawwill nearly complete use of his hand. Not only was he able to ride and race again, but McQueen covered what was likely an expensive doctor's bill.

723. For a short period, Steve owned and rode a titanium-framed Husqvarna off-road motorcycle in addition to his often-photographed 1971 400CR. The 189-pound motorcycle was made famous by Swedish racer Lars Larsson who rode one to four victories in six races in the European motocross series, leaving other Husky riders scratching their heads.

724. The key to the 25-pound-lighter machine was a host of titanium parts such as the frame, fork crown, handlebar, and axles as well as the use of aluminum and thinner-than-usual plastic. Steve didn't have quite so much luck with his, the brittle metal on the fork crown cracked upon a hard landing, and that was the last time he used that bike.

725. After *Le Mans* was released in Europe, the German magazine *Bravo* ran a sweepstakes to promote the film. The grand prize was a brand-new Porsche 914, which sparked entries for driving-age teenagers and adults from all over the country.

726. One such teenager who was keen on winning the 914 got stuck with the second-place prize: Steve McQueen's racing suit, helmet, and fire-retardant underwear. Surely, the disappointment was catastrophic.

727. The boy stored the suit away, but used the helmet when he rode his motorcycle. About 46 years later, his widow uncovered the nearly original suit, helmet, and underwear and consigned them at auction in 2017. The package sold for $336,000, or about $320,000 more than a 1971 Porsche 914 would be worth. Talk about a case of having the last laugh!

728. Steve often used the pseudonym of Harvey Mushman when he entered off-road races. As usual, other racers and fans expected to see McQueen at racing events, and it didn't take them long to figure out who he was. The alias is mentioned in the film *On Any Sunday* when he enters the Elsinore Grand Prix as Harvey Mushman and also in a 1971 *Sports Illustrated* article called "Harvey on the Lam."

729. Steve McQueen's closest friends were those in the motorcycle world, and he became especially close with Mert Lawwill during the filming of *On Any Sunday*.

730. There was one instance in which Lawwill had a race in Southern California and was invited to stay with the McQueen family the night before it. Upon waking, he headed to the kitchen in search of coffee when he stumbled upon Neile and actress Natalie Wood making breakfast. They nonchalantly asked if he wanted some and there he sat, a flat-track motorcycle racer, having two famous, beautiful actresses make him breakfast.

731. In the Elsinore Grand Prix racing scene in *On Any Sunday*, director Bruce Brown shows race leader, and one of the film's stars, Malcolm Smith, appearing to exit the course through a barbed-wire fence in order to skip the treacherous muddy section before returning to the course. To race fans watching the movie, it looks as though he's cheating as he laps a handful of other racers who are on the course, even though he's obviously so far in the lead. In actuality, Brown doesn't mention that race officials cut the fence to route riders around the muddy section that had become a dangerous motorcycle graveyard by the second lap.

732. Unfortunately, although the film got it right with Smith winning the race, because of mud on his number plate and lapped traffic in the way, his second lap was never recorded. Even though he finished six minutes ahead of "winner" Gary Bailey, he was given a DNF for the race.

733. Like most other race car drivers of the day, McQueen kept his blood type written on the back of his helmet, which is seen clearly in the movie *Le Mans* as "Group O, reh D neg." This practice was so that first responders would know what blood would be safe for a transfusion in an emergency when every second counts. Even though this information is more easily accessed today, many racers and motorcyclists still keep their blood type and an emergency contact written somewhere on their helmet, jacket, or boots.

734. At the time of his divorce to Neile, Steve blamed racing as the root cause of the split, and it likely was a big reason as she didn't want to see him get hurt. The speeds attained while filming *Le Mans* were the fastest he had yet driven, and in his words, "I don't think Neile ever got the image of me hot-assin' the 917 down Mulsanne at 200-plus out of her mind." A Solar crewmember noted that after that particular scene Neile "looked real grim and tight-faced" before driving away in her car, never to return to the circuit for the remainder of filming. Neile even told reporters that racing was the cause of the separation. She said, "Some men drink. Steve races."

735. For the 1970 running of Le Mans, the Solar crew physically brightened the entire Le Mans circuit by repainting the pit area in shades of light colors rather than the original darker colors. They also brightened many sections around the track with both paint and additional lighting to make it more visually appealing for filming. That must have confused drivers and fans who attended the event the year before!

736. To create the best re-creation of Le Mans, the Solar crew contacted various manufacturers about leasing or buying factory race cars for the movie. When they reached out to Enzo Ferrari, a notorious stickler for who was "allowed" to buy the cars with his name on them, he simply asked which car won the race at the end of the movie. Of course, a Porsche wins the race by edging out a

Ferrari. Upon hearing this, Mr. Ferrari refused to allow any factory cars to be used in the movie. Private owners were then contacted about leasing their Ferraris to Solar.

737. The Solar Racing Porsche 908 was set to be auctioned off at Bonhams' Quail Lodge sale during Monterey Car Week in 2008. The hammer price was estimated at $1.5 to $2 million; however, the car was pulled from the sale.

738. Steve insisted that there be dead bugs on the drivers' helmets for the filming of *Le Mans* because after hours of racing, there would be dead bugs in real life. An artist first attempted to draw them on, but that didn't look real enough for Steve. Then, the costumer added some material to give them a three-dimensional effect. Still, this wasn't good enough. The costumer then spent all night holding a helmet out a car window until enough dead bugs had been collected to make Steve happy. Even then, he could tell the difference between a bug splat at 50 mph and a splat at 150 mph and deemed the helmets still not worthy.

739. How much would you pay for a piece of racing and cinema history? One of the most recognizable Steve McQueen movie costumes is his Gulf racing suit worn in *Le Mans*. Because the suit would become dirtier throughout the course of the 24-hour race, and the film was shot out of order, McQueen had several identical racing suits in his wardrobe, three of which are known to be in collections today. Just how badly would you want to become the persona of Michael Delany? An authentic suit sold at auction in 2015 for $425,000.

740. In 1971 the Porsche Club of America honored Steve McQueen at an event in Los Angeles for his "continuing care of the marque." The previous year saw McQueen winning a major race at Holtville in his new 908 after lapping the entire field and, of course, just a few months later he took second at Sebring in one of the most memorable endurance racing finishes of all time. But his representation of the German sports car in the movie *Le Mans* had to be a favorite of the club's members.

Chapter 7
1976–1980

PERSONAL LIFE

741. Steve McQueen spent a long time at the top of the box office bank, but in 1976 a new star named Burt Reynolds took his place and held on to the title until 1980. Interestingly, Steve sensed something in young Burt Reynolds when he came across him a few years earlier at a wardrobe fitting and told him, "It's all yours kid . . . Number one, kid. It's yours. I'm stepping down."

742. With Steve and Ali virtually separated, McQueen was living at the Beverly Wilshire Hotel where he took on the persona of "Fat Joe." With scruffy beard and disheveled appearance, he'd sit at the hotel bar and talk to the other patrons, none of whom had any idea that the man they were speaking with was actually the famous Steve McQueen.

743. He took on the make-believe role of a construction foreman who embarked on motorcycle adventures around the world in his free time. He and writer Louis L'Armour sometimes had lunch at The Beverly Hills Hotel, but since they pulled up in one of Steve's old pickup trucks, the parking attendants motioned them around back to the delivery area, having no idea who was in the car.

744. In early 1977, Ali MacGraw was offered a role in a film called *Convoy*, set to be directed by Sam Peckinpah. She was offered $400,000, and even though she didn't much like the script, her agent compelled her to take the job for the money, considering the condition of her failing marriage and the fact that she hadn't worked in five years. When she told Steve, he threatened to divorce her if she took the job and would even pay her not to take it. She took the role, and traveled to New Mexico for filming.

745. Steve noticed a 23-year-old model in a Club Med advertisement and pitched her agent on having her play the role of the Indian Princess in *Tom Horn*. At the time, there was no Indian Princess character in *Tom Horn*, so the model and her agent flew to Los Angeles to meet with McQueen and figure it out. The young woman's name was Barbara Minty, and she noted after their two-hour meeting that something clicked between them and that one day she would marry the shaggy, bearded man sitting across from her.

746. Ali and Steve filed for divorce on October 10, 1977, after a disastrous family trip to a hunting lodge in Montana. Steve was livid after Ali spent the night speaking in Italian with another hunter and spent the entire drive back to Malibu berating her about it. She and her son, Joshua, moved out a few weeks later when they found a rental home not far from Steve. However, that was the last straw for the relationship, and by October 1978 they were officially divorced. McQueen's pre-nuptial agreement held up, and Ali left the relationship only with what she brought into it.

747. Unlike McQueen's usual tendency to steer well clear of cameras, he had no problem when Barbara Minty photographed him early on in their relationship with her 35-mm camera. It's not surprising that a model would be a photography enthusiast, but according to McQueen's friends, it was surprising that he allowed her such unfettered access. Nobody else had been able to photograph Steve in natural settings for years, and it showed the trust that he had for Barbara.

748. McQueen knew that he needed to get back into his typical movie star shape if he ever wanted to get back into good graces at the box office and likely to keep up with his 25-year-younger girlfriend. He quit smoking cigarettes by enrolling in a five-week program at the Schick Center for the Control of Smoking and Weight using Pat Johnson's name. Part of the treatment included electric shock therapy, which introduced a mild current from a 9-volt battery to his body. The process worked, and although Steve quit smoking cigarettes, he continued to smoke cigars and use chewing tobacco.

749. Steve McQueen's favorite beer was Old Milwaukee. He'd start every morning with a cup of coffee, followed by a can of Old Milwaukee. Friend and fellow actor Lee Majors recalled taking a cooler of the stuff when he and Steve visited antique stores up the

California coast. The only problem, Majors noted, was that Old Milwaukee gave Steve gas.

750. The McQueens' next-door neighbor in Trancas was The Who drummer Keith Moon, nicknamed "Moon the Loon," who added a bit of color to the otherwise serene neighborhood. Steve actually saved Keith's life one morning when he discovered his body floating face-down in the ocean after drinking all night. Steve pulled him out of the ocean, dragged him up the beach, and deposited him at his front door.

751. Things turned sour with the rocker next door when he barged in on Chad McQueen while Steve was away, leading Steve to get his lawyer and the district attorney involved. The feud ended not only with Moon's death in 1978, but when McQueen blasted a hole in his stained-glass window with a shotgun one night after repeatedly asking Moon to turn of the light in the room because it shined brightly into their bedroom.

752. When it came to raising his children, McQueen felt strongly about making them earn their own money and not falling into the usual Hollywood attitudes. Chad remembers having to earn everything by doing chores around the house, and when he was older and needed more money, he took a job at a nearby gas station pumping gas. The regulars who knew him got a kick out of having their gas pumped by Steve McQueen's son.

753. According to Chad, one of his father's proudest moments came when he got home at 5:30 in the morning after being at a Hollywood club all night (as an underage youth) and then reporting to work on time a couple of hours later.

754. Steve dreamed of opening a General Store near his ranch in Ketchum, Idaho, and call it Queenies. He wanted to be a part of the old-fashioned western community where people could gather over a cup of coffee and an open fireplace. He wanted to decorate the store with all the antiques he'd collected over the years.

755. Steve even had a location picked out with an interesting Hollywood history. It was the North Fork Store on Highway 75, just north of Ketchum, which served as Grace's Diner in the Marilyn Monroe movie, *Bus Stop*. Local politics got in the way and prevented him from buying the town's famous landmark.

756. McQueen, along with girlfriend Barbara Minty, purchased a five-acre parcel in Ketchum, Idaho, in early 1978 with plans to build a log cabin on the property. The couple fell in love with the wilderness area and later that year purchased a 400-acre property at 100 Creek Cove Road in Hailey, Idaho, just south of Ketchum. McQueen planned on building a compound including a main cabin, guest cabin, and private runway and call the ranch the Crazy M.

757. Steve took his first solo flight on May 1, 1979, in his recently purchased, bright-yellow Stearman biplane. He had been training for a couple of months with legendary aviator Sammy Mason and his son, Pete, in Santa Paula, California, and trained for hours to prepare himself for solo flying. On his first flight, he was accompanied by several other pilots as well as friend and actor Lee Majors.

758. Steve and Barbara moved to Santa Paula, California, in the early summer of 1979 after falling in love with the quiet town about an hour's drive north of Malibu. Until they could purchase a property to live in, they cordoned off a section of the 3,000-square-foot hangar and lived there.

759. On July 8, they purchased what became Steve's final home, a four-bedroom Victorian built in 1892 sitting on a 15-acre ranch. The couple remained in the hangar until necessary renovations were completed on the house.

760. Steve and Barbara wasted no time in becoming a part of the community of Santa Paula, and got along especially well with the other aviation enthusiasts at the airport.

761. Steve even volunteered to babysit his friends' seven children five days a week when the husband was diagnosed with cancer and the family couldn't find anyone to watch that many kids for that many hours. McQueen often took pizza to the house when he came, much to the delight of the kids.

762. With the spiritual guidance of his flight instructor and father-figure Sammy Mason, Steve and Barbara began attending the Ventura Missionary Church nearly every Sunday. Steve enjoyed going to church, a process made easier by a congregation that gave him his space without asking for autographs or discussing his movie star life.

763. Steve McQueen officially became a born-again Christian three months later, after a lengthy conversation with Pastor Leonard DeWitt.

764. When he arrived in Chicago to film *The Hunter*, Steve engaged in philanthropy projects around the city. His first mission was to ask the local Catholic church about any immediate financial needs it might have. Upon hearing the amount, he wrote out a check to the priest, then asked producer Mort Engleberg to match the donation.

765. One day, he noticed boys in a poor part of the city using a football stuffed with rags because it wouldn't hold air. He handed a few hundred dollars to stuntman Loren Janes, who went out and bought 100 footballs, as well as a slew of baseball equipment. He had everything delivered to the boys playing in the dirt lot while they watched from a van.

766. Steve and Barbara made a special connection on the set of *The Hunter* with a 15-year-old extra named Karen Wilson. Karen lived in a nearby tenement with her family, and something about the feisty tomboy struck McQueen; perhaps he saw himself in her. It turned out that she was missing school to participate in the movie in order to make money for her family, including her mother who was dying of alcohol poisoning.

767. When filming wrapped up, Steve and Barbara took Karen back to California and enrolled her in a private school in nearby Ojai. When Karen's mother died in June 1980, they became her official legal guardians.

768. The first sign of a health problem for Steve came on December 10, 1979, when his friend's doctor ran X-rays and found a spot on his right lung. A week later, McQueen checked into Cedars-Sinai Medical Center under the name Don Schoonover for further testing, which revealed that a substantial tumor had developed in his right lung. Doctors scheduled exploratory surgery for December 22, when they discovered the tumor to be mesothelioma, or cancer of the lining of the lungs.

769. The initial treatment consisted of experimental chemotherapy and the implantation of radioactive cobalt in McQueen's chest. He was told that mesothelioma was incurable, and after five days of testing, was released on December 29, 1979.

770. Mesothelioma was still a relatively new illness, with the link between it and asbestos having only been discovered a decade earlier. By the time of Steve's diagnosis, there had only been 24 other cases, with all victims succumbing to the disease.

771. Looking back on his life's work, McQueen had been exposed to asbestos nearly every step of the way, primarily from his time in the Navy when he had been ordered to clean asbestos-lined pipes for a month, but the stuff was also used on soundstages and in fire suits and motorcycle helmets.

772. Steve McQueen and Barbara Minty were married on January 16, 1980, in the living room of their home in Santa Barbara by Reverend Leslie Miller, the associate pastor at the Ventura Missionary Church. Sammy Mason and his wife, Wanda, served as witnesses to the 10-minute ceremony.

773. After the ceremony, Steve called friend and stuntman Loren Janes and told him, "This is the greatest thing to happen to me." Interestingly, just three days later, his first wife Neile was also married.

774. Steve McQueen's cancer officially became public on March 11, 1980, when *National Enquirer* ran a story after securing an interview with one of the surgeons. The article mistakenly referred to the cancer as lung cancer rather than mesothelioma, which was either a mistake, or because few people knew about mesothelioma at the time.

775. After the story broke, the magazine also sent a young man disguised as a college photography student to Santa Paula to befriend McQueen and take photos of his private life. Since McQueen had a soft spot for young people, he took him to the hangar to see all the vehicles. There, under the guise of a school project, he photographed the inside of the hangar and took pictures of Steve as he was in poor health. A new age of celebrity journalism was being ushered in, and Steve McQueen was the guinea pig.

776. Steve's self-defense instincts of carrying a firearm for personal protection hardly faded away when his cancer kicked in. On April 7, 1980, he filed paperwork with the city of Santa Paula for him and Barbara to each carry a Colt .45 automatic for "business protection."

777. Late in 1979 Steve became aware of a story about an 8-year-old boy suffering from terminal brain cancer. The *Los Angeles Herald-Examiner* ran the story, noting that it was unlikely he would live until Christmas, so his family had put together a Christmas party for him to be held on Thanksgiving Day. Upon hearing the story, Steve called the family and arranged for a limousine to take them to Disneyland for two days and put them up in a suite in the Disneyland Hotel. Special gifts for each family member were waiting for them in the suite when they arrived.

778. The boy's grandmother was so touched by Steve's gift that she told a reporter about it. When the story hit the papers, Steve was upset by the publicity. He had just wanted to do something special for the family and didn't want anyone but them to know about it.

779. Can you believe that a restaurant actually turned Steve McQueen and supermodel girlfriend Barbara Minty away because of their casual attire? Steve tried to bribe the maître d', offered to meet with staff and customers, even sign autographs to be allowed to eat there, but to no avail. Rather than find another place to eat, Steve and Barbara ran to the mall to buy the tackiest formal wear they could find and, upon their return, were seated.

780. McQueen's first attempt to fight the cancer was actually an illegal injection that had to be administered by Barbara. The seven-week process required daily injections that lasted six hours a day and had to be given five days a week.

781. Rather than have to appear in public at the San Fernando Valley doctor's office, he rented an RV and left it parked outside. A nurse taught Barbara how to perform the procedure, since legally, neither a doctor nor nurse could do it. The nurse stayed with them the whole time in case any problems arose.

782. McQueen first met with Dr. William T. Kelley in mid-April under the guise of a honeymoon with Barbara in Winthrop, Washington, where Kelley had an organic farm. Kelley walked the couple through his all-natural cancer remedy system that included vitamins, coffee enemas, organic food, massages, and other body-cleansing techniques. Steve took a liking to Kelley's simplified, holistic approach to treatment, while Barbara, years later, admitted her doubts, thinking that "Kelley was kind of a weirdo, a little off."

783. The newly married Barbara and Steve McQueen left for their actual honeymoon on April 29, 1980, which consisted of a cruise from Long Beach to Acapulco, Mexico, followed by a stay at the Las Brisas Hotel.

784. The cruise ship was named the *Pacific Princess* and happened to be the inspiration for the TV show, *The Love Boat*. Whether they took that particular ship on purpose or not, *The Love Boat* happened to be one of their favorite shows.

785. While staying at the Plaza Santa Maria, McQueen quickly grew tired of the monotonous diet planned out for him that largely consisted of raw vegetables. Against his doctors' wishes, he asked friends and fellow pilots Pete Mason and Art Rink to fly his favorite foods from Santa Paula down to Brown's Field in California, near the Mexican border once a week. From there, ranch hand Grady Ragsdale collected the food and drove it across the border and past the resort guards.

786. Pie, cake, ice cream, and soda were among the treats delivered, but McQueen's favorite came from his friend Pat Johnson's wife: blueberry pie and thin-cut, breaded pork chops. When it came to the sweets, he would usually just take a bite of each to satisfy his taste buds.

787. On September 27, 1980, Steve McQueen, with the help of business manager Bill Maher and attorney Kenneth Ziffren, drafted his last will and testament. The process took about two hours for them to figure out how to best to divide McQueen's massive fortune, properties, vehicles, and other possessions. When the two men came from Los Angeles, they brought Steve two chocolate cakes that Neile had made for him.

788. On October 2, 1980, Steve McQueen, through publicist Warren Cowan, issued a statement to the press confirming his cancer and announcing the holistic treatment he was undergoing. He had been going back and forth for several weeks about whether to make a statement, with Dr. Kelley pushing him to do it in support of the Plaza Santa Maria and his cancer treatment approach. Finally, reporters began to poke around the hospital and the decision was made to release a short, to-the-point statement to the public before a reporter broke the story.

789. After the announcement, a $50,000 bounty was offered to anyone who could secure photos of the actor undergoing treatment, and the area around the Plaza Santa Maria swarmed with reporters and news crews.

790. The last recording of Steve McQueen's voice is an interview with former Mayo Clinic doctor turned spiritual teacher Brugh Joy who visited the Plaza Santa Maria for a sit-down with the actor in mid-October. Joy's interview is more of a philosophical conversation that clearly indicated McQueen's doubts about his treatment and whether it was the best use of his remaining time. Until then, he hadn't considered that his time had an expiration date. On October 23, he announced that he was leaving the Plaza Santa Maria, and the next day, Steve and Barbara headed back to their beloved home in Santa Paula.

791. On November 3, 1980, the legendary Reverend Billy Graham visited Steve McQueen at his home in Santa Paula before he departed for Mexico for his cancer removal operation. They prayed together, and Reverend Graham read several passages to him for strength over the coming days. Reverend Graham gave Steve a bible in which he noted the passage Philippians 1:6. Graham accompanied Steve to his waiting Lear Jet and blessed the plane, pilots, and flight path before they took off.

792. Steve McQueen died on November 7, 1980, which was officially declared by doctors at 3:54 a.m. after a heart attack caused by an embolism. His tumor-removal surgery the day before was technically successful, but he had suffered a major heart attack while under anesthesia. Happily, he was able to spend a few joyous, optimistic moments with his wife and children before they returned to the hotel for the evening. The official cause of death was cardiac arrest. Steve McQueen was 50 years old.

793. Early on in their relationship, Steve and Barbara Minty took a road trip to Missoula, Montana, to stay at a rustic cabin near some hot springs. When they arrived, the lodge manager and his family were eating dinner. Even though the lodge was closed for the season, he still gave a room to the nice couple who had just showed up and invited them in for dinner.

794. Steve and Barbara dined with the family every night during their stay and got along so well that they were invited into town for coffee with some of their friends. One of their friends stood in shock at meeting Steve, as he was the only one to recognize the long-haired, bearded actor with the supermodel girlfriend. The lodge manager turned to him flabbergasted, having not realized over the previous few days who the man having supper with his family really was.

795. Can you believe that Steve's appearance around the time of *An Enemy of the People* actually got him escorted out of White-fish, Montana, by the police? He looked so mangy when he and his gorgeous young girlfriend rolled into town on a road trip that locals started to eye him suspiciously. When he pulled out a wad of $100 bills to pay for gas, someone called the police on the mysterious traveler. Officers pulled over the old truck, and not recognizing the name of Terence Steven McQueen on his driver's license, escorted them to the town limits and told them never to return. Not wanting a repeat of his Anchorage mugshot uproar for drinking and driving, he politely left town.

796. Although he put on a bit of weight to play Dr. Thomas Stock-man in *An Enemy of the People*, McQueen lost it quickly by continuing his martial arts and exercise routine.

797. Many nutritionists agree that eating healthy is half the battle in addition to working out, but they never met Steve McQueen! He started each day with a cup of coffee, an Old Milwaukee beer, and a piece of chocolate cake. One of his favorite foods was mashed potatoes and gravy, and he'd often order and eat two meals when dining out.

798. When you're famous like Steve McQueen, every little detail in your life faces public scrutiny, down to your choice of beer. McQueen was always an Old Milwaukee drinker, but in 1979 a study was released saying that Coors was actually better for you. Apparently, this study caused the fitness-minded actor to consider switching beer brands. An executive heard that he was considering a switch and sent cases of Coors to Steve's Chicago hotel room while he was filming *The Hunter* with a note that read, "Here you go. Now you're drinking Coors."

799. Steve was always a keen money saver and throughout his life went through great lengths to find tax deductions and savings. Steve and Barbara's house-sitter, Jodi Moon, quickly became a friend to the couple and even played a part in *The Hunter*. When Steve and Barbara went out for lunch they often invited Jodi, who would pretend to be an actress, or any number of other professions, so that Steve could claim lunch as a business expense!

800. It's hard for fans to believe, but McQueen was indeed human like the rest of us. While honeymooning in Mexico with bride Barbara, they made the age-old mistake of drinking tap water one morning with breakfast. Montezuma's Revenge struck both hard and fast, and they had to cut the honeymoon four days short. They returned to Santa Paula by plane and required several days of rest and replenishment.

801. When *National Enquirer* first broke the story, in its own unsavory way, about Steve's cancer, they approached Barbara Walters about being featured on her show. Because the story was leaked by one of Steve's nurses, and not official, Walters not only turned down the magazine's request, but put a call in to McQueen's press agents informing them of the pending story. Thanks to her call, McQueen's reps were able to get a handle on the story, even if they weren't successful in flat-out killing it.

802. During their only direct phone conversation, Al Toffel, Neile's husband, promised Steve that if something should happen to him, his children would always be loved and cared for.

MOVIE FACTS

803. In 1978, Goldie Hawn and Chevy Chase starred in the comedy *Foul Play*, which was a virtual spoof of *Bullitt*. The San Francisco–based movie was a hit, playing nearly opposite the stern thriller on which it was based. And yes, there was even a car chase with jumps and crashes.

804. While McQueen was on hiatus from his film career, rather than flat-out retire, or announce a break, he simply charged exorbitant prices for his services. To read a script, he charged a $50,000 fee, which greatly reduced the number of scripts coming his way.

805. He even met with Francis Ford Coppola to star in his epic film *Apocalypse Now* and was offered $1.5 million. He countered, saying he'd take $1.5 million up front, and another $1.5 million when filming was complete. Coppola then offered him the smaller role of Colonel Kurtz, but McQueen stood strong at $3 million. Coppola decided to pass, going with Martin Sheen for the lead role and Marlon Brando for the smaller part.

806. McQueen also passed on major hits *First Blood, One Flew Over the Cuckoo's Nest, The Gauntlet,* and *The Bodyguard*.

807. Still under a three-film contract with First Artists, and having only completed one film, McQueen began to be hounded to fulfill his contract in the allotted timeframe. He hated the idea of being forced into a film, especially a low-budget one; First Artists projects were capped at $3 million budgets.

808. He was offered lead roles in *Tara: The Continuation of Gone with the Wind, Raise the Titanic!, Raid on Entebbe, The Driver, The Towering Inferno II, Superman,* and *Close Encounters of the Third Kind,* most of which went on to be highly successful and popular films.

809. Because he was forced to do a film, and it didn't matter which one, he simply grabbed a book from Ali's sophisticated bookshelf, took a quick look through the pages, and announced that he would make a movie about it. The book was Henrik Ibsen's *An Enemy of the People*, and a bearded Steve McQueen went on to play a scientist who takes on the corrupt local government of a small Norwegian town when he discovers the medicinal spa is polluted.

810. *An Enemy of the People* featured the longest single dialogue of Steve's career, taking up three pages of the script.

811. At first, McQueen didn't bother to learn the entire speech, but when he showed up on set high and forgetful, director George Schaefer let him have it in front of the entire crew. No director had ever angrily called McQueen out in front of others, but Steve knew he was in the wrong. After the public admonishment, he memorized the entire speech.

812. Warner Brothers decided not to distribute *An Enemy of the People* after it tested poorly in a number of focus groups. McQueen set himself too far away from his usual character, and the executives didn't think anyone would want to see a heavy-set, bearded Steve McQueen playing a scientist. Rather than make a serious investment in the marketing and distribution of the movie, the studio cut its losses and placed *An Enemy of the People* on the proverbial and literal shelf.

813. Steve McQueen's biggest movie deal (the biggest in Hollywood history at the time) ended up falling apart because of a late payment. The producer was late with McQueen's second payment, which nullified the contract. Steve walked away with a cool $1 million just for signing his name. Although it may seem a bit odd that they couldn't have worked something out, the fact was that the producer had raised $18 million in foreign presales, largely using Steve McQueen's name.

814. *Tai-Pan* was set to be a two-part epic backed up by a $40 million budget. McQueen's deal delivered $1 million to him up front, followed by deferred payments totaling $9 million, and on top of that, 15 percent of the profits. No movie star had ever been payed $10 million, and the deal was a reminder that McQueen was still a box office hit.

815. To prepare for his role as Tom Horn, McQueen and Barbara actually went to the Old Pioneer Cemetery in Boulder, Colorado, to visit Tom Horn's grave. McQueen wanted to see if he could pick up on Horn's "vibration." Steve and Barbara picked up different vibrations at the site, with Steve getting a feel for the side of legendary frontiersman while Barbara picked up on the evil side of Tom Horn who had been hung for murdering a 14-year-old boy in addition to 16 others as a gun-for-hire.

816. Against the producer's wishes, McQueen refused to shave his beard to play Tom Horn. He agreed to trim it to look somewhat presentable, although he failed in that attempt. The day before filming started, a fan walked up to a stunt double standing right next to McQueen and asked for his autograph, completely ignoring the unrecognizable bearded man standing right there. After that, Steve understood why producer Fred Weintraub wanted him clean-shaven for the film, and showed up the next day as such.

817. Three days into the filming of *Tom Horn*, McQueen fired director James William Guercio and took over the position himself. He was quickly informed of a Director's Guild rule that an actor, or anyone else associated with the film, could not take over as a director.

818. Rather than fight the ruling, which could be time and energy consuming, William Wiard was hired to essentially sit in the director's chair and collect a paycheck while McQueen continued to direct the film. *Tom Horn* ended up with five different directors, if you include McQueen, during the course of the production.

819. The only stunt that McQueen ever declined to do, after years of trying to push his way into doing stunts, was the hanging scene at the end of *Tom Horn*. The fabricated gallows consisted of a series of pulleys, counterweights, rope, adjustable water containers, and a special trapdoor that was operated by the one wearing the noose. The rig bothered McQueen, as it likely would anyone, and he wanted to play no part in operating it. This wasn't one of the more exciting stunts in his career, no match for jumping motorcycles and racing prototype cars anyways, and the concept of being put to death wasn't appealing to him.

820. McQueen's friend, stuntman Chuck Bail, wrote a screenplay called *The Last Ride*, which he had already been in talks with Columbia about getting made. When he asked Steve to read the screenplay as a friend, Steve said that it was one of the worst screenplays he had ever read in his life, but that he would do the movie if the studio hired a seasoned writer to redo it. Offended, Bail said he didn't need him and that the movie was already being made. But then he remembered the McQueen box office phenomenon and agreed. Bail's salary was increased, and he was given the title of director/producer.

821. Filming for *The Last Ride* was set to begin in the spring of 1980, but by then, McQueen had been diagnosed with mesothelioma. *The Last Ride* was never made.

822. Steve was so disgusted with the original director for *The Hunter*, Peter Hyams, that in order to kill the bad aura he brought to his hotel room at The Beverly Wilshire, he asked the director to get out of the chair he was sitting in and blasted a hole in it with a .45 caliber revolver. Afterward, McQueen told Hyams that he would have shot him if he could have gotten away with it and then told him to get out of his sight. Meetings continued to be held in the hotel room although no one else sat in the high-backed Victorian chair with a hole through the middle and stuffing strewn all over the floor.

823. When the cast and crew of *The Hunter* arrived for filming in Chicago in September 1979, McQueen discovered that although he had been given a luxurious suite in the famed Drake Hotel, the rest of the crew was shacked up at a Holiday Inn. He refused to accept the suite at the Drake, opting to stay with the rest of the crew during filming.

824. Steve's last movie line he ever said was, "God bless you." At the time, the scene where he looks into his newborn baby's eyes and says those words was meant as a lighthearted ending to the film. The reality was much more chilling when examined in the context of his life and the fact that he passed away shortly after the film's premier. From having been abandoned by his own father has a baby, to becoming by all accounts a wonderful father to his own children, to babysitting and even becoming a needy teen's guardian later in life, so much can be read into this one simple scene.

825. Steve McQueen made his last official public appearance at the Hollywood premiere of *Tom Horn*. With cancer rumors running amok, and McQueen wishing to keep the matter private, the premiere was the perfect vehicle to show off to the public how healthy he was in order to get the press off his back. He and Barbara showed up in his pickup truck to an army of press photographers. When asked, he denied the cancer, repeatedly saying, "Do I look like I have lung cancer?" By design, the answer was no, but in reality Steve and Barbara had to sneak out of the theater before the closing credits, and he was exhausted for a week after the affair.

826. When Francis Ford Coppola began to finally put together his vision for *Apocalypse Now*, he turned to *The Sand Pebbles* for inspiration. *The Sand Pebbles* was the last film to be predominantly shot on location in East Asia, not to mention the fact that it shared many of the same general themes such as a group of soldiers adventuring upriver on a boat. Many of the problems Coppola ran into during the filming process also haunted the crew of *The Sand Pebbles*, which was a large part of why Steve turned down a role in the film when offered.

827. Steve McQueen received one of his most personally important awards late in 1976 when he was made an honorary member of the Stuntmen's Association of Motion Pictures as "an actor who has the courage and ability to perform his own stunts."

828. His entire career had been about proving his mettle and pushing the limits when it came to performing his own stunts. Whether it was driving a race car alongside the sport's greats at Le Mans, blazing across the German countryside on a motorcycle, or dodging incoming aircraft at San Francisco International Airport, he strived to live up to the ideals of the proverbial Hollywood stuntman.

829. Steve actually had the chance to meet Ralph "Papa" Thorsen, the bounty hunter who's life story he portrayed in *The Hunter*. Thorsen filled Steve in on what the job entailed and how he got started in it. He told him stories that weren't all that glamourous but allowed Steve to add a hefty dose of realism to the role. It also made Steve so excited to play the part that he called his agent right after the meeting to set up the deal.

830. In real life, 52-year-old Papa Thorsen was married with two children, even though the character in the film was written with a pregnant 29-year-old girlfriend. The movie character's unwillingness to have children was an added character point that emphasized the dark world in which he lived and worked. He and his girlfriend, played by Kathryn Harrold, disagreed on having a child, which added a tense human conflict to the film. Because she wasn't pregnant in real life, Harrold had to wear padding under her clothes throughout the production.

831. If you're wondering what the real-life Papa Thorsen looked like, well, all you have to do is watch the movie, *The Hunter*. Thorsen appears in a cameo as a bartender who serves McQueen.

832. In fact, it was after shooting the Papa Thorsen cameo scene that the two went out for drinks and Steve found Thorsen to be a bad driver. The bad driving was immediately written into the script and became one of the film's enjoyable satiric aspects.

833. Did you know that actor Robert Redford was working on a *Tom Horn* film at the same time as Steve McQueen? The Redford film was to be called *Mr. Horn* and produced by Wildwood Productions, Redford's company. In fact, they announced their intentions on the same day.

834. To top it off, both production company offices were located on the first floor of the Warner Brothers lot, leading many of the staff there to wonder if a real Wild West showdown would take place down the building's corridors.

835. Filming *Tom Horn* allowed Steve the opportunity to create a fake character in order to entice his future wife, Barbara Minty. The character was the "Indian Princess," a nonexistent role.

836. When Barbara's agent brought it up to her, she told her she'd be meeting the star of *The Towering Inferno*. "The one with the blue eyes," was her exact wording. Remember, McQueen's co-star in *The Towering Inferno* was Paul Newman, who actually had been unofficially bestowed the nickname of "Old Blue Eyes." Barbara went into the meeting expecting to be introduced to Paul Newman!

837. *Tom Horn* writer Tom McGuane owned a ranch in Livingston, Montana, not far from a ranch owned by Peter and Becky Fonda. When initially looking for a ranch property, Steve and Barbara visited Livingston. Although McGuane was out of town, he allowed them to use his ranch. Just a year earlier, his screenplay had been optioned by First Artists to be turned into a Steve McQueen movie.

838. If you're thinking of great ways to win over a girlfriend's or boyfriend's parents, giving them roles in a movie is a great start. Barbara Minty's parents, Gene and Wilma, came to visit their daughter and her boyfriend on the set of *Tom Horn* on the first day of shooting. In fact, they were invited there by Steve himself, who less than a decade earlier kicked Dustin Hoffman's friends and relatives off the set so he could focus on shooting *Papillon*.

839. Steve gave Gene and Wilma roles as background extras in the film. When the casting director saw Gene, standing at 6 feet 2 inches, weighing in at 220 pounds, and carrying a shotgun, he was assigned a role as one of the sheriffs escorting Tom Horn to the gallows. He probably didn't have to reach too deeply to get into character for that one.

840. Every time Steve and *Tom Horn* co-star Linda Evans had to kiss for a scene, Steve's girlfriend, Barbara, left the set and drove to the horse corral to spend some time.

841. During their time together, Steve became Linda Evans' mentor and taught her to truly become her character rather than play her character. Throughout her successful career, Linda Evans credited Steve McQueen with giving her the confidence she needed to play popular future roles.

842. The rifle used by Tom Horn in the film is a Winchester Model 1876 chambered in .45-60 and equipped with a custom sight. It's believed that the rifle Tom Horn used in real life was a .30-30 Winchester Model 1894.

843. *Tom Horn* was the only Steve McQueen film to receive an R rating.

844. The classic green jacket that Steve wears in *The Hunter* is an MA-1 flight jacket produced by Alpha Industries. That jacket was originally produced specially for the US Air Force.

MOVIE AUTOMOBILE FACTS

845. McQueen served as an uncredited stunt rider in the 1976 Warren Oates and Christopher George film *Dixie Dynamite*. Friend Gary Davis mentioned to him on the phone one day during McQueen's break from filmmaking that he and Bud Ekins were scheduled to do a motorcycle scene and couldn't go riding in the desert with him the next day. Davis jokingly invited McQueen to join them on set as a fellow stunt rider for the daily fee of $172, to which he agreed.

846. For the only time in his career, Steve McQueen had to play a bad driver when he took on the role of Ralph "Papa" Thorson in *The Hunter*. The pale yellow 1951 Chevrolet Styleline Deluxe convertible's manual three-speed transmission and Stovebolt straight-six engine proved to be difficult for the character, yet it was loved by McQueen who added it to his collection after filming.

847. Unfortunately, the 1951 Chevy was his last movie car, although it couldn't touch the level of fame many others did. It was sold in the 1984 Steve McQueen auction, restored in the early 2000s, and sold again at auction in 2013 for $84,000.

848. Think Burt Reynolds is the only actor to rock a black and gold Trans Am on the silver screen? Think again. Steve McQueen drove one in *The Hunter*, although unlike The Bandit, he struggles with driving the high-performance automobile. The car in *The Hunter* lacks the classic Trans Am T-top, but it does have the WS6 suspension package and 400-ci V-8. And rather than driving off with Sally Field in the passenger seat, McQueen's Trans Am is blown in half by a stick of dynamite after being chased through a corn field. Admittedly, the car's scenes where McQueen overly struggles to drive it is seriously laugh-out-loud funny.

849. While filming *Tom Horn*, the area was hit with some serious weather in the form of rain, sleet, and wind, which led to a lot of mud. Equipment had to be moved regardless of the weather, so the crew used four-wheel-drive vehicles to get around. At one point, a vehicle became stuck in the mud, so the crew called in a bigger 4x4 to pull it out. But then, that truck became stuck, and an even bigger truck pulled up to help free it. Before long, nearly a dozen vehicles were stuck, each trying to get the one before it out of the mud. At some point, someone realized that the effort was going to be fruitless and called the Army Corps of Engineers who brought in their massive, military-grade trucks and tractors to pull out the film crew's vehicles.

850. For the three-month stretch of *Tom Horn* that was filmed in Patagonia, Arizona, the studio rented Steve and Barbara a luxurious house with a swimming pool not too far from the set. A hotel suite in Tucson was on standby for the couple in case the house wasn't to their liking. Well, the house was not to their liking. In fact, they opted to stay much closer to the set in a 28-foot Winnebago RV. What it lacked in creature comforts it made up for in privacy and peacefulness.

851. For much of the mid-1970s, Steve attempted to find and purchase the primary *Bullitt* Mustang that he used in the film. In 1977 he made his final attempt with a letter to then-owner Robert Kiernan asking to buy back "his" 1968 Mustang. He even offered to buy him a similar car in exchange "if there is not too much monies involved in it." Kiernan denied the request as he and his family used the car regularly and enjoyed it.

AUTOMOBILE COLLECTION

852. Chad McQueen's first car was a restored 1949 Chevrolet pickup truck that his dad located for him. The 3100 Chevy had been painted British Racing Green and cost the younger McQueen $2,500, which took him two years of working at the gas station to pay his dad back. Chad still has the truck today.

853. Steve flew his Stearman plane to the 1979 Watsonville Fly-In and Air Show, and although Barbara went with him, she was flown there by veteran pilot and friend Chuck Bail. McQueen wasn't 100-percent sure of his flying skills, so he wasn't comfortable completing the trip with a passenger yet.

854. Upon landing, he had to register his antique plane in the show, and he used the name "Bob Minty" to stay under the radar. He also wore a lady's red bonnet over his head and face to avoid being seen; not exactly his "coolest" moment.

855. McQueen purchased a 1941 Boeing Stearman PT-17 biplane in March 1979 after discovering it in the classifieds one morning while looking for bargains. The $35,000 price tag was a great deal for the bright yellow plane, and he purchased it immediately.

856. In July 1979, Steve bought his famous Santa Paula hangar that went on to store much of his car and motorcycle collection, in addition to his antiques and aircraft. The owner of the hangar had paid $37,000 for it in 1967 and had no interest in leaving, so he played Steve McQueen at his own game, asking way more than what the hangar was worth: $180,000. After initially walking away, McQueen called back an hour later to say that he'd take it.

857. In April 1980, McQueen asked his friend Bud Ekins if he would go to Boston with him to inspect and appraise a collection of motorcycles that he might be interested in buying. Ekins told him he would go only if McQueen bought them first-class tickets, to which he begrudgingly agreed. He ended up buying the entire collection, which surely took his mind off his terminal cancer at least for a little while.

858. On the return flight from Boston, Steve told Bud that "if anything happens to me," an obvious allusion to his cancer, he wanted Ekins to pick out the two best motorcycles in his collection and keep them.

859. At first, Steve wanted Bud to have every motorcycle in his collection after he died, but Ekins denied the request. He said that the money from selling the bikes should go to Steve's children, and Steve couldn't help but agree.

860. McQueen could feel he was becoming physically worse, but he longed for another, most likely his last, flight. He knew that he couldn't handle the controls on his own, so he asked his friend and instructor Sammy Mason to take him up. The day they had scheduled a flight, Mason showed up at the hangar, but McQueen never did.

861. After receiving news from doctors at Cedars-Sinai that his cancer was indeed terminal, Steve called ranch hand Grady Ragsdale and told him to fill the silver Ford truck with gas. The following day, July 31, 1980, Steve and Barbara (with Steve at the wheel, of course) drove the silver Ford to the Plaza Santa Maria in Rosarito Beach, Mexico, where he began his holistic cancer treatment.

862. If you were Steve McQueen, what would be your Sunday car for driving to church? For him, it was his 1952 Hudson Wasp. The large, chrome-covered American automobile was perfect for him and Barbara to take on a casual cruise in Santa Paula.

863. The Wasp is equipped with the rare combination of Twin-H dual-carb engine and automatic transmission. It currently resides in the Petersen Automotive Museum, which purchased it at auction on its own premises in 2006, for $50,000.

864. The last car Steve McQueen special ordered and had customized to his unique tastes was a 1976 Porsche 930 Turbo Carrera, which was incidentally the final year of that car's availability in the United States.

865. Upon taking ownership, he swapped in a new set of wheels that were 1-inch wider in the front and back and had a switch installed that instantly killed the rear driving lights. The reason for the switch was that if he were being chased by the police down Mulholland Drive, his favorite go-fast street, he could cut the lights and lose them.

866. The third owner of the car was Dino Martin, son of actor Dean Martin, who was dating figure skater Dorothy Hamill at the time.

867. Like any normal 15-year-old boy, it was difficult for Chad McQueen not to get in trouble with a brand-new Porsche 930 Turbo sitting in the driveway. With his dad out of town, Chad pushed the Porsche out of the driveway, fired it up, and took it for a spin down the street at least once a day. That is until Julia, the brave woman whose job it was to keep an eye on him, found out and told Steve.

868. Steve called Chad to tell him he'd be gone for a couple more days, so Chad continued to take the Porsche out at the usual times. Except it was a trap. Chad noticed a taxi cab drive by him and, "Inside that cab, I see two of the biggest blue eyes in the world" staring back at him. Although Steve was upset, he certainly understood the 5-second 0-60 mph Turbo's appeal.

869. It's one thing to be forgetful, but could you imagine forgetting that you bought a brand-new Rolls-Royce? Steve McQueen did until he got a call from a dealer one day telling him his black Corniche convertible was ready, but he didn't believe it until the dealer read him his credit information. When he and Barbara had walked past the Rolls-Royce dealership in Los Angeles, he decided to buy the car on a whim.

870. McQueen's favorite song to cruise to was "Stayin' Alive" by the Bee Gees. The penultimate disco-era song came out in 1977 and was made famous by the John Travolta film *Saturday Night Fever*, which also happened to be one of McQueen's favorite movies. He kept the soundtrack cassette permanently lodged in his Rolls-Royce's radio and liked to crank up the volume when that song came on. Barbara remembers ducking under the dash whenever it happened so that nobody could see her.

871. McQueen's last of his six aircraft was a blue and silver 1945 Boeing Stearman similar to his first one, and the two are often confused. Just like his famous vanity license plate, he gave the former US Army trainer a tail number of N3188 and commissioned a rebuild, which was completed after his death. This was the last plane that McQueen flew. The plane is currently owned by Californian Bill Allen, who flies it regularly.

872. Steve bought one of the six original PA-8 Super Mailwings that were built in the 1930s for use in the early air-mail system. The plane was in rough condition when purchased, although it's one of two known survivors from the original six.

873. When Steve wanted to get that old Hollywood feeling, his motorcycle of choice was his white 1941 Indian Chief. He always had an affinity for the Springfield, Massachusetts, brand that produced its last motorcycle in 1953. He had the Chief restored after purchasing it in 1977 and rode it regularly until his death.

874. The Chief was first sold at the 1984 McQueen auction and most recently sold in 2009 for $99,450 including premium. Interestingly, it now wears the original gas tank emblem rather than the 1942–1946 emblems that Steve had.

875. Did you know that Steve McQueen owned an Indian chopper that he nicknamed "The Blob?" The bike's nickname is almost as interesting as the bike itself considering he never liked talking about his first major film role. Of all his motorcycles, this was the only long-fork chopper. He bought the 1947 Chief-based custom in 1977 and usually kept a rolled-up sleeping bag on the front forks to complete the gypsy look. Even when he owned it some 40 years ago, it carried a rough-and-tumble, ratty patina that could have let him pass for any other long-haired biker of that period.

876. At some point in the 1970s, Steve purchased a rare 1929 Scott Super Squirrel, a motorcycle prized by collectors for its many advanced features, such as its frame design and water-cooled two-stroke engine. As with many of his motorcycles, he tasked Von Dutch with the detailed restoration of the machine that included a top-notch paintjob.

877. Since the Scott Super Squirrel was meant to be a showpiece and not a rider, Steve wanted a number plate on the front fender with the bike's year, make, model, and basic information. Unfortunately, when Von Dutch painted the number plate, he accidentally painted 1929 instead of 1926. The bike sits just like that today, to correct the mistake would be to eliminate the motorcycle's story.

878. When Chad McQueen was 15 years old, his father gave him his 1947 Indian Chief with sidecar, just like the one that he had at the beginning of his motorcycling career.

879. Although Chad couldn't legally drive on the street, that didn't stop him and his father from riding together. Sidecar motorcycles have a much lower tendency of getting pulled over or even looked at with a curious eye, which made the classy Indian the perfect street machine for Chad. Oftentimes, Barbara accompanied them, riding shotgun in Steve's sidecar. Looking back, even though Chad was riding without a license, it allowed the father-son pair to ride together for at least a short period of time before Steve's death, something both were certainly thankful for.

880. In 1977, Steve's massive collection of motor vehicles garnered some interest from the *Los Angeles Herald-Examiner*. The newspaper assigned a reporter to visit the McQueen residence and count the vehicles that Steve owned. He found an eclectic collection of trucks, military vehicles, motorcycles, luxury cars, and European sports cars with racing pedigrees. He returned to his editor with a final tally of 53 vehicles.

881. In recounting the story to biographer William F. Nolan, McQueen laughed at the reporter's count, which was an impressive number. "I had a lot more than that," he said. "This guy didn't know about my whole warehouse full of antique bikes. He just counted what he found."

882. Steve's dear friend Sammy Mason instantly fell in love with Steve's 1950 Hudson Hornet. Mason had owned a car similar to the cream-colored one Steve drove one day to the airport, and was blown away when he got to drive it. A week later, Steve drove to the airport in a beautifully-restored black Hornet and showed it to Sammy. He told him that he didn't have any room for the car and would his flight instructor and friend mind holding on to it for him? In return, he could drive it all he wanted.

883. Sammy Mason drove the car and continued to fall in love with it, so Steve suggested that he buy it. When Mason balked at what he assumed was a heavy price tag, Steve told him that the car would only cost him $1. So Sammy Mason handed Steve a one-dollar bill, and Steve signed over the title to him.

884. Many of McQueen's friends and fans pictured him leaving this world the way he lived in it: full throttle and in a blaze of glory. Toward the end, one of his friends even suggested that rather than this slow, drawn-out, painful march toward death he was embarking on with surgery, that he simply get in one of his planes and fly until he couldn't anymore. Master automotive fabricator Von Dutch understood why Steve couldn't do this. "He loved machines too much. Couldn't bear to destroy one on purpose."

885. Steve was one of those guys who could just get into a car and drive for hours on end just for the thrill of it. Considering the stable of vehicles he had to choose from, this might not be entirely a surprise. What may come as a surprise is that he so often found himself having driven so far that he needed to stop at a hotel for the night! Because of this, he always carried a toothbrush and a spare t-shirt in the car.

886. Living on the Pacific Ocean in the town of Trancas Beach was soothing, peaceful, and beautiful, but beachfront property doesn't allow for all that much parking. Although Steve had warehouses full of cars and bikes in storage, he parked his favorite and most-used ones on the private street that his and several neighboring houses shared.

887. After neighbor Keith Moon's death in 1978, a big-wig attorney bought the house and moved in. He constantly complained at the number of cars and motorcycles crammed all over the exclusive street. McQueen eventually punched him during an argument.

888. Steve once drove 700 miles from Southern California to Salt Lake City to see a rare 1915 Power Plus Indian and sidecar rig. He and Barbara set out on the trip armed only with the knowledge that the bike existed somewhere in Salt Lake City. When they arrived they asked around and were quickly led to the owner's house. The motorcycle wasn't listed for sale, and although Steve surely wanted to add it to his collection, after meeting the owner and his family decided that the bike was too special to them to even put an offer on it. Respectfully, Steve posed for some pictures with the family and their motorcycle then got in his truck and drove the 700 miles back home.

889. Although Steve was an excellent pilot, he failed his pilot's license exam not once but twice! The dyslexic grade-school dropout could fly, but he couldn't take tests! On his first attempt the administrator even sneaked him the exam ten minutes early so he could study the exact questions, and he still failed. To make matters worse, Barbara passed with flying colors on her first attempt, and they threw a party for her at the hangar. Steve finally passed on his third attempt in July 1979.

890. McQueen owned more than 100 motorcycles, most of them from varying early-American manufacturers. Although he loved them all, his favorite, comprising the bulk of his collection, was Indian.

891. To help maintain his motorcycles, he hired legendary Indian mechanic and restorer Sammy Pierce as his full-time technician. Pierce was responsible for originally piecing together, fixing, and restoring many of the Steve McQueen Indians that reside in collections all over the world today.

892. It's no secret that Steve loved anything with an engine, whether it was a car, plane, motorcycle, or even a bulldozer. When he and Barbara purchased their 450-acre Crazy M Ranch in Idaho, Steve purchased a bulldozer to grade and clear the land himself! Somewhere in Idaho there's a big red bulldozer probably still being used by someone who unknowingly has a valuable ex-McQueen vehicle!

893. After his first long-distance flight in the Stearman, Steve called ex-wife Neile's new husband, Al Toffel. An accomplished Air Force test pilot in his own right, Al was one of the few people who would understand the feeling Steve was experiencing, and it gave them an opportunity to bond over their common love of aviation.

894. It is reported that the last motorcycle Steve McQueen ever purchased was a 1929 Harley-Davidson model DL. The first year for Harley's 45-ci flathead V-twin was 1929, and the engine went on to be one of Harley's longest-running powerplants, seeing its swan song in 1973. Few changes were made to the engine itself over the years, although iterations of it found their way into racing motorcycles, affordable cruisers, and three-wheeled Servi-Cars used by businesses and police departments. The year 1929 was also special for the DL because it was not only Harley's first flathead V-twin, but it featured a four-muffler exhaust and dual-headlight arrangement unique to several of Harley's 1929 models only.

895. Steve was able to buy his old Jaguar XKSS back in 1977, likely for a whole lot more than he sold it for. The car next sold at the Steve McQueen estate auction in 1984 for $147,500 and is believed to be worth well into the millions today.

RACING

896. One of the race bikes Steve owned had originally been campaigned by legendary racer and AMA hall of famer Charles "Red" Wolverton, whom he ran into at a swap meet. It turned out that Steve owned one of Wolverton's old Ace racers, so he invited him to Santa Paula to ride the bike. Steve even payed for his plane ticket!

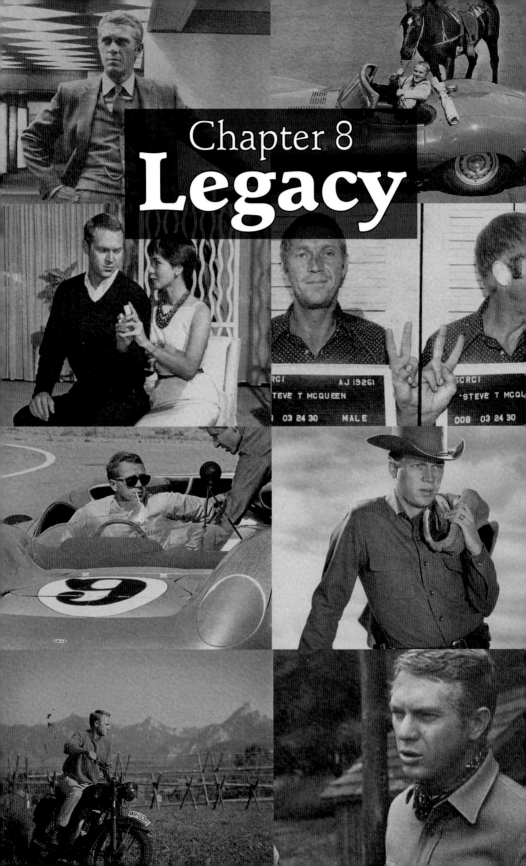

Chapter 8
Legacy

PERSONAL LIFE

897. Teena Valentino, who worked for Dr. Kelley as a metabolic technician, kept a detailed diary of Steve McQueen's stay at the Plaza Santa Maria. The 800-page tomb, entitled *99 Days to God*, chronicled not just McQueen's health regimen and day-to-day treatment but also his emotions, thoughts, and fears as he engaged in battle with his cancer.

898. Following Steve McQueen's death, the Mexican government, through the local police and mortician, refused to release his body until a massive ransom was paid. Attorney and former Secret Service agent Bill Carter was called to negotiate the release and discovered that it would take $160,000 to make it happen. Carter used the tough talk he learned in the Secret Service to threaten a "major international incident" that would involve the State department, Bureau of Customs, and the Immigration and Naturalization Service (INS) if the body was not released immediately.

899. McQueen's body was released shortly after Bill Carter's intervention and taken to the airport without so much as a question at customs. Two Lear Jets waited to take McQueen's body, his family, and friends back to the United States before the press could overrun the airport.

900. On the way from El Paso to Santa Paula, the plane carrying McQueen's body made a ceremonial low pass over the airport before landing at Ventura County Airport. About 50 of Steve and Barbara's friends and neighbors gathered to wave and say goodbye as the plane passed 100 feet above Runway 22. "God bless you, Steve," came through the radio as the plane flew by.

901. Steve McQueen's November 9 memorial service at his home in Santa Paula was the first time all three of his wives were together. Barbara invited Neile and Ali to sort through Steve's jewelry box so that they could take anything that they had given him during their time together. Steve had kept his earlier wedding rings, which Neile and Ali reclaimed as something to remember him by.

902. The memorial service concluded with Steve's fellow pilots flying overhead in the missing man formation before lead pilot Larry Endicott scattered his ashes into the Pacific Ocean.

903. Terry and Chad McQueen were left the bulk of their father's estate, which included an unknown sum of money and the majority of his possessions.

904. In November 1984, after years of cataloguing everything Steve owned, most of it was auctioned off to the tune of $2 million.

905. He left $2 million to Barbara, in addition to their 480-acre ranch in Idaho.

906. Steve left $200,000 to Boys Republic, the school that he credited with putting him on the right track during his troubled teen years and whose students he continued to care about throughout his life. The school built a recreation center in his honor, which officially opened on April 21, 1983.

907. Steve also left $100,000 to the Ventura Mission Church, which has used the money to provide scholarships for underprivileged children, not unlike himself.

908. Steve's daughter, Terry, passed away on March 19, 1998, from hemochromatosis at 38 years of age. Both of her parents were carriers of the disorder, although they never displayed symptoms of the disease.

909. Terry had undergone a successful liver transplant operation just five months earlier, and was airlifted from Malibu to UCLA hospital after having breathing difficulties associated with a blocked airway. The official cause of death was respiratory failure. In lieu of flowers, the family asked that donations be made to either the JoAnn Transplant Foundation at UCLA or to Boys Republic.

910. Chad McQueen and the McQueen estate control the licensing for Steve McQueen's name and likeness, which to this day is still highly sought after by companies around the globe. Although the potential for great riches is there, Chad discriminately chooses to work with brands that embody his father's spirit and that his father would have been likely to use himself. All sorts of products have been approved for licensing from automobiles to liquor, computer games, fashion accessories, and others.

911. The McQueen estate takes in between $5 and $10 million per year from licensing fees used primarily in advertising. In addition, because Steve had the wherewithal to push for profit points on top of his salary, anytime a film is shown on TV, a DVD is sold, or a digital version is rented, his estate earns royalties.

912. Forbes ranked Steve McQueen as one of the top-ten posthumous celebrity earners, right up there with Elvis Presley and Marilyn Monroe.

913. On June 12, 1986, Steve McQueen's star was added to the Hollywood Walk of Fame on Hollywood Boulevard. His was the 93rd star laid down and currently resides at 6834 Hollywood Boulevard, near the prime intersection with North Highland Ave. Although they weren't there at the time, it's fitting that his star now rests between a lingerie store and a Harley-Davidson store.

914. In 2008, Boys Republic began holding the annual Friends of Steve McQueen Car Show at the Chino Hills, California, campus to raise money for its cause. The event attracts all sorts of cars and motorcycles, several of which are usually ex-McQueen machines. The car show, silent auction, and banquet raise hundreds of thousands of dollars every year for Boys Republic, to the tune of more than $2 million in its first ten years. Each year has a different Steve McQueen movie theme, and to lend support to his father's favorite charity, Chad McQueen co-chairs the event.

915. Immediately after his death, the Jake Holmen/Steve McQueen wax statue at the Hollywood Wax Museum had to be removed due to the onslaught of fans descending upon it. Fans brought flowers and gifts as they paid their ceremonial last respects to a man who had touched millions of lives around the globe. Fearing that the statue could become damaged or destroyed, museum officials took it off the floor and placed it in a secure location. It was the first time in the museum's history that a statue had to be removed from public display for this reason.

916. Beginning in 2007, Beech Grove, Indiana, has held the annual Steve McQueen Days festivals. The inaugural event saw several previous co-stars and his wife Barbara attend. The events included car and motorcycle shows, movie screenings, and a parade.

917. In 2019, the old McQueen house on Solar Drive, left mostly intact from the McQueen ownership, was listed for rent at $25,000 per month. That would have been quite the investment had they decided to keep it!

918. After Steve's death in 1980, Barbara kept the ranch until 1999. The Crazy M Ranch, now called the Pioneer Moon Ranch and encompassing around 500 acres, was listed in 2013 and subsequently sold for $7.4 million.

919. In 2005, TAG Heuer released the Monaco Vintage Limited Edition watch to celebrate what would have been Steve McQueen's 75th birthday. The watch sports the same red, white, and blue bands on the face and the Gulf Oil logo as the one worn by Michael Delaney in *Le Mans*. There were 4,000 examples produced.

920. The GAP used an image of McQueen in his signature khakis for a 1993 print ad campaign for, you guessed it, khakis! The campaign was entitled "Who Wore Khakis?" and the ad read, "Steve McQueen Wore Khakis." Several other iconic celebrities were featured in the campaign, such as James Dean, Marilyn Monroe, and Andy Warhol.

921. The fashion company Vintage 55 at one point created an entire collection of clothing based on several Steve McQueen films. The collection included a number of race-inspired shirts featuring the Gulf Racing treatment from *Le Mans*, a short sleeve polo shirt with McQueen's signature embroidered on the left side of the chest, and a graphic Frank Bullitt T-shirt. Shirts based on his 1964 International Six Day Trials appearance and even the chinos worn by Virgil Hilts in *The Great Escape* were available.

922. The 2005 book *Denim: From Cowboys To Catwalks, A History of the World's Most Legendary Fabric* used a photo of Steve on its cover. The book notes many of his contemporaries including John Lenin, Paul Newman, Elvis Presley, Lee Marvin, Marvin Gaye, and Miles Davis, but throughout the history of denim, apparently, the editors felt no one better represented the fashionable fabric than Steve McQueen.

923. One of Steve's favorite watches was his 1967 Rolex Submariner, which he was often photographed wearing. His watch sold at auction in 2009 for $234,000.

924. Luckily, McQueen did allow one writer into his world toward the end: William F. Nolan, with the intention of writing his biography together someday. Nolan brought out the deeply personal feelings Steve had from his childhood all the way up to his death.

925. During a series of interviews that started in 1970 with a profile piece in *Road & Track*, Nolan continued his work until he received a call from Steve in late 1980 when he was told, "I'll never live to write the damn book. . . You do it, okay?" Nolan's 1984 biography stands today as one of the best primary sources on Steve McQueen.

MOVIE FACTS

926. In 1987, 29 years after the original version premiered, *Wanted Dead or Alive* was remade into a modern-day movie featuring

Josh Randall's great-grandson as the main character. Along with the release of the new film, Four Star also released a color version of the original series, which became popular in syndication across Europe and introduced a whole new generation to Steve McQueen.

927. *Bullitt* continues to be recognized even to this day as a fan favorite. In 2005, a British television show awarded it the top spot. *Bullitt* usually falls in first or second on varying lists online, jockeying back and forth with Gene Hackman's *The French Connection* and Robert DeNiro's *Ronin*. For someone who always made sure never to be outdone by his co-workers, even Steve McQueen couldn't envision a car stealing the show. *Bullitt* was even voted into the National Film Registry in 2007, cementing its iconic status in cinema history.

928. The movie *Tai-Pan* was eventually made and released in 1986, eight years after it fell through with Steve McQueen. An unpublicized aspect of McQueen's original contract stated that if the deal fell through, not only was he guaranteed $1 million, but also the rights to the film. Steve's last agent, Marvin Josephson, brought this issue up with McQueen's estate in 1986, but considering that the film was such a massive commercial failure (losing around $20 million), no action was taken.

929. An episode of *Star Trek: Deep Space Nine* called "The Siege of AR-558" aired on November 18, 1998, that follows a similar story to *Hell is for Heroes*. Several characters are named for those in *Hell is for Heroes,* and the plotline is similar.

930. In the TV series reboot of *The Magnificent Seven,* which ran from 1998 to 2000, Vin Tanner (played by Eric Close, originally McQueen's character) carries a Winchester Model 1892 Mare's Leg rifle that McQueen used as bounty hunter Josh Randall in *Wanted Dead or Alive.* Although *Wanted* and *The Magnificent Seven* have nothing to do with each other, nor did Steve carry the Mare's Leg in the movie, it's still a fitting tribute to the actor rather than the characters he played.

931. In the final years of his life, Steve gave no interviews about his personal life to journalists, even going so far as to cut conversations short and send anyone who asked packing. Journalists were instructed to only ask about movies or racing, with a narrow emphasis on those subjects.

932. In 2006, the sunglasses believed to have been used in *The Thomas Crown Affair* were sold at a Bonhams auction for $70,200 including buyer's premium. Interestingly, the 1967 Rolls-Royce Silver Shadow from the film fetched the exact same amount.

933. A 2006 issue of *GQ* magazine ranked the most stylish movie characters of all time that had a lasting impact on the way people dress. *Bullitt* ranked ninth with McQueen's classic turtle neck and blazer combo that he reportedly picked out for the character himself.

934. A video game version of *The Great Escape* came out for XBOX, Playstation 2, and PC in 2003. Gamers could play as Virgil Hilts in his attempt to escape the German POW camp. You could even go on the motorcycle escape! Unfortunately, the game never found any significant popularity at the time.

935. The Henry Repeating Arms rifle company makes a real Mare's Leg lever-action pistol so *Wanted* and Steve McQueen fans can channel their inner Josh Randall. Several configurations are available including .22, .357 Magnum, .44 Magnum, and Colt .45. No .44-40 rifle-round version is available.

936. *The Magnificent Seven* was reprised as a TV series that saw two seasons of action from 1998 to 2000. McQueen's character of Vin is played by Eric Close, and Robert Vaughn, who played Lee in the original, played Judge Oren Travis in the show.

937. A remake of *Papillon* was released in 2018 starring Charlie Hunnam as the Steve McQueen character and Rami Malek as the Dustin Hoffman character.

938. The actual rifle used by Tom Horn, played by McQueen in 1978, is currently in the collection of the National Cowboy Hall of Fame in Oklahoma City.

939. A remake of *The Blob* was made in 1988 starring Kevin Dillon and Shawnee Smith. The story follows a similar path although with significantly more modern special effects and a massively higher budget at $19 million.

940. Chad McQueen was originally offered the lead role in *The Blob* remake but turned it down because he didn't want to take on roles related to or inspired by his father's work. Plus, he didn't like the script.

941. *The Great Escape II: The Untold Story* was released in 1988 starring Christopher Reeve. In this version, the allied prisoners managed to escape return to Stalag Luft III to enact vengeance on the Nazis who killed their fellow escaped prisoners.

942. *The Getaway* was remade in 1994 starring Alec Baldwin and Kim Basinger as husband and wife bank robbers on the run. The remake gives a nod to the original when Baldwin (as Doc McCoy) is playing with a remote-controlled Volkswagen car at the dump, the same type that Steve and Ali sit in at the dump in the original.

943. *The Thomas Crown Affair* was remade in 1999 starring Pierce Brosnan and Rene Russo, this time around with Crown as a Billionaire art thief. Faye Dunaway is also in the film as the psychiatrist. The film contains a number of nods to the original such as the golfing scene in which Crown hits an excellent shot out of the bunker. Rather than a polo match as in the original, director John McTiernan felt that a high-speed catamaran race would lend more action and excitement to Crown's character, rather than just wealth.

944. In 2019, the film *Chasing Bullitt* was released, which was the first major fictional work to be based directly on Steve McQueen. He is played by look-alike Andre Brooks, and the film occurs in 1971 after the flop of *Le Mans*. The backstory is that McQueen won't do another film until his agent can locate and buy back the Mustang used in *Bullitt*. But the film itself covers quite a bit of McQueen's life through a series of flashbacks, giving it a hint of biopic quality.

MOVIE AUTOMOBILE FACTS

945. Steve McQueen posthumously starred in the 2004 Ford Mustang commercial entitled "Cornfield." By using a body double and a computer to superimpose McQueen's character from *Bullitt*, the commercial actually shows what appears to be Steve being tossed the keys to a newly-designed 2005 Mustang and driving it around on a paved track in the middle of a cornfield. The commercial says, "The 2005 Ford Mustang. The legend lives." That second part could easily be applied to either the car or the actor.

946. Sean Kiernan inherited the original *Bullitt* Mustang in 2014 after his father, Robert, passed away. By that time the car was in pieces in his father's garage, although luckily nothing had been touched, fixed, or altered from the original movie car. By mid-2016 the car was mostly back together again and ready to be unveiled to the public.

947. Sean Kiernan enlisted the help of automotive industry experts to get the car on the National Historic Vehicle Register and contact Ford to help with the public unveiling.

948. Ford and Sean Kiernan launched their respective *Bullitt* Mustangs alongside each other at the Detroit Auto Show in January 2018. After the public launch, Kiernan and his Mustang traveled around the country displaying the car to hordes of onlookers at major automotive events and museums.

949. In August 2019, as this book is receiving its finishing touches, it was announced that the original 1968 *Bullitt* Mustang would be crossing the auction block at Mecum Auctions' January

2020 sale in Kissimmee, Florida. The car will continue traveling to automotive events leading up the sale, where it is expected to fetch well into the millions of dollars.

950. The whereabouts of the two Bud Ekins-built Triumphs used in *The Great Escape* are unknown; but wait, isn't there one positioned mid-jump at The Petersen Museum in Los Angeles? That motorcycle, pictured readily around the Internet, is actually a perfect replica built by Triumph collector Sean Kelly around 2007. He started with a 1962 Triumph TR6, just like the original, and outfitted just like the Triumphs in the film. Rather than give his creation a "new" appearance, it sports a wonderfully vintage patina that represents what the bikes would look like today.

951. The original bikes built for the film were bought back from the studio by Bud Ekins who then reconverted them to their original appearance and sold them.

952. Most of today's car enthusiasts are familiar with the use of Steve McQueen in advertisements for Ford's Mustang, but did you know that the actor's first commercial appearance for the Blue Oval was for the 1997 Puma? It wasn't available in the United States, so using McQueen's likeness to sell a front-wheel-drive two-door hatchback wasn't quite as taboo as you might think. The one-minute commercial features a digitally super-imposed Steve McQueen driving the Puma around San Francisco before backing it into a garage spot (past a Faye Dunaway look-alike, although a Jaqueline Bisset type would have been more accurate) between a Highland Green 1968 Mustang and a green Triumph scrambler.

953. The 1968 *Bullitt* Mustang replica used in the Ford Puma commercial was Dave Kunz' oft relied-upon GT. His car is a near-exact replica of the original, which caused a problem the day of the commercial shoot when the director noticed that it correctly lacked a Pony emblem in the grill. Ford's creative team wanted the famous Mustang emblem in place to promote the brand cohesiveness between the Mustang and the Puma. Plus, international audiences might not be as quick to recognize the classic Mustang.

Luckily, a local parts vendor had one for sale and was given more than it was worth to bring it to the set immediately. After the shoot, Dave Kunz pulled it off his car and gave it to a crewmember who owned another Mustang.

954. In 2000, Ford released its first Bullitt concept car based on the newly-redesigned Mustang. The Highland Green paint, black leather interior, and American Racing Torq-Thrust wheels looked right at home on the new Mustang, and audiences and media at the Los Angeles Auto Show couldn't get enough of it. A production car was quickly developed and released as a 2001 model. Buyers could choose between the classic green, black, and dark metallic blue paint offerings, although most went straight for the Highland Green.

955. Although only good for an additional 5 hp, Ford upgraded the 4.6-liter engine with a larger throttle body and high-flow mufflers, which gave it that classic V-8 rumble. The 2001 Bullitt was available for one year only, and unlike the movie car and later Bullitt editions, it wore a Pony grille badge. A total of 5,582 *Bullitt* Mustangs were built that year with 3,041 in Dark Highland Green, 1,818 in black, and 732 in True Blue.

956. Anybody walking the streets of San Francisco in 2005 might have been shocked to see a newly-launched black Charger being chased around by a Highland Green Mustang with black Torq-Thrust wheels. Ford had yet to announce another run of *Bullitt* Mustangs when the editors of *Motor Trend* had the idea of customizing a 2005 Mustang GT to look like a Bullitt edition and use it for an article mostly showcasing the all-new Dodge Charger. Apparently, the camera crew and cars caused a scene in the City by the Bay, leading to a widespread conspiracy theory that this car was actually a Ford prototype.

957. The following year, 2006, Ford actually announced the development of a *Bullitt* Mustang, which was released in 2008. The first production unit went to none other than Chad McQueen for his collection.

958. Fifty years after the release of *Bullitt*, the Dark Highland Green special-edition Mustang is still as popular as ever as Ford released the latest *Bullitt* Mustang in 2018. The first 2019 *Bullitt* Mustang, sporting VIN 001, was auctioned off at Barrett-Jackson's 2018 Scottsdale auction for $300,000 with all of the proceeds benefitting Boys' Republic.

959. Although the name of the *Bullitt* Mustang and the McQueen family charity of choice haven't changed since McQueen's time, the car itself has. A 475-hp V-8 engine gives the latest iteration of the *Bullitt* Mustang a 163-mph top speed, and the 12-inch LCD instrument cluster and dash screen are luxuries that Steve likely could never have imagined. Chad was on stage to help with the sale alongside his father's original 1968 *Bullitt* Mustang.

960. Greenlight released three editions of the *Bullitt* Mustang and Dodge Charger starting with its first issue in 2010. The 1/64-scale diecast models featured opening hoods, detailed engines, rubber tires, and were officially licensed by Ford, Chrysler, Warner Brothers, and the Chadwick McQueen and the Terry McQueen Testamentary Trust. There were 5,000 examples produced, the success of which led to two more releases. The second release used essentially the same cars, but this time they featured chase damage such as dents, missing hubcaps, and bullet holes just as in the movie.

961. The Gulf Porsche 917K driven by Steve in *Le Mans* sold for $14 million at a Gooding & Co. auction in Monterrey, California, in 2017 after sitting in a barn for nearly two decades. When the hammer dropped it became the most expensive Porsche to sell at auction.

962. The 1970 Porsche 911S driven by Michael Delaney in the opening scene of *Le Mans* sold at RM Auctions in 2011 for $1.375 million. Similar models without the Steve McQueen provenance sold for less than $200,000 at the time.

963. The second *Bullitt* Mustang, which was used primarily for the hard-hitting jumping scenes and was far too damaged to sell post-production, was found in a Mexican junkyard in 2017. Little of the original car remains, but it carries the correct VIN and had undergone a significant dose of restoration work over the years.

964. A 2012 episode of the television show *Alcatraz*, which took place in San Francisco, featured a near-recreation of the *Bullitt* chase scene in which a suspect in a new black Dodge Charger is being chased by a cop, with green turtleneck and leather shoulder harness, in a new Mustang. In this version the Mustang is blue, but the green Volkswagen Beetle that is seen several times throughout the original chase appears several times in the reproduction as well.

965. The 1988 remake of *The Blob* starring Kevin Dillon featured a distinct nod to McQueen in its use of Triumph motorcycles. Dillon rides a 500-cc Triumph Tiger T100R on the street, and a 200-cc Tiger T20 Cub is used for the jumps.

966. The remake of *The Thomas Crown Affair* sees a nod to Steve McQueen's *Bullitt* as Pierce Brosnan drives a dark green Shelby Mustang around his island retreat on Martinique.

967. For the first time in quite a few years, the dune buggy from *The Thomas Crown Affair* will make its public appearance when it hits the auction block at Bonhams' Quail Lodge sale in August 2020.

AUTOMOBILE COLLECTION

968. McQueen willed a handful of specific vehicles to his friends and loved ones whom he knew would enjoy them best. First and foremost, he left Barbara his 1978 Rolls-Royce Corniche and a 1958 GMC pickup truck, the perfect vehicles for roaming the ranch in Idaho or cruising the streets of Los Angeles. He left her three of his antique motorcycles as well.

969. Pat Johnson, and his wife, Sue, received the beastly 1972 Mercedes 300SEL 6.3.

970. Friends Sammy Mason and Chuck Bail were left the PA-8 Pitcairn and MCMD Stearman aircraft, respectfully.

971. Chad McQueen took ownership of Steve's Porsche 1600 Super after his father's passing, and aside from minor restoration and mechanical work, has left it exactly as his father had it. In its current condition the bumpers are back on, but the trim pieces had been removed between the time that Steve originally owned it and the time he bought it back. He must have liked it like that because, when he freshened it up after the repurchase, he left them off.

972. In 1997, the owner of McQueen's 1964 Ferrari 250GT Berlinetta Lusso sold it to restorer Mike Regalia. Oddly enough, in addition to cash, Regalia also gave up a .45-caliber black-powder pistol handmade by Steve's old friend and customizer Von Dutch.

973. McQueen willed his 1969 Porsche 911S to his daughter, Terry. After she passed away, Chad took ownership of the Porsche and treated it to a meticulous detailing and mechanical servicing, as the car hadn't been used much over the years. It currently resides in his collection today, alongside his father's 1958 Speedster; the two cars that Steve felt should belong to his children.

974. After McQueen's death, one of the motorcycles that Bud Ekins chose for himself was the 1926 Cleveland Fowler four-cylinder. It changed hands a couple of times since Ekins sold it in the mid-1980s, with the most recent public sale being in 2006 when it sold at auction for $104,500.

975. One of Steve's most historically interesting motorcycles didn't come to be understood until about 25 years after his death. Dale Walksler, owner and curator of Wheels Through Time Museum in Maggie Valley, North Carolina, had owned Steve's 1917 Harley-Davidson that was likely used in World War I. Over the years, Dale also added a World War I pigeon carrier to the museum's collection and, since they matched up with year and paint color, decided to try putting them together. To his complete surprise, several brackets that were missing from the Signet pigeon carrier were already on the McQueen bike! The bike and carrier currently sit prominently on display at Wheels Through Time.

976. In 2006, the largest Steve McQueen auction since 1984 was put on by Bonhams & Butterfields at the Petersen Automotive Museum in Los Angeles. The bulk of the sales came from Barbara's property and included furniture, tools, clothing, photos, and toys in addition to several cars and motorcycles. Other collectors also consigned ex-McQueen vehicles and other celebrity collectibles.

977. The highest-selling item at the 2006 Bonhams auction previously belonging to Steve McQueen was his 1934 Indian Sport Scout, which sold for $177,500, or about ten times the Bonhams estimate. Although anything with Steve McQueen's name behind it typically sells for one or two multiples of a similar machine, the massive discrepancy in the 1934 Scout was a complete surprise to everyone attending the auction.

978. What's the best way to buy an ex-Steve McQueen vehicle at a reasonable price? Buy it from someone who doesn't know what they have. Several times, McQueen's old vehicles have shown up on the Internet auction site eBay listed without any mention or knowledge of the vehicle's provenance.

979. On one such occasion, vintage Husqvarna enthusiast Rob Phillips saw a well-used 1972 Husky 400 Cross for sale and purchased it. He knew that Steve had owned several just like it, but when he checked the serial number with a records keeper, the bike turned out to have been sold to Solar Productions. Rather than restoring the bike to new, he left it aesthetically as-is, but he restored all the internals and wear parts to make it run like new again.

980. For the 2012 model year, Triumph announced a limited run of special-edition Steve McQueen T100 Bonnevilles built in conjunction with Chad McQueen's McQueen Racing. Only 5,000 motorcycles were built, all of which sold quickly, in a special dark metallic green paint scheme with Steve's autograph on the side cover.

981. The military lettering "Triumph" on the gas tank, the black knee pads, solo seat, and luggage rack is reminiscent of the Triumphs built for *The Great Escape*. Other than that, the general look of Triumph hasn't changed a whole lot since Steve was riding around, and that's a good thing!

982. The last remaining Steve McQueen vehicles that were still owned by Barbara were sold in 2006 at a Bonhams auction. The three motorcycles were a 1929 Harley-Davidson Model B single-cylinder flathead that sold for $37,440, a 1934 Indian Sport Scout that sold for $177,500, and a 1920 Indian Powerplus Daytona racer that sold for $150,000. The Harley and the Powerplus were restored under his ownership by his personal mechanic Steve Wright.

983. Steve's 1952 Chevrolet 3800 camper, nicknamed "Dust Tite," sold at Barrett-Jackson's 2016 Scottsdale auction for $60,500. This is credited as being the last vehicle he ever rode in, having to lie down on the way to the airport. When sold, it still had the original mattress that was used by Steve McQueen.

984. There are actually two Cobras with the CSX2174 VIN running around today, believed to have been built using key parts from the original that Steve drove for several months.

985. In the early 2000s Ferrari used Steve McQueen's image and persona to markets its new cologne Passion. This was Ferrari's first attempt at a fragrance brand extension, which notes that McQueen's "passion for life and racing make him the perfect figure to drive Ferrari's new cologne." Point of sale displays featured images of Steve driving or posing with his Ferraris.

986. Would you believe that of all the incredible cars that Steve McQueen owned Corgi Vanguards decided to create a limited-edition 1:43-scale diecast model of his 1961 Austin Mini Cooper S? Just 2,200 examples of the brown get-around car were produced by the English firm.

987. Steve McQueen's 1976 930 Turbo exists today just as he owned it, selling at auction in 2015 for $1,950,000.

988. The Pitcairn PA-8 airplane is currently owned by The Woodlands Toy Store in Pennsylvania and has been restored to its original silver and green livery. It still flies in airshows, usually in New York.

989. Steve's Indian Chief chopper, nicknamed "The Blob," is currently owned by the National Motorcycle Museum in Anamosa, Iowa, where its condition and history will likely be maintained for the years to come.

990. Steve's 1929 Harley-Davidson DL was originally sold at the 1984 Steve McQueen auction and most recently in 2009 for $39,780.

RACING

991. In 2010, Chad McQueen formed McQueen Racing, which works with custom car and motorcycle builders to build high-performance limited-edition vehicles and accessories. The firm has also been involved in developing Steve McQueen documentaries and merchandise.

992. TAG Heuer reintroduced its Monaco line of watches in 1998, which included a replica of the one Steve wore in *Le Mans*. In addition to the blue face/black strap model, a limited Gulf Oil racing edition with the familiar blue and orange logo and stripes was released in 2006.

993. Multiple versions of the Monaco were made available and McQueen's image was used in a number of ads promoting the line.

994. The new Monaco lists for $5,900, which is a bargain considering one of the two watches Steve wore in the film sold at auction in 2012 for $799,500.

995. If you want to relive the 1964 International Six Day Trials by motoring about just like Team USA did, reproduction gear is available. The first available product was released in 2009, a specially-painted Bell 500 replica helmet produced by the company Grand Prix Legends. It is an open-faced helmet with modern protection certifications and comfort but with the original Von Dutch style. A bonus if you're name is also Steve: "Steve" is pinstriped on the back just as on the original and also on the sides.

996. To complete the ensemble, Barbour came out with the Steve McQueen Rexton Jacket in 2013, which is an exact replica of the one Team USA wore with the addition of an American flag liner and McQueen's picture on the inside left. It even came pre-distressed so you wouldn't have to actually ride a motorcycle to get it to look like Steve's.

997. In 2005, Metisse Motorcycles, a new venture taken up by Geri Lisi, teamed up with Don and Derek Rickman, and Chad's McQueen Racing brand to develop the Steve McQueen Desert Racer. The Desert Racer uses an original Triumph 649-cc engine, and everything else is an exact replica of McQueen's Rickman-Metisse desert bike.

998. Only 300 of the special-edition machines were built, and each came with a certificate that it had been endorsed by the McQueen estate.

999. Even though Steve's bike was originally meant for off-road purposes only, in the 1960s and 1970s he could get away with some on-road action. The 2005 Metisse could be ordered with street-legal equipment, passenger seat, and a registerable VIN so owners could enjoy their piece of history without getting it dirty.

1000. Even though Steve McQueen wore a Barbour jacket for the 1964 International Six Day Trials, Belstaff, another high-end English designer, released the Steve McQueen Celebration jacket in 2007. Belstaff's version lived up to all the performance characteristics necessary for ISDT competition and included a special patch inside honoring McQueen and explaining his connection to Triumph and enduro racing.

1001. The FLY slot-car company produced a Steve McQueen collection of 1:32-scale slot cars that came in collectible boxes. The most popular was the Le Mans Porsche 917K, but several other cars were also available, including the 1969 Porsche 911S from the film and the Porsche 908 that McQueen campaigned to a second-place finish at Sebring that year. The blue number 29 908 used as the camera car for *Le Mans* was also treated to a slot-car version.

AMERICAN IRON MAGAZINE PRESENTS 1001 HARLEY-DAVIDSON FACTS
by Tyler Greenblatt
American Iron magazine editor Tyler Greenblatt has compiled 1,001 Harley-Davidson facts into this single volume, with subjects ranging from the historic powertrains to pop culture to Harley-Davidson as a company and manufacturer. 6 x 9", 352 pgs, 106 photos, Sftbd. ISBN 9781613252963 Part # CT575

CARROLL SHELBY: A Collection of my Favorite Racing Photos *by Art Evans with Carroll Shelby*
This final work from Carroll Shelby is a personally curated collection by the legend himself that is filled with images that have never been seen in print, as well as images not published since the 1950s and 1960s. It is packed with photos selected by Shelby himself, and the captions are quotes from Shelby's commentary on the action in the photo, as well as his memories. 9 x 9", 256 pgs, 295 photos, Sftbd. ISBN 9781613254608 Part # CT650

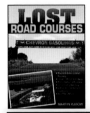

LOST ROAD COURSES: Riverside, Ontario, Bridgehampton & More
by Martin Rudow
Road racer and road racing expert Martin Rudow retraces road racing's glorious past and visits the defunct classic road courses across the United States and Canada. Rudow recounts the breathtaking races and fascinating history of more than 16 tracks through period photos and digs beneath the surface to reveal the story behind the story. 8.5 x 11", 176 pgs, 358 b/w and color photos, Sftbd. ISBN 9781613252222 Part # CT549